DISCARDED

Confederates
against the
Confederacy

Confederates
against the
Confederacy

Essays on Leadership and Loyalty

JON L. WAKELYN

PRAEGER

Westport, Connecticut
London

Library of Congress Cataloging-in-Publication Data

Wakelyn, Jon L.
  Confederates against the Confederacy : essays on leadership and loyalty /
Jon L. Wakelyn.
      p. cm.
  Includes bibliographical references and index.
  ISBN 0–275–97364–6 (alk.paper)
  1. Confederate States of America—Politics and government.   2. Confederate States
of America—Social conditions.   3. Confederate States of America—Military
policy.   4. Politicians—Confederate States of America.   5. Upper class—
Confederate States of America—Political activity.   6. Unionists (United States Civil
War)—Confederate States of America.   7. Allegiance—Confederate States of
America.   8. Political leadership—Confederate States of America.   9. United States—
History—Civil War, 1861–1865—Public opinion.   I. Title
E487.W25 2002
973.7'17—dc21   2001055155

British Library Cataloguing in Publication Data is available.

Library of Congress Catalog Card Number: 2001055155
ISBN: 0–275–97364–6

First published in 2002

Praeger Publishers, 88 Post Road West, Westport, CT 06881
An imprint of Greenwood Publishing Group, Inc.
www.praeger.com

Printed in the United States of America

The paper used in this book complies with the
Permanent Paper Standard issued by the National
Information Standards Organization (Z39.48–1984).

10 9 8 7 6 5 4 3 2 1

Contents

Preface and
Acknowledgments

Many associates in the scholarly community have encouraged me to publish my thoughts on the dilemmas and divisions in the Civil War South
that led Confederates to oppose other Confederates. Why leaders of importance went along with secession and the formation of the Confederate
States of America and then in many different ways and for different reasons
turned against that new government certainly reveals much about what
that society was all about. To be sure, some of them never admitted their
disloyalty, and history certainly either has ignored or has covered up their
actions and the reasons for them. Nevertheless, their story needs uncovering and I have attempted to think through the lives of those important
leaders. The results of my thoughts are the seven related essays that make
up *Confederates against the Confederacy*.

Chapter 1 on James Henry Hammond was published in the *South Carolina Historical Magazine*. I have added some current biographical information and sources in the notes and created a short new conclusion for
this volume. I thank the editors of that magazine for long ago publishing
it and allowing me to reprint it here. The theme of Chapter 2 in part comes
from the introduction to my book, *Southern Pamphlets on Secession*. I am
grateful to the University of North Carolina Press for allowing me to steal
some of my own thoughts. The essay, however, is new and incorporates
many additional findings building upon the ideas and interests of those
antisecessionists who reluctantly supported the Confederacy. Chapter 3

appeared in Lawrence Lee Hewitt and Roman J. Heleniak (eds.), *Leadership During the Civil War*. It was delivered at the Deep Delta Civil War Symposium in honor of the late T. Harry Williams and Frank E. Vandiver, two good friends and two outstanding students of the Civil War. Vandiver was my major professor, and I am pleased to honor him once again with a show of my appreciation for all that he has done for me and the other Vandiverians over the years. He shows again and again why he is known as "The Great Man." I am uncertain how he will take this wilting of Confederate loyalty. I am indebted to Larry Hewitt for the invitation, for the editing, and for years of friendship. He has also given me permission to republish this article here. I have made only a few minor adjustments to place the piece in line with the others in this volume. Some of the ideas for that essay came out of my long study of the speakers of state legislatures during the war era and after, *A Biographical Directory of Speakers of the State Legislatures, 1850–1910*.

Chapter 5 also was first delivered at a Deep Delta Symposium at Southeast Louisiana State University. It has been greatly revised in my attempts to come to grips with the many disputes among historians of the frail Episcopal Church. Although I remain unconvinced that Bishop Thomas Atkinson of North Carolina was evangelical, I will go along with the current arguments. I do insist on seeing him as institutionally hierarchical. Again, I have Larry Hewitt to thank for the invitation and the many good comments on the piece. An early version of Chapter 7, the concluding overview of the actions of disloyal Confederates, also first was given as a talk at Southeast Louisiana. That most sophisticated audience of experts, including a mind-stopping question about Bobby Lee from Stephen Woodworth, made me rethink my arguments and certainly dissuaded me from including much on the high command in this volume. I am also grateful to Alan Kraut for inviting me to give a seminar at the American University on another version of Chapter 7, and for the searching questions emerging from that rousing session. All those questions and comments assisted me in the revisions of this chapter.

As the book unfolded I found the necessity to include other supporting essays. Chapter 4 on Henry Stuart Foote is completely new, although I first began to face the life and writings of that brilliant, tormented, and underrated leader when I worked on *Union Pamphlets in the Confederacy*. Foote cannot rightly be seen as a unionist, or Tory as they were called, but he certainly turned on the Confederacy to the point where he was the only sitting congressman expelled from that body. I can't say that I found Foote appealing, but I did see him as a most important political leader against the Confederacy. Chapter 6 also is new for this volume. It stems from my close reading of that most political of memoirs, Mary Chesnut's *Diary from Dixie*. Perhaps better than any other Confederate, Mary Chesnut recorded its leaders dividing. Her brilliance, style, and perceptions have been of great benefit, as in her own right she contributes much to this story.

Gathering the written word in publications, letters, and the press for analysis is laborious, as is the digging into personal lives and their surroundings for context. Fortunately, many librarians, archivists, and friends have eased this burden. To Dave Kelly of the Reference Division of the Library of Congress, once again I am indebted. I am also grateful to an unnamed archivist in the Library's Manuscript Division, who saw fit to honor a historian's request that he preserve a disintegrating newspaper article that contained a major commentary on one of my leader's writings. To the staffs at the Southern Historical Collection in Chapel Hill; the Virginia State Library in Richmond; the Alderman Library in Charlottesville; and the Barker Collection in Austin, Texas, I owe a great debt. I am pleased to acknowledge the splendid digging capacity of former students John Allen and Clayton Jewett.

My editor and friend, Heather Staines, of Greenwood-Praeger, has encouraged this work from its inception. My other editor, Beverley Jarrett of the University of Missouri Press, has generously foregone her usual demands and freed me to expand this work. Colleagues elsewhere, Arthur Bergeron and Larry Hewitt of the Deep Delta Symposium, have encouraged me to publish what they have read. Other colleagues and friends, Randall Miller and Catherine Clinton, have also encouraged my musings. Bill Freehling's professional friendship and discerning eye have been of much help. That his most recent work, *The South Versus the South*, touches on my own work only led him to encourage my book even more. Alan Kraut has had perhaps greater hopes for what the theme of this book tells us about the Old South than I. I thank him especially for his support, for years of excellent talks, and for more than twenty-five years of friendship.

Joyce Bogardus Walker never asked why I wasted so much time on dissidents, malcontents, and hateful leaders. She put up with my trips to dig further into the lives of those leaders. Her busy duties at the Trinity Cathedral did not keep her from answering my arcane questions about the church. As a partner in the enterprise of learning, she is magnificent. It is because of all this and more that I dedicate this book to her.

Introduction

This volume has emerged from two concerns that have perplexed me for much longer than I would want to admit. The first is that the defining moment of the Old South, the Civil War, has been studied in great depth, but not always in connection with the defining characteristic of that region. Simply put, slavery influenced the character, behavior, and values and the material concerns of those people, but its role in the Civil War has until recently rarely received attention. Now that historians have begun to study how slaves actively undermined the Confederacy, perhaps we can see the complicated role that slavery played in how that society's white male leadership self-destructed. Slavery divided white leaders, not because they did not unite behind their system, but because they differed over how to support and defend their way of life. The second is that, as I began to investigate those leaders who remained in the Union and worked actively against the Confederacy, I found them often lumped, when studied, with those Confederates who opposed the Confederacy. This was especially made clear to me when going over that great work of Carl Degler's, *The Other South*. Anti-Confederate leaders like Parson William G. Brownlow and William W. Holden, who hardly supported one another, have been seen as part of one cohort. But then Degler himself says that he ignored the wartime activities of the leadership class in his concern with other Southerners. My principal concern until now has been to write a book on one group of anti-Confederates, the Tories or southern Unionists. To do so, I have had to uncouple them from those Confederate leaders who turned, in their own ways, against the cause they had embraced either reluctantly or with verve. The result is this separate book, *Confederates against the Confederacy*.

As will be seen, the great leaders, private and public, political and economic, clergy and other propagandists are the prime movers in this story. Recent excellent work on the small farmers and ordinary soldiers who left the Confederacy have obviated the need to consider them other than as constituents and allies of the great leaders. Likewise, Bill Freehling's and Ira Berlin's seminal works on the slaves as resisters has led to my separate study of that resistance's influence on the master class of leaders. That slavery undermined the cause is apparent in the works on slaves as self-liberators. That story is the most magnificent one of the entire Civil War, and our profession is enhanced by the efforts of those scholars. The second, and sadder, great story is how some leaders worked against their own cause, largely because of slavery. Certainly, they disagreed over how best to defend slavery. In that slavery influenced the values and the behavior of those leaders, perhaps it is time to consider once again the context of action and thought of the leader class so as to understand their world even better.

In this case texts are a means to understand the thoughts of some Confederates who turned on the Confederacy. Of course, first, as Degler says needs doing, we must see how they undermined the cause. Their actions against the Confederacy, policy and procedure, set in different regions and over conflicting issues, must first receive full treatment, not the least because those leaders were men of action. To fail to understand how those men—often reluctantly, hesitatingly, and even in denial—spoke against the cause is to diminish their actions. Why they said they turned, or merely opposed, requires a detailed textual analysis of their works. Fortunately, they left behind, if studied carefully and with suspicion for revisionist qualities, a body of writing that reveals much about their opposition. I say "carefully" because I am aware of Richard Hofstadter's valuable admonition, "Look at their feet, not at their mouths." Well, the task is to see just how they put their feet in their mouths.

There is another problem with studying these leaders against the cause. They often did not act in consort. Many of them seemed quite wary of speaking out against the Confederacy, often out of real fear. They were political leaders, men in public and private life who hoped to continue in power or authority. If they appeared too far in front, too hostile, would they have a political afterlife? So, aside from the difficult task of uncovering their actions, there is the equally arduous duty to uncover their mendacity. They, their families, and their associates even down to now have participated in a great cover-up, or a revision of their actual record, which has confused their place in the story of a new republic at war with itself.

To uncover them is to attempt also to explain just what it meant to oppose the Confederacy when so many of the leaders claimed to support the cause. Policy issues such as how to fight the war, where to fight the enemy and protect the home front, who to include in the fighting, and how to pay for the war cut to the heart of an independent people. Confederates differed on those matters, often to the detriment of the cause. Besides, over time a number of them became disenchanted enough with the Confederacy's war that they talked of peace and even did something about it. That their loyalty ebbed and flowed over time and from place to place requires more than the bald belief that some leaders merely ran out of steam. Those issues and actions must be looked at on the state and the federal level, and they require familiarity with such concepts as the writ of habeas corpus, and what it meant to those leaders and their constituents and society. Also required is what public life meant to them and how it worked. Many of the leaders had grown up in the hothouse of proslave governance. They were brutal slaveowners, supersensitive to any slight. They were men, in other words, whose society had formed a belligerent but controlled and nuanced world of leadership. That experience in pride and ownership certainly influenced the language they employed against one another as well as that sense of personal honor that often resulted in true political violence. Last, though few were political thinkers of the quality of John C. Calhoun, James Henry Hammond, or even Henry Stuart Foote, they all were guided in their thought and thus their politics by a grand contradiction. As Confederates, they were revolutionary defenders of personal liberty, a principle informed by their hostility to any interference with their slave society. On the other hand, as owners of people who did not want to be owned, they were supersensitive to all threats to an ordered existence. Social control, political order, quite conservative political constructs, are at the core of their beliefs. Was there then another struggle between liberty and individual rights and conservative order? What kind of rebels did that make of those leaders?

To understand, or at least begin an understanding, of that group of disloyal Confederates, I offer here seven essays. Chapter 1 on James Henry Hammond is about the depths of conservatism (and a peculiar kind of liberalism) and the importance of personal possession that led one man to oppose secession and then, though he claimed not to, to turn on the

Confederacy. Chapter 2 builds on the Hammond essay by asking what there was in the arguments so many antisecessionists made against breakup and formation of the Confederacy that would make them eventually turn on the Confederacy itself. In short, those who came to oppose the Confederacy had worries about its ability to defend their way of life before they took to the barricades. Chapters 3 and 4 deal with procedure or the actions of the politically powerful. Chapter 3 considers the anti-Confederate activities of the states' most powerful leaders, the speakers of the houses. Localism and complex attitudes toward personal freedom thus replaces that hackneyed theme of states' rights. Chapter 4 confronts the opposition in the national Congress to the administration's policies. The most outlandish, most outspoken, and most hostile anti-Confederate leader was Henry Stuart Foote. Accused of ambition or blind hatred of the president has been used to explain the actions of a man ostracized. It will be shown that Jefferson Davis, rather than a lightning rod of individual hate, represented policies that anti-Confederates found anathema. Chapter 5 looks at the relationship between southern religion and morale, or the decline of morale, in the Confederacy. It goes beyond fundamentalist theology of good and evil and God's will to the institutional activities and beliefs of the church. Since really only the Episcopal Church had a fully developed hierarchical set of beliefs, despite its small numbers, it has been singled out for study. Besides, many of the Confederacy's most important leaders belonged to that church. Chapter 6 looks at the uses of political gossip to undermine the Confederacy's government and will to fight. But it is more, because Mary Chesnut, more than any other Confederate, chronicled who opposed the cause and even why they may have opposed it. The last chapter brings the actors together to understand their opposition, its nature, and its cause. Taken together, these chapters reveal a leadership against itself. The key issue was the defense of slavery, and they fell out over how best to do it. Moreover, slave society defined those leaders in many ways, and thus their behavior was based on what slavery had done to them. At the last, the Confederacy died of slavery, just as it was born of that system.

I say died, and that implies an interpretation of why the Confederates lost the war. But that conclusion is neither my interpretation nor my assumption. That dissent and disruption among the leaders reflecting their personal views and those of their constitutents undermined the cause to some extent is a given. That the Confederacy was a flawed nation from the beginning is also a given, and those flaws take preeminence in this volume. I must, however, agree with the view of the late Thomas L. Connelly. When asked to comment about localism, personal resentments, the loss of morale, and poor public policy as factors in the defeat, he rose up and said, "Dammit, they lost on the battlefield."

A final word of regret. I have had great admiration, if worry, for the Old South. A lifetime of studying one's own past elicits pride in many of one's forebears' qualities, if unforgiveness for what they did to others and to themselves. They did try to break up their own country. That is unforgiveable. But they acted in brave, if foolhardy, ways, and that is a marvelous story for the nation. In no way do I seek to diminish the sacrifice so many made, the giving up of their lives, even for a wrongheaded cause. But the task has been to understand them, especially those who were disloyal in their many ways, and to break the ideology of those who claim the South to have been a monolith. I do subscribe to the central theme of U.B. Phillips. I just think that he had it not quite right. Southerners have never agreed on how to do what they wanted to do. The great tragedy of that Old South society and maybe even its later society is that to defend slavery and to maintain racial control they undermined themselves. Not only had their prejudice and desperate need for control and personal freedom undermined them, but they also were left confused and in disagreement over how best to protect their way of life. This book is the story of some of those wartime representatives of the people as they struggled to do what they believed was best for their South.

1

The Changing Loyalties of James Henry Hammond

Although a number of South Carolinians either opposed secession or equivocated until it became too late to take a positive stand against it, historians have been more interested in evaluating the political activities and in understanding the motivations of the vast majority of Carolinians, who supported cooperative or single-state secession. Early historical works detailed political behavior and studied intellectual and propagandistic pro-secession writers, while current scholars have dealt with the complex internal racial and psychological motivation and attempted to grasp the meaning of the total material culture.[1] When historians have applied their methods to the so-called Unionists, they have concluded that similar reasons, especially planter fear of losing economic and social status, motivated the Unionists of South Carolina.[2] A reconsideration of those political leaders who questioned the *means* used to achieve secession, especially a reconsideration of the interaction between political activity and the political deal, could put the complex secessionist movement in South Carolina into sharper historical perspective.

While the actual political power of the planter aristocracy remains debatable, historians have justified their concentration on planters with fifty slaves or more, because so many of that number led the state's secession movement.[3] Certainly the slaveholders and those rising young politicians who sought planter status felt that they had the most to gain or lose from the disruption of the Union. The planters also had a set of values that

placed a priority on political service and duty, although few of them bothered to articulate those values in any works on political theory or to ra-
tionalize secession in political terms. They seemed more activists than
thinkers. Indeed, their actions dominated the South Carolina secession
convention. Half the 120 delegates owned at least fifty slaves, and at least
twenty-four owned more than a hundred slaves. More than 450 South
Carolina planters owned more than 100 slaves and, though many reasons
existed for them to avoid election at the convention, if service and vested
interest in loss of status were major factors in leading planters to secession,
then perhaps there should have been a larger contingent of planter aristocrats active in the secession movement. At least three of the 450 have
been described as so-called Unionists, and many other planters either
equivocated or refused to participate in any of the political events that led
to secession.[4] Undoubtedly, some of those planters feared any change
whatsoever, but did that make them Unionists?

The most perplexing behavior of any South Carolina planter-statesman,
whose career shall serve as a model for the other Unionists, was that of
James Henry Hammond, a lifelong secessionist who, as United States senator from 1858 to 1860, established a reputation as an equivocal Unionist.
A tall, handsome, arrogant man, given to portliness in old age, Hammond
had been a precocious student, having rushed through South Carolina
College by the time he was nineteen, who had turned to law and newspaper editing on the eve of nullification. He quickly caught the notice of
John C. Calhoun and George McDuffie, became an adviser to those radical
leaders, and then made a fortunate marriage to an heiress and retired to
the pleasant contemplation of a lifetime fortune in planting. Calhoun requested that he resume public duty, and at the age of twenty-eight, Hammond was elected to Congress, where he made a reputation as an
opponent of the abolitionist petitions. In the midst of his success, Hammond developed an illness that required him to travel abroad, where he
sharpened his political views and bought wine and paintings in the manner
of a wealthy planter. In 1842 Hammond was elected governor and joined
another secession group, Robert Barnwell Rhett's Bluffton Movement,
which had been precipitated by Texas annexation and the tariff struggle.
Hammond's faction lost the battle for a state secession convention to the
now more moderate Calhoun, and because of a personal scandal Hammond again retired from public life. As a delegate to the Nashville Convention of 1850, a movement for unified Southern opposition to
compromise over the extension of slavery, Hammond again found himself

on the wrong side of a secession struggle, though he had finally moved from the single-state position to become an advocate of united Southern secession.[5]

During five years of semi-retirement, Hammond continuously lectured throughout the state on agricultural and political topics. He also studied history and added to his writings on political theory, though much of his work was disorganized. A dogmatic, self-praising, and self-deceiving individual, Hammond had acquired a reputation as the ablest political mind and most statesmanlike politician in the South after the death of Calhoun. In the fall of 1857 South Carolina's legislature elected Hammond to the United States Senate because of his intellectual status and because he represented a compromise between disputing factions in the state. Neither James L. Orr's National Democrats nor Robert Barnwell Rhett's radical secession faction was certain of Hammond's position, but each thought that he favored its respective views.[6] Hammond served in the Senate until November 11, 1860, when he resigned his seat after cautioning the state legislature against precipitous action. He then refused to serve in any public capacity for those who wanted to achieve secession. Hammond's senatorial service had acquired a mixed reputation back in South Carolina; for a few he was a dedicated Secessionist, for many a confirmed Unionist, and for some a practical Cooperationist. Though this author largely agrees with those scholars who have evaluated Hammond's Senate career as that of a cautious but committed Secessionist, a reconsideration of Hammond's exact political behavior from 1857 through 1860 should place his motives and his indecisiveness into clearer perspective.[7]

Hammond went to Washington early in 1858 as a committed Southern consolidationist, determined that a unified South could rule the Union or "send it to the devil." Though he immediately developed a distaste for the poor quality of the Southern leaders whom he found in Washington, Hammond realized that he had to overcome a personal reputation as a radical as well as to reform the radical image of his own state before he could hope for a united South.[8] To head off any radical movement in South Carolina, he became involved in a scheme to purchase the Rhett-owned *Charleston Mercury*. This scheme, which never succeeded, nevertheless gave Hammond an opportunity to advise young radicals in Congress such as William Porcher Miles and helped to moderate the radical posture of both Miles and the Rhett family.[9] Hammond voted for the Lecompton Constitution, which would have admitted Kansas as a slave state, and he spoke against Stephen A. Douglas's squatter sovereignty program in hopes of defusing a volatile issue that divided Democratic leaders in Congress.

In his "Mud-Sill" speech, which claimed the need for a servant class to free the leaders to pursue their governmental duties and the ordinary whites to have better jobs, Hammond angered many Northerners. At the same time, he favored recommittal of the entire Kansas bill in order to calm those Southern congressmen who had begun to talk of civil war because of the territorial issue. For doing this, Hammond gained the respect of many Northern Democrats and other moderates. Making a direct pitch for Southern harmony, Hammond boasted that the South already controlled the Mississippi River, and he affirmed that common economic and social institutions united and prepared the South to control the economic direction of the Union.[10]

Some Southerners seemed to understand that Hammond was advocating moderation in order to give the rest of the South an opportunity to solidify, but most South Carolinians grew incensed over his views and demanded an explanation for his apparent Unionist behavior. Back home at Beech Island, in the summer of 1858, Hammond claimed that the Kansas climate could hardly tolerate slave labor and that unplanned expansion negated the more important issue of unifying the Southern people. He compounded his felony by discounting the Republican party as a threat to the South at that time.[11] His friends felt that he had erred on the side of Unionism, and they advised him to clarify his views with another public appearance. Speaking at Barnwell Courthouse in October, Hammond took the offense against those who feared attachment to national parties as he condemned all local politicians whose desire for personal gain divided the South. He declaimed that he had once believed that the South's only safety lay in dissolution of the Union, but he had come to feel that "we can fully sustain ourselves in the union and control its actions in all great affairs." In an attempt to conciliate the radicals, he concluded that he had always regarded the Union as a "policy rather than a principle."[12]

South Carolinians reacted with mixed emotions to their new senator. Miles alleged that even the Cooperationists had begun to doubt Hammond's veracity. Radicals such as Governor John Adams and Maxcy Gregg felt betrayed. The Unionist Benjamin F. Perry said that the senator had dealt the death blow to disunion and revolution.[13] In contrast, a handful of astute politicians discovered a pattern of behavior that led them to believe that Hammond was correct in claiming "that our fellow Southern States are not yet ready to move." When the moderate James Chesnut gained election to the Senate through Cooperationist support, the *Mercury* noted that Hammond's strategy of achieving unity and calm in South Carolina had succeeded.[14] Hammond, who hardly had cause to show confidence in Southern leadership, was advocating their cooperation, which would lead the South to secession.

Early in 1859 Hammond explained much of his practical behavior by saying that while a private man could hold extreme views, a representative man, forced to work with national politicians, had to present a moderate position "so as to maintain flexibility for future action." He had found Southern leaders ignorant, cunning "Blackguards whom the vulgar had placed in high places," who were in no position to discuss united action. Therefore, though he had always loathed national parties and had resented South Carolinians' joining any national caucus, he called for Southern politicians to work with the National Democrats. His proclamation of patriotic Democratic fervor for expansion into Central America must have sickened even his loyal supporters.[15] South Carolina's radicals schemed to keep Hammond from joining the Douglas Democrats, but there was never a reason to believe that the senator had any intention of supporting Douglas. Orr and his Democratic cronies knew this because Hammond had opposed their attempts to elect a moderate congressman from Charleston by defeating the radical anti-National Democrat William P. Miles.[16] Hammond's support for the Democratic party seemed based on his desire to use that party as an instrument for sectional unity, and it in no way signaled his capitulation to Unionism.

Upon returning home from Washington after the 1859 session, Hammond discovered that most Carolinians continued to believe him too vociferous a defender of the Union and too little concerned over the election of a Republican president. Letters published in the *Mercury* denounced his loyalty to the Democrats and questioned his value to the South.[17] In the wake of such criticism, and after learning that the fall session of the state legislature had turned into a series of meaningless debates rather than being devoted to the development of serious plans for action, a sick and tired Hammond resolved to forego the 1860 congressional session. All the same, he was a leader whose sense of duty, especially after the furor raised over the John Brown raid, forced him to reconsider and to return to the Capitol to politic for the election of a Southern Democrat as president.[18]

Hammond's public political behavior during most of 1860 should have put doubt in the minds of those who insisted upon calling him a Unionist. He worked actively against Douglas's nomination and attempted to unite Southern congressmen around the candidacy of either Robert M.T. Hunter of Virginia or John C. Breckinridge of Kentucky. Though he publicly stated that the Democratic party could serve as an instrument for uniting the South, behind the scenes Hammond instructed the South Carolina dele-

gation to the Democratic convention to leave the convention after a sizable
and unified delegation from other Southern states had resigned.[19] Unable
to attend the Charleston meeting for the election of delegates to the Richmond convention, he telegraphed the members to forsake any pretense of
cooperation with the National Democrats, and he advised Southerners to
form their own party behind Breckinridge. When the senator discovered
that most Southern congressmen still distrusted Rhett, he asked the newspaper editor to avoid any open support for Breckinridge in the *Mercury*.[20]
In his last Senate speech, countering Douglas's attempt to divide Southern
Democrats on the issue of a territorial slave code, Hammond reminded
Northerners that South Carolina's failure to secede in 1850 had resulted
in the movement for Southern cooperation.[21]

When Hammond returned home from Washington, he wanted to retire
from the political life of coercing and educating the South's leaders, but
his constituents demanded his views on pressing public issues. His request
that those who urged disunion create a positive program probably resulted
in a secret meeting at his plantation to discuss the best means of achieving
secession.[22] Most significant was Hammond's long letter in response to a
request from the state legislature for his views on secession, in which he
flatly stated that he would follow his state, "whenever she determined to
dissolve the union," though he was convinced that the election of a Black
Republican president would not result in secession. He feared that the
internal squabbling of unprincipled politicians in search of the spoils of
revolution made secession over the election of 1860 impossible. Strategi-
cally, he cautioned that the rest of the South had never forgiven South
Carolina's irresponsible radical leaders of the past, and he advised his own
state to follow rather than lead. When South Carolina's radical leaders
debated plans to disrupt the upcoming presidential inaugural in Washington, Hammond told the legislature that "I fear in the organization of a
new Government our own Demagogues at home, more than our enemies
abroad." To that end Hammond insisted that South Carolina's secessionists
meet in a Southern convention and adopt the United States Constitution
for the Confederacy without any modification. He concluded his letter by
saying that the American Revolution had required years of work by intel-
ligent leaders who had never submerged their judgments to the popular
excitement.[23] When it was finally time for action, Hammond's analysis of
the poor quality of Southern leadership had led him to believe that the
South hardly seemed prepared for secession.

Yet less than a week later, on November 11, 1860, upon hearing that
Robert Toombs of Georgia and James Chesnut had resigned from the

Senate, Hammond also resigned, perhaps in the belief that such a symbolic act would unite the South.[24] After that, Hammond refused service in the secession movement, although he did advise South Carolina's secessionists to make certain that other cotton states were planning conventions and were prepared to secede. He suggested to a delegation of Georgia radicals that Georgians meet in convention and decide for secession before South Carolina met on December 17. In a letter to the *Mercury*, he was adamant about South Carolina following the others, his practical reasoning being that his own state could not secede alone. When friends asked him to stand for election to the secession convention, he again refused.[25]

Hammond's final behavior, a combination of headstrong impulse and practical action, left many of his friends with the feeling that he had equivocated when he was most needed. For many Carolinians his actions were at best conservative; for others he was so cautious that they thought he had become a Unionist. His personal analysis of his actions revealed some confusion; without any explanation he confided to his diary that the Union was worth more than slavery, though publicly he declared that he preferred secession.[26] However, his practical political activities revealed a man who had spent his Senate career trying to unite the South, only to be frustrated by what he had considered to be faulty leadership. Hammond's continual carping about irresponsible politicians and his fears about the consequences of secession are clues to understanding his vacillation between secession and union. Perhaps a look beyond Hammond's practical behavior to his political theory and the code of service by which he lived could additionally clarify Hammond's changing loyalties.

Parallel to the contention that men like Hammond opposed secession because they were disestablished by a new political elite is the theoretical argument that Hammond's political philosophy was so conservative that he could not bear change of any kind. In another view, a scholar has asserted that Hammond's political theory was based on a desire to control the massses, so that when his class was threatened, he had no choice but to support secession. Another, after studying Hammond's proslavery writings, has concluded that Hammond was a member of the new political elite and therefore sought to please the established planters by lamenting the decline of aristocratic values.[27] Most, however, have judged Hammond a conservative theorist without carefully evaluating the relationship between government and order, leadership and duty in Hammond's philosophy of politics. A look at his political theoretical writings and speeches should give better perspective on his activities in those crucial days leading to South Carolina's secession.

Hammond considered the people the source of all power; their desires and needs formed the basis of his political philosophy. The instrument for controlling this power was ordered government. Therefore, people formed government to function as security for themselves and their property. If society created government, the history of Western politics proved that government always became too strong, thus provoking a continuous battle for balance between freedom and security. Hammond also studied the science of human nature and found that the people often lacked reason and therefore were susceptible to coercion by those who would distort the true purpose of government. Popular government, for him, required responsible leaders to guide the people to their true interests.[28] In other words, government was important as an instrument of order imposed by the people on their society. Their leaders were to set the standards of compromise between freedom and order.

The fact that Hammond's governing order was adapted to the social system calls for comment on the contribution of slavery to the structure of government. Hammond called slavery a cornerstone of representative government. His most succinct statement of the role of slavery was in his Mud-Sill speech of 1858, where he related the leaders to the menials who "constitute the very mud-sill of society and of political government." The menials were called slaves, fortunately black and part of an "inferior" race. Every freeman was considered an aristocrat, and the dichotomy provided for the best organization of society. In Hammond's system, then, slaves had no political influence, nor did their existence determine the structure of government. Rather they freed whites to recognize their political interests in preserving a stable and well-ordered government.[29]

If slavery in Hammond's theoretical system freed whites to compete for office, this did not imply a democracy of leadership. Throughout most of his life Hammond believed in an aristocracy of political leadership, based on intellect and ability rather than on wealth and status. His old college professor, Thomas Cooper, had taught him that throughout history, intelligence and aptitude made harmony in leadership, and Calhoun's dedicated and brilliant public service seemed to epitomize the essence of high-quality leadership. Hammond's system allowed for the self-made man of talent, and he prided himself on recognizing that in a world of opportunity, knowledge was king.[30] With the death of Calhoun and the subsequent scramble for political gain, Hammond grew pessimistic about the quality of the rising leadership class. He was most disturbed that members of established planter-aristocratic families, as they felt competition from the intellectual leaders, relied on fawning and demagoguery in order to gain political power.[31] His reputation as a conservative probably stems from the fact that at times he faulted republican institutions for succumbing to such leaders. Given the ideal characteristics of officeholders for his system of government, is it any wonder that Hammond became fearful of faulty leadership in the late 1850s?

Hammond found fault with the leaders, but did he, as most scholars who have looked at his actions during the secession movement believe, blame the ignorant masses for the general decline of quality? He had always believed in a natural variety of classes based on ability, but he had also considered universal suffrage "a necessary appendage to a Republican system" of government. As a student of history, he recognized that the previous two centuries had brought the great middle class to a knowledge of its rights and hopefully of its duties.[32] He quibbled over how far the popular vote should be extended, but in most cases he believed that the people, when properly led, made correct decisions. During his term as governor, in line with his theory that government should provide for the security of its constituents, Hammond offered a comprehensive reform for the state's educational system. His plan was to provide a thorough education for every child, rich or poor, who possessed energy and worth. As one who had risen from the ranks, he wished to keep those ranks open. He also believed that an educated electorate was in a better position to elect the ablest candidates.[33] Although he finally faulted popular pressure for undermining the political leverage of qualified leaders, he blamed irresponsible politicians for using the people.

The question of leadership quality certainly affected Hammond's fear of what the political revolution (for so he regarded rapid change in government) of secession would do to the South. While constructing his own argument for secession, he had always felt that the South's government and people were steady in principle and reluctant to change. His own firsthand observations of the results of the French Revolution left him with the feeling that no state had much to gain from anarchy and revolution. Only, he rationalized, when the enemy attempted to upset the governmental system by showing utter disregard for principles of political justice would he condone secession. But the movement that was growing in the South during the 1850s was ill-conceived, leaderless, and prone to disrupt social order. In short, it was revolutionary and hardly secessionist.[34] In 1860 the fear of failed revolutions caught up to Hammond, and if the theory of an ordered governmental system had entirely determined Hammond's code of behavior, he would never have been able to support secession.

There was one essential ingredient in Hammond's political code that temporarily forced him to allay his trepidations over change and largely explains his resignation from the Senate. His concept of the leaders as servants of the state and of the people made Hammond overcome his fears of the poor leadership that had caused such damage and a changed governmental system. Simply, Hammond believed that a statesman's foremost responsibility was to guide and also to respond to the will of his constituents. Years earlier he had explained a foolish duel as part of the painful need to force an elected official to assume his duty. Time and again, despite personal anxieties and his desire to retire to his study, Hammond had accepted public office. He had even served in the United States Senate in spite of severe illness and family misgivings.[35] In 1860 Hammond's code left him no choice but to follow his state, because he could never default on that public trust.

James Henry Hammond was a practical politician who believed in his own political phlosophy. He was hardly class-motivated, nor was he fearful of loss of personal political status in any conventional sense. He believed in an aristocracy of ability and integrity, of leaders being duty-bound to serve their government and the people. His reverence for the past was hardly based on the self-deception of one who revered a mythical romantic aristocracy. He studied past political leaders because they, and especially those of eighteenth-century America, set a standard for behavior, intelligence, and obligation. Hammond's final indecisiveness resulted from his acquaintance with the flawed leaders of the secession movement, whom he had found woefully unqualified to organize the South and to achieve its goal. History had taught him that precipitant revolution produced political chaos. He was also uncertain whether he wanted to live in a governmental system controlled by an ignorant, ambitious, demagogic aristocracy. Certainly he was too critical of the secession leaders, but he was hardly motivated by love of the Union. Unless one regards vacillation as action, Hammond's (and perhaps many other so-called Unionist planters') inability and unwillingness to influence the secessionist leaders deserves to rank as one of the tragic events of the Old South.[36]

As his state rushed headlong to secede from the Union, Hammond remained in seclusion. Uninvited to bring his experience and talent for governance to Montgomery to assist in forming the new Southern Confederacy, before long the aging leader would question the powers of that government. When Confederate government authorities, men for whom he had little respect, asked him to plant corn rather than cotton, the old conservative refused.[37] In the face of a hungry army of the Confederacy,

Hammond had stood on his own kind of principle. Indeed, from the time of the secession crisis Hammond belonged to the group of planter leaders who claimed out of duty to be part of the Confederacy, but who never really had faith in it. He was one of the wealthy conservative planters who opposed the Confederacy.

Until the day he died, despite evidence to the contrary, Hammond maintained that he supported the Confederacy. In late 1861 Hammond traveled to Richmond, where, along with a number of other South Carolina leaders, he attempted to persuade government authorities to use cotton as the basis of Confederate credit. Furious when refused, Hammond went into opposition. He joined a group headed by Congressman William W. Boyce to oppose the policies of President Jefferson Davis. Hammond even caucused with Senator Louis T. Wigfall, a Davis opponent, over how to resist the Confederate government's plans to confiscate food crops to feed the army. Certainly the old man had turned against the government, as he was obsessed with its inefficiency and oppressive behavior. But his son Edward Spann, in a letter to his brother of November 13, 1864, after their father's death, explained that Hammond had died of a broken heart as "he seemed to succumb at the fall of Atlanta." Edward went on, "he never lost confidence in the high qualities of the people, and the resources of the South."[38] One wonders if Edward's revision of the wartime activities of his father failed to acknowledge that Hammond was a man too conservative to be a Confederate.

2

Fears for the Future: A Consideration of Reluctant Confederates' Arguments against Secession, the Confederacy, and Civil War

A number of historians who study the Civil War era belong to the so-called revisionist or repressible conflict school. Their concentration on the events leading to the war has profoundly influenced all who have studied that momentous event. They have suggested that the war need not have been fought, that blundering leaders without real justification made a war when more able men might have avoided the wasteful bloodshed.[1] For some years the revisionist argument has receded before those who believe that slavery so divided the North and the South that war was inevitable, or that the conflict was irrepressible. But recently the repressible conflict historians have had a revival. Neorevisionist post-Vietnam historians have contested those who insist that the problem of slavery could not have been reducible to adjudication. Daniel Crofts, the most thoughtful of the neo-revisionists, has written the well-researched and generally convincing *Reluctant Confederates*. In that book, actually two books in one, Crofts focuses on Northerner William H. Seward's struggles to ameliorate the secession crisis, and on the Upper South Unionists who opposed secession but joined the Confederacy after Abraham Lincoln called for troops to put down insurrection.[2] In that section of his work in which he studies the antisecessionist Upper South Unionists, Crofts makes a contribution to those who believe that conflict repressible.

Crofts has, however, overlooked prewar events crucial to irrepressible conflict historians, events that led some of those reluctant leaders to turn against the Confederacy during the war. Because of his focus on Upper South antisecessionist plans to bring the Lower South back into the Union and on Lincoln's failure to assist them, Crofts generally ignores why Southern Unionists opposed secession and the new Confederacy. Only briefly in chapter 6 does he explore the Unionists' hostility to the secession movement.[3] The Lower South's effect on the Upper South's defense of slave society, and how the crises of secession and of the formation of a new nation made the Upper South worry about slavery's future, are left out almost entirely. Yet those tensions between and within the conflicting slaveholding regions surely reveal the irrepressibility of the internal sectional (as well as the national) conflict and suggest problems that Confederates would have had in working together.

Crofts' important book concludes before the Upper South ex-Unionists marched off to war or to government office. The wartime careers of those peacetime leaders disclose a group of men who remained confused about what actions to take to save the way of life for which they had reluctantly joined the Confederacy. In fact, many of Crofts' ex-Unionist leaders betrayed or undermined the Confederate cause one way or another.[4] Why this was so relates to the reasons they opposed the Confederacy in the first place.

The wartime behavior of ex-Unionist leaders in the Lower South, those who claimed fealty to the cause, is similar to that of their Upper South counterparts. A small number of Lower South antisecessionists, often ones in important places with numerous friends and followers, insisted on their loyalty but actually harmed the Confederacy. Examples from Florida and Georgia of leaders who rejected the Confederacy are useful. Former Florida governor and antisecessionist Richard K. Call offered his services to his state's war leaders, only to be turned down because they did not trust him. Call gave no more of his considerable talent to the cause. Another former longtime national congressman and antisecessionist, Georgia's Alexander Stephens, also turned his back on the government in Richmond and rarely performed any duties of his office as Confederate vice president. Instead, he lived much of the war at home intriguing with his brother and with Governor Joseph E. Brown of Georgia to resist Confederate national government encroachment on his home state's rights. Some of Stephens's closest antisecessionist allies, including Hiram P. Bell and Herschel V. Johnson, also harmed the Confederacy. Johnson served in the Confederate Congress, where he opposed all wartime financial measures and some military initiatives, asserting that those war needs injured the people back home. Bell entered the Confederate House of Representatives in 1863 and kept a journal, which he eventually published. In his marvelous journal, Bell explained why he opposed wartime policies, especially the laws of impressment, and why he supported a peace movement.[5]

Alabama, too, produced a number of ex-Unionists who turned against the Confederacy. Former Whig congressman and author William R. Smith of Alabama eventually became an opponent of the Confederate government. He had opposed Alabama's secession and questioned the Confederate constitution. Yet he held the rank of colonel in the Alabama state militia, served in western Virginia, and became a member of both permanent Confederate congresses. In congress he voted against much of the administration's wartime policies, including a vigorous dissent over the use of armed slaves for military service. His political play, the *Royal Ape*, analyzed elsewhere in this book, was an antiadministration work of art. He rejected accusations in Confederate Congress that his peace initiative undermined the cause, and in January 1865 he resigned from the Congress. Smith's prewar Alabama Unionist friends, Robert Jemison, Jr., and ex–supreme court justice John A. Campbell, also turned against a Confederacy they believed was rotting from within. A former Whig congressman, Jemison entered the Confederate Senate in 1863 as a peace candidate. Jemison and Smith, who talked often, supported a negotiated honorable peace. Like Smith, Jemison insisted that government taxation and confiscation were punitive measures against private citizens. Alabamians Smith, Jemison, and eventually Campbell belonged to that small but vociferous group of political leaders who regarded the president as incompetent and demanded his removal. In June 1864, Jemison left for Alabama, never to return to Richmond, and in effect became a Confederate dropout. Another prewar Alabama Unionist, former Democratic congressman Williamson R.R. Cobb, gained election to the second Confederate Congress, only to be expelled for Unionist activities even before he took office.[6]

The wartime actions of the Lower South's reluctant Confederates compare with those of leaders from the Upper South, specifically those from Virginia, North Carolina, and Tennessee. Upper South ex-Unionists, too, espoused loyalty to the Confederate cause during the war, but some did not practice it. For example, Tennessee's prewar Unionist congressman Robert Hatton joined the Confederate army, served ably, and rose to the rank of brigadier general, but he soon wanted out of the army altogether. His death in May 1862 in Virginia, so far from home, remains a tragic moment of the misplaced loyalty of a man who believed that the Confederacy had done much damage to the people of Tennessee.[7]

Other Tennesseans who were prewar Unionists, such as former congressmen Meredith Gentry and James H. Thomas, went into the provisional Confederate Congress and voted against many war measures. Both of them refused election to subsequent congresses and opted to drop out; they gave no further support to the Confederacy. The loss of their talents, especially their strong voices back home, was indeed great. Yet another Tennessee Unionist, the influential Episcopal Bishop James H. Otey, also early on endorsed the Confederate war effort. He preached to the troops and assisted many poor people in his state. But before he died in 1863, Otey regarded the cause as futile, opposed continuation of the conflict, and supported Tennessee's return to the Union.[8]

North Carolina's contingent of former Unionist leaders who joined the Confederacy deservedly have received closer study than any other equivocal Confederates. Antisecessionist and former Whig federal congressman Zebulon B. Vance ably served in the Confederate army and as his state's wartime governor. But as governor Vance opposed the use of North Carolina troops in Virginia, refused to help finance the war with state taxes, and by 1864 supported a separate North Carolina peace movement. Fellow Unionist Whig and later committed Confederate, *Raleigh Standard* editor William W. Holden, spoke out against Confederate war policies, damned the president's aggressive anti–North Carolina comments, and early called for a Southern peace convention to bring the Confederacy back into the Union, all the while espousing loyalty to the cause. Holden and Vance's sometime ally, the former peace Democrat and state leader, Bedford Brown, also initially supported the war. But by 1862 he advocated peace, if necessary even a separate peace for North Carolina.[9]

Three other influential North Carolina ex-Unionists joined the war effort and became reluctant wartime Confederates. Former Whig congressman John Gilmer had been a famous prewar Unionist, so well known that President Abraham Lincoln had considered him for the cabinet. During the war Gilmer served in the second Confederate Congress. Like other anti–central government leaders, he resisted outside interference in the state's defense of its citizens. He supported the Hampton Roads peace initiative. In February 1865 the Virginia wartime Unionist John Minor Botts went to Washington at Gilmer's behest to reopen peace negotiations. Likewise, the prewar Unionist leader, Whig congressman and former governor William A. Graham, claimed to ably serve the Confederacy in the second Congress. But Graham spoke against the oath of loyalty for all Confederate leaders and insisted that the oath violated individual rights important to the defense of the Southern way of life. In the second Congress he opposed all the president's legislative programs, called Davis a despot, and with others demanded that the president resign. He refused to vote to arm the slaves and insisted that such a vote undermined what Southern people had been fighting to protect. Graham became a peace advocate and, in March 1865, he supported North Carolina's separate negotiations for reconstruction. Perhaps no North Carolina ex-Unionist leader revealed the contradictory behavior of Confederates more than Episcopal Bishop Thomas Atkinson, once a leading Southern rights advocate. Atkinson too sought an early peace. As soon as the war had ended, he led the unseemly hurried movement to bring his church back into communion with its northern branch.[10]

Even though they lived in a state constantly under Federal siege, many of the former Unionist leaders from Virginia nevertheless became reluctant Confederates during the war. One, former congressman Samuel M. Moore of Rockland, served for a time in the army. But he accomplished little there and soon retired to private life. Norfolk ex-Unionist John Millson returned home and refused to assist the Confederacy in his beleagured section of the state. Prewar Unionist John Brown Baldwin supported the Confederate cause and became inspector general of Virginia state volunteers and a colonel in the army. Baldwin also served in both Confederate Congresses. But there he opposed impressment and insisted that his Valley constituents bore an unequal burden of the war effort. He resisted all attempts to suspend the writ of habeas corpus and opposed what he called the excessive powers of central government. Another ex-Unionist who aided the Confederacy, the former United States senator, diplomat, and James Madison biographer William Cabell Rives, at first was rejected for membership in the Confederate Congress, despite his political skills, because of his Unionist proclivities. The old, ill, and often disappointed leader hoped to drop out of public life. He did gain election to Congress in 1863, but he seldom attended, yet he insisted he supported President Davis. Nevertheless, in 1864 Rives endorsed peace and attempted to persuade the president to hold the Hampton Roads peace meeting. Rives also openly resisted any attempt to arm the slaves, because he knew slave soldiers would become freemen. Defeated and crestfallen, in March 1865 that symbol of Virginia's fidelity to the cause resigned from the Confederate congress.[11]

Most of the leaders Crofts studied, as well as a number of the Lower South Unionists, then, supported the Confederacy after Lincoln called for troops. Many of them had insisted, even when they appeared to desert the cause, that they remained Confederates. Still, their votes against government war policies were damaging. Others fomented antigovernment sentiment back home, or at least encouraged their people to resist the war effort, doing further damage to the cause. A number of those wartime congressional, state, and federal government antisecessionist leaders supported various peace initiatives. Of course, desire for peace as the Confederacy began to crumble may have been true devotion to their region, or a means to salvage that for which they had fought and sacrificed.

Why had these ex-Unionists become such fragile or reluctant wartime Confederates? Perhaps what they had in common in their prewar careers explains their wartime behavior. Most, but not all, had been Whig nationalists. In their home states, at least those from the Upper South, some semblance of a two-party system allowed for an organized antisecession movement on the eve of the secession crisis.[12] Many of them also supported John Bell or Stephen A. Douglas in the presidential canvas. But John Gilmer and a number of others had been Democrats. Most of them had business ties to a new trade, transportation, and factory South, as well as to their Northern counterparts. But others did not. Most, though not all, owned slaves. Then, too, a number of them came from parts of their states with declining slave numbers, and their constituents did not share their same commitment to slavery. Enough differences existed among the South's Unionist leaders to negate any prewar career or interest patterns as explanations for their opposition to secession, let alone their anti-Confederate behavior during the war.

Perhaps their reasons for prewar Unionism and hostility to forming the Confederacy explains their wartime behavior. Most of them had had years of public service and a real following back home who listened to them. Those who remained in the federal Congress up until their states seceded often had spoken out and then sent home their views in pamphlet form. Those who served in their state's conventions, and those who gained election to the Montgomery convention and created the new government, recorded their views and shared them with their fellow leaders and the people. Therefore, in correspondence, in speeches, and in pamphlets they left a clear record of their prewar views, a record to explain their wartime behavior.

I say clear, but often those leaders were purposefully unclear. They were, after all, political animals with careers at stake. They had to weigh their words quite carefully if they wanted to influence an often hostile audience. In debate, in correspondence, and to the press they appeared circumspect. Opposition to Southern secession they advocated, to be sure, but no fondness for Northern antislavery forces marked their discourse. No one reading their words about the North would believe the sectional conflict repressible. No one listening to them talk about divisions within the slave states would believe that internal conflict repressible during the war. Their opinions, views, and values as Southern Unionists, what they had to say about the crisis and the actions of their fellow slave state leaders, sometimes purposely vague or circumspect, often similar in tone and content, when taken together, tell why those reluctant Confederates turned on the Confederacy.

Some of those prewar Unionist leaders from the Lower South who eventually opposed the Confederacy reacted adversely to their state's secession movement and to the formation of the Confederacy. Florida's Richard K. Call stands out as a thoughtful opponent of his state's secessionists. In a remarkably brave, widely circulated letter to a Northern friend, John S. Littel, Call explained why he rejected secession.[13] Written in February 1861, from his home on Lake Jackson, Call's letter is a lament on the dismemberment of his nation. All the pathos of former national glory, surely a stock story to set a mood, is summoned as Washington, Franklin, and Madison's patriotism are invoked to upbraid the Southern rebellion. Their history in a unified nation that overcame despotic Europe linked the American people, he said. The greatness of republican government and an economically successful people, he claimed, had depended on slave society. Call said that the entire country should unite in defense of Southern slavery because all benefited from it. Of course, he attacked Northerners for undermining slavery and provoking such reaction against them in the Lower South. But Call also demanded that Lower South secessionists compromise with the North.

What had caused this loss of support for a united nation and what would be the results for the defense of slavery, Call asked? He answered that mad, rash, unreflective leaders, a new generation of men, had acted without thinking of the consequences for their region. The frustrated old man obviously wished to put brakes on those demagogic actions. "Oh, that I had the genius to lead," he wrote his friend. He next asked what those radical, unthinking leaders had created. Chaos! he exclaimed. Some secessionists even wanted to reopen the slave trade. Call opposed this action as dangerous to civil order. Civil order certainly was at stake, for lawless radicals had forced a crisis. To protect slavery, they had launched a "calamitous, desolating, ruinous" confrontation that surely would lead to civil war. Civil war, far from protecting slave society, would create situations ripe for slave rebellion. For Call, slavery would be the victim of those crazed demagogues. Of course, he believed disunion a last resort if

the sections could not settle their differences. Nevertheless, he had predicted the results of disunion and he did not like them. No wonder that
confused former leader proved useless to the Confederate war effort.

As Call acknowledged his fears for slavery in disunion, so too did Alexander H. Stephens in his pivotal November 1860 Unionist speech before
the Georgia legislature. Stephens's fellow Unionists, including his ally Herschel V. Johnson, had persuaded him to speak to that body in opposition
to the secessionist leadership of Robert Toombs, Howell Cobb, and Governor Joseph E. Brown. Speak he did, and splendidly prepared he was for
all the personal attacks on his loyalty. Combinations of patriotism and
logic, hopes and fears, stirred in Stephens qualities of logic and reason as
he commented on the consequences of calling a convention in that climate
of hatred and resentment.[14]

That famous Georgia leader began with the admonition, lest anyone
doubt his loyalty to Georgia, that he planned to speak about rights, interests, honor, and also peace. Stephens then compared the dictatorial actions
of mediocre revolutionaries, who wanted to secede and make a new government, with a federal system that was too powerful to allow the next
president, Abraham Lincoln, to take control of events. The government of
the United States, created by America's brilliant forefathers to protect the
interests of the people, had made Georgians prosperous, this old Whig
advised. Evil and faulty leadership, he claimed, emerged out of a surfeit
of unorganized and chaotic liberty. Indeed, he went on, he feared the
unwise, the yielding to passion, because the many secessionists "at no
distant day [will] commence cutting one another's throats." He then attacked the members of the legislature who wanted to call a state convention. Instead, Stephens argued that Georgia secessionists should call for a
southernwide convention, but they resisted, uncertain of their powers.
Without "united cooperation" of all the southern states, that wise leader
concluded, each slave state would be vulnerable to opponents.

Stephens also discussed what he expected to be the results of secession.
He feared hasty action would exacerbate the differences among the slave
states. He demanded wisdom, justice, and moderation, lest hotheads so
divide the slave states that they destroy what was of most value to them.
The results of this division would be border war, as the cautious Upper
South slave states would never join a radical secessionst movement. Once
Georgia and other Lower South states had forced civil war, that old politician insisted, they would then fall out among themselves. "The greatest
curse," therefore, "that can befall a free people is civil war." Civil wars
would destroy the South and its way of life, he said. No wonder, when

asked later to speak before the Georgia secession convention, a disgruntled Stephens refused.

Of course, like so many other antisecessionists, Stephens eventually supported his state. He went as a delegate to the Montgomery convention. But there he worried over the weakness and divisiveness in the proposed Confederate States constitution. Some of those who chose him as vice president expected him to lead in the movement to reconstruct the Union, but he proved a temporary disappointment to them. Back home in Georgia, he delivered an argument for a permanent Confederacy and explained why the people were willing to fight a civil war.[15] Indeed, the "cornerstone speech," so called, on the surface depicted a people of patriotic solidarity and firm interests. In that speech Stephens seemed almost frantic to bring the Upper South into the Confederacy. Without those states, he knew the Confederacy would not have the necessary forces to defend itself. Without a united Southern front in defense of slavery, slavery itself was threatened. That was why he called the Confederate constitution conservative and welcoming to Upper South slave states. That was why he had promised the upper South that the Confederate government never would interfere with the rights of the individual states. But what if the new government did? In that speech, Stephens also told Southerners there would be no war and that a successful Confederate government would protect its people. Contained in those words were seeds of resentment that soon made him oppose what he had helped to construct.

In other parts of the Lower South, especially in the Gulf Coast states, a few Unionists also spoke out on what worried them about secession. United States Supreme Court justice John A. Campbell from Alabama told friends at home that those Southerners who favored insurrection had failed to convince conservative businessmen and planters there that their interests would be protected. To Jefferson Davis he wrote that the only way for slavery to survive was if the Union could be reconstructed along the basis of the slave protection clause of the Confederate constitution. No wonder some Confederate leaders were skeptical about his loyalty and opposed his appointment to the War Department. Likewise, Alabama congressman W.R.W. Cobb, later to be expelled from the Confederate congress, spoke in Washington about the future as he prepared to resign and go home to his fate. He told his constituents that their rights could best be protected by the Federal government and not in a newly constructed, fragile nation. Besides, untrained, weak, corrupt, and selfish Southern politicians would never be able to protect popular rights or society's interests. In Mississippi, the Rev. G.H. Martin preached about why he feared secession, yet said he opposed using the pulpit for political speechmaking. He began with a prayer in which he called on all in authority to keep peace. Listen to God, the uniter, he said, and do not break up a successful and protective government. Over the upcoming Mississippi secession convention he prayed for wisdom, moderation, and prudence. He warned that an untested country would have few funds for houses of faith, and thus could hardly expect assistance from the churches. In short, for Rev. Martin, war meant the institutions that held society together, including the churches, would be broken and unable to help in the effort to defend their country. No wonder he asked that his parishioners pray to God to sustain the union and avoid civil war.[16]

Another voice of Unionism, the novelist, chronicler, and political leader William R. Smith of Tuscaloosa, Alabama, resisted the secession of his state and the formation of a new nation. Smith had begun his public career as a Whig and then turned Democrat and served in the United States Congress during the 1850s, where he observed the increasingly belligerent and uncompromising attitude of fellow Southerners. He sought to head off sectional divisions, and he used his most important novel, *As It Is*, published in 1860, to portray derisively those who wanted to break up the Union. In Alabama Smith campaigned with Robert Jemison, Jr., for election to the secession convention as Unionists. They published a campaign leaflet about their intentions. As a delegate to the convention, Smith spoke forcefully to preserve the Union, and he discussed the consequences of secession for Southern society. Smith also took notes on the convention's proceedings and maintained an almost daily correspondence with his wife about the politics of secession. He attended the birth of the Confederacy at Montgomery and there spoke out against what he found worrisomely divisive in the proposed Constitution. The state's secessionists invited him to edit the journal of the secession convention, published as *The History and Debates of the Convention of the People of Alabama*, which gave him additional opportunity to address his concerns. In that memoir and in his other writings, perhaps more keenly than any other Lower South Unionist, William R. Smith revealed what he believed wrong with secession and the Confederacy.

In *As It Is*, Smith's mid-nineteenth-century version of *Tristram Shandy*, he wrote of the problems of flawed leadership among those prepared to destroy the Union. Weak talent, political corruption, and demagogues contest the young, brilliant man of letters and statesman, the protagonist Jack Sterling—Smith himself no doubt—who fights to save the Union. Jack's major adversary is the corrupt congressman Polydorous Blunderbuss, a blowhard and inveterate gambler who paid his debts in political favors, thus rendering him useless to the proponents of sectional compromise in those trying, contentious days. Another caricature is Mr. Clodhead; his name says it all, a Northerner who sought the speakership of the house, and when elected, was incapable of holding radical Southern Democrats in check. It is the failed politico, but perceptive Southern congressman, Ponderous Pustleponch, who grasps the real dangers to the Union from partisan politics and the poor quality of leadership. Unless something is done to unite Northern and Southern conservatives, Pustleponch said, "we shall be severed into fragments." "And what would we be without the Union?" he exclaimed. "A poor benighted people; worse than the Grecians in their worst degradation! Greece united was the scourge of tyrants, the dread of Persia. Greece divided, was the toy of demagogues, the sport of ambition, . . . the grave of liberty." Summing up the political chaos, Smith's surrogate Jack Sterling proclaimed that poor leadership would destroy his beloved South.[17]

In their joint circular letter, Smith and his ally Robert Jemison, later a Confederate senator and a peace advocate, elaborated on the antisecessionist themes in *As It Is* and went further. To their constituents they described their fears that Alabama would never be able to defend itself outside the Union. Because the state was broke and unable if part of a separate nation to protect insolvent banks, private money would flee. The result, they said, would be internal warfare, as many in the state would never reconcile themselves to business chaos. That meant Alabamians would divide just when they needed to protect themselves. (Of course, that very internal financial chaos befell Alabamians during the Civil War.) Smith and Jemison predicted a similar plight for all of the Confederacy. Secession would, they said, destroy the United States, the only true protector of the South's values, economy, and people. A separate Confederacy, understaffed and underfunded, then, would hasten the demise of all that Southerners cherished.[18]

The convention itself, a chapter in "the life of liberty," turned into a nightmare for the Unionist Smith. The convention's poor treatment of the state's Unionist minority meant all recent settlers in Alabama faced a bleak future, and he believed this to be a harbinger of continuous internal division. That is why Smith spoke eloquently in support of naturalizing loyal immigrants. In addition, the majority opposed popular ratification of secession, thus antagonizing the minority further. Both Jemison and Smith argued that after the vote to secede a plebiscite should be held to ratify secession. "Lodge it in the hearts of the people," said Smith, or face uncontrollable dissensions. Smith also worried that the new Confederacy divided the people, yet expected to make new allies. Over secessionists' claims that England would join them in war, he exploded, "How does one trust the abolitionist English?" For Smith, the Confederacy would have to negotiate emancipation if it aligned with England.[19] These issues of Southern unity and new allies were of great importance to this Unionist, who nevertheless went along with the majority in his state.

The new secessionist also found much to worry about in Montgomery that late winter of 1861. Again, Smith wanted the leaders to persuade the public to support the new government. He advocated sending the Confederate constitution to the people of the slave states for ratification. Smith also wondered whether parts of the Constitution were unfriendly to potential allies. Those who wanted an amendment to reopen the slave trade he believed had offended the Upper South. Smith wrote angrily to his wife about those clumsy actions. Thus, while present at the formation of the new nation, he worried again whether the South had enough leaders of quality with which to defend itself. As to the new president, sadly Smith found Jefferson Davis tired, old, ailing, and lacking in confidence. Smith also feared whether courage alone could make up for the absence of powder mills and gun factories in a Confederacy certain to have to defend itself. Without the Upper South, without goods, without talent, without harmony, he predicted annihilation of the Confederacy and, along with Jemison, warned of the death of slavery itself.[20]

Editing *The History and Debates of the Convention of the People of Alabama* gave Smith additional opportunity to address his concerns for the new Confederacy. In that book he "hoped to lift the veil of the uncertain future." But Smith also trumpeted, as only a worried Unionist could have done, the minority who "rose to the heights of moral sublimity as they surrendered their long cherished opinions for the sake of unity at home." His fellow Unionists, Smith wrote, made no "effort to disguise" their worries and fears as "the speeches on this occasion were uttered in husky tones, and in the midst of emotions that could not be suppressed."[21] Smith no doubt spoke out about that group of Confederate leaders who soon would go into opposition, because he feared the new government's inability to defend and protect the interests and values of the Southern people.

Upper South antisecessionists joined Smith and the others from the Lower South in their worries for society's future, because of the poor planning of mediocre personnel in the secession movements and at the Montgomery convention. They skillfully used Lower South Unionists' analysis of events in the cotton states to resist the secession movements in their own states. In addition to the fears that Lower South antisecessionists had, Upper South Unionists added their own worries that the new Confederacy planned to exploit their economy and control them and neglect the needs and interests of their region.

Few of them projected more graphically the results of secession and the formation of the Confederacy for the Upper South than congressman Robert Hatton, who tragically became a victim himself as the Civil War engulfed his beloved Tennessee and he was killed. From Washington and on the hustings back home Hatton spoke frankly to his friends and constituents about how radicals, North and South, had forced a crisis that had dragged the border states into the conflct. He singled out the Northern personal-liberty laws and Republicans' failure to address those insults to slave society's pride. If Hatton faulted the North for creating sectional tensions, he also accused friends in South Carolina of acting "most precipitately." Hatton said the Lower South's incautious leaders were bound to make their own people suffer. "Hearty destruction" of the national government was the fault of both sides, and both would be hurt. The future Confederate general also insisted that secession meant civil war. War for the Upper South, if it joined the cotton states, created an exposed frontier sure to bear the brunt of any confrontation with the North. For him, civil war meant youth would die, cities burn, fields be lost, and throughout the land would be heard "weeping widows and wailing of their children."[22]

What had brought the slave states to the brink of disaster? Hatton asked. He answered that to protect slaveowners' honor, radicals in South Carolina had put all slave society in danger. Hatton said that the Lower South's inept leaders threatened the Upper South's slave economy. Lower South leaders wanted to reopen the slave trade, which would lower the price of slaves in the Upper South. In addition, Lower South free-traders raised revenue through direct state and Confederate government taxation, but the protection-oriented Upper South regarded taxation as destructive to its economy. Already, he said, reckless secessionists had reduced the value of Upper South property. Even worse, those Lower South secessionists used fears for the future of slavery to coerce and bully the border slave states into joining them.

Hatton's frustrations with secessionists' threats spilled over into worry that the new Confederacy would harm slavery. Especially were the border states' slave economies potential losers in the secessionist cause. Of course, secession had already devalued slave property. Worse, a mobile slave population would rapidly flee the Upper South to freedom, and Northerners would entice them to do so. Who will stop the John Browns from coming into the slave states now? asked Hatton. Other fears for the future of slavery were that the West would be lost as a safety valve for slavery's expansion from the Upper South, as the new Confederacy "shamefully surrendered all the territories to the North." Convinced that the cotton South planned to expand into Latin and South America and desert the Upper South, Hatton said there would be no room for his people to grow. He spoke of the folly in the policy of negotiating with anti-slave England to expand southward. Indeed, Hatton insisted, similarly to a number of antisecessionists from the lower South, that Confederate policies would lead to the death of slavery.[23]

Another Tennessee antisecessionist affirmed many of Hatton's fears. Rt. Rev. James Hervey Otey, Episcopal bishop of Tennessee, added his own views of the Lower South's folly. Otey, who eventually supported his friend Bishop Leonidas Polk's joining the Confederate army, nevertheless had serious problems with radical clergy. He told many friends that some clergy, the "false teachers," had helped to incite irrational mob violence. That violence, for Otey, created a climate of radical and unreasonable behavior. The result would be a broken Union, and a Southern society unable to perpetuate its great material succcess. The bishop also seized on what he believed was a fatal flaw in the new Confederacy. False and mediocre leaders or prophets were to become the future leaders, and those men could not protect the Southern way of life.[24]

If Tennesseans opposed Lower South secessionists, so too did North Carolinians. Both in Congress and at home Unionist leaders rejected a state convention for fear of secession. In early 1861, ex-Whig congressman Zebulon B. Vance, later to become governor of his wartime state, in a letter to his constituents excoriated both the Northern abolitionists and South Carolina's plot to destroy the nation. He demanded, obligatorily, guarantees from the Republican party to protect slavery if North Carolina was to remain in the Union. But he also scorned an extravagant and hasty South Carolina. To his constitutents he said that South Carolina and its cotton state confederates had made no plans to protect slavery in the Upper South. Like Tennessee and other border compatriots, Vance believed that a separate nation encouraged North Carolina slaves to escape to the North. He also was convinced that the West would be lost as a place for the Upper South to send slaves. Like Hatton and others, Vance was certain South Carolina had designs on Mexico, which meant the Upper South would have to fight in that foreign land. Then Vance launched into his fears for North Carolina business, as he insisted that South Carolinians had already begun to abuse the taxing power. Would that tax, he wondered, eventually affect slave prices in the Upper South? "Think of that, farmers of North Carolina," its future governor said, "when you hear some talk flippantly, of a dissolution of the Union as a blessing greatly to be *coveted.*"[25]

Another North Carolinian who understood that "coveted" blessing to be a curse was the state's Episcopal bishop, Thomas Atkinson. Soon to accept secession, and later to become a reunionist, Atkinson spoke often in those harrowing days before war started of the costs of joining the Lower South in a separate Union. In a sermon, *On the Causes of Our National Troubles,* delivered in January 1861, he warned that "family hatred is the most vehement of all hatred, and civil war is the most cruel of wars." Because of an anticipated wilful destruction of people's lives, the otherwise pastoral cleric cursed the Lower South for its abuse of authority. He concluded that sermon with another warning to his people if war ensued. Loss of the legal structure and loss of civil authority, he predicted, would follow revolutionary secession.[26]

Atkinson's friend and fellow Unionist, Congressman John A. Gilmer, repeated those fears in his own argument against secession. Gilmer spoke about his worries in a January 1861 speech in Congress that he then circulated widely among his constituents.[27] According to this wise and conservative lawmaker, the Lower South had too many extremists, and those deranged leaders would lead a southern Confederacy to chaos. He insisted a conspiracy was afoot among deluded and ambitious North Carolina politicians to align with those Lower South radicals. When friends said to him that only a separate Confederacy could reconstruct the Union, he called them mad, and questioned how they could lead such a thoughtless movement. Gilmer himself became a wartime reconstructionist, but that was only after he had employed his considerable talents to assist leaders he knew, and had confirmed, were incompetent.

This learned and able political leader embellished his attack on mediocre leaders with particularly fretful comments about cotton South economic activities in the event of civil war. The old-line Whig questioned the very interests of the agrarian cotton states as being removed from those of the more capitalistic Upper South. First, he was certain that war meant the disruption of the Upper South's trade with the North and Europe. All shipping on his state's coast would be blockaded, or worse, destroyed. Then, a powerful invading army would plunder and burn the growing cities and towns of the Upper South. This Northern success would arise because a poorer and weaker Lower South could provide little financial aid and no military protection for the Upper South. Then, along with economic ruin, all institutions of learning, and all churches, echoing Otey and Atkinson, that had made the Upper South powerful and peaceful, would close and wither away. Gilmer's description of what the future would hold for his people surely influenced his life as a reluctant Confederate.

Like Gilmer, ex-governor William A. Graham feared sectional confrontation. Graham's friend Bartholomew Moore said to him that if North Carolina joined the Confederacy, slave society would come to an end. Secessionist radicals at war, he predicted, and Graham believed, would do anything to maintain a separate existence, even confiscate civilians' property. In February 1861, Graham told Alfred Waddell that he planned to follow his constituents. But he feared that a separate Confederacy would never be able to protect citizens' freedom, property, and safety. In Graham's private papers there are talking points for a February 1861 "Speech Given As a Candidate for the Secession Convention" that confirmed what he was saying to his friends. He opposed secession because if it failed, and it would, slavery would end, as North Carolina's slaves would escape north through Virginia. Another of his points focused on what war would bring. Virginia, he believed, could neither protect border state slavery nor defend itself if war came. Also, Lower South assertions that Northerners couldn't fight were mere bravado. He had seen well-trained Federal troops in action. Then, however, in his April 27, 1861, "Speech upon the Political Situation," Graham, even though he predicted catastrophe, acknowledged that he had to follow his state into war. All the same, he couldn't help comparing his own support of the popular will in his state with a Lower South that he maintained had stifled public opinion and thus endangered popular support for the cause.[28]

Graham concluded that speech with the admonition that North Carolina would go along with secession, but he warned that it eventually must go its own way. Nevertheless, he said, "let us postpone any differences which may separate us." Soon, however, those differences so riled Graham that the new Confederate leader spoke out. On December 7, 1861, he delivered a withering *Speech . . . on the Ordinance Concerning Test Oaths and Sedition*, a fitting capstone to this North Carolinian's continued suspicions about the Confederacy, and a speech that all who believe unity existed among Confederates must read. In it he discussed the meaning of disloyalty. The Confederate constitution and the new state laws, by demanding that all in public life take an oath of fealty to the Confederacy, he believed, had made a mockery of what loyalty meant. He insisted that the test oath was an act of government "desperation." True Confederates didn't have to sign it;

anti-Confederates could sign it with glee. Added to the burden of excessive taxation that had already made slaves of the people, this new form of slavery, or control of the people, this demand for testamentary loyalty, led him to predict that "an internal war" over values would destroy the Confederacy.[29]

In his response to demands for conformity, to what he called attacks on personal pride and liberty, Graham surely agreed with the many Virginia leaders who resisted secession and worried about flaws in the new Confederate national government. Three important future Virginia Confederate leaders, John Millson in the congress, and Samuel M. Moore and William Goggin in the state convention, all spoke forcefully about their concerns. Millson defended South Carolina's right to secede, but he wondered, if Virginians followed, would they be ceding their own rights to a more radical Lower South? He feared that a Lower South–dominated Confederate government would swallow the rights of the Upper South. Goggin of Bedford on the east coast argued that Northern Republicans had behaved badly. But he also rejected the overtures from Lower South emissaries to his state's convention as threatening Virginia's interests. Goggin insisted that the cotton states would take slaves south and leave Virginia without the labor necessary to grow wheat and herd livestock, thus starving the Upper South. Virginia's diversified economy, he said, will be destroyed by fighting to protect cotton. In addition, for Goggin the constitution of the Confederacy damaged Upper South trade interests. In short, "Virginia will be placed in a position to perform the office of a baggage master upon a railway train, who has no interest in the general luggage, except to perform the bidding of those who employ him." ·

Moore gave a major address, *Substance of a Speech . . . on His Resolutions on Foreign Affairs*, to the state convention in February 1861, in which he combined Millson's and Goggins's fears most eloquently. Earlier, in a series of letters to a fellow Lexington lawyer, he stated that Virginians had little in common with the incompetent, radical leaders of the Lower South. Those Lower South leaders, he claimed, had threatened to reopen the slave trade and refuse to buy slaves from the Upper South. In other words, they didn't care what happened to the complex, diversified slave society of the upper South. In his convention speech he described for all Virginia's leaders the "conflict of interest between Virginia and the seceded states." He accused leading South Carolina radical William L. Spratt of demanding an amendment to the Confederate constitution to reopen the slave trade, and Moore worried the result would be a lowering of the price of slaves in the Upper South.

But it was the coming civil war that Moore most feared. King cotton, the Lower South's economic defense, would be bottled up in blockade, leaving the Upper South to pay for a war it had not wanted. Virginia, he insisted, would be taxed more heavily than any other slave state because it was the richest. Virginia white workers in the factories would have to pay taxes for the war, and if they refused, men like Spratt surely would replace them with slave labor. The other border slave states, Maryland, Kentucky, and Missouri, all growing wealthy through northern trade, recognized what would happen to Virginia and thus, Moore said, had refused to join the Confederacy. Last, since the Lower South was unprepared to fight a civil war, the Upper South, particularly heavily populated Virginia, would have to shoulder the burden of military defense, especially along the northern border. All these fears—taxation, excessive payments, loss of the border South, and war on Virginia land—Moore concluded, meant that civil war would destroy slavery and slave society.[30]

Another Virginia Unionist, John Brown Baldwin, agreed with his anti-secessionist peers, and said so at length in speeches that lasted three days in March in the Virginia convention. Of course, he too chastised the North for opposing the spread of slavery. But as a Whig political leader, he knew that Southerners had little to fear from the national executive, because Congress was the stronger governing body. He also said that he would not denounce the seceded states, but he felt no need to leave the Union. The Lower South states, he insisted, were guided by resentment, and resentment was a poor rationale for action. Therefore, as Lower South states talked of a violent remedy for Northern antislavery, Baldwin suggested that the Upper South reconsider its relationship with them. Virginians, he said, must not become dependent on the cotton states, neither physically, morally, nor commercially. Some of his colleagues, he stated, wanted to believe that the Lower South states would abandon fanaticism and make common cause with the Upper South because the former needed a food supply. Baldwin warned that war would drain to the cotton South all the wealth of the Upper South.[31]

Those resentful leaders' voices and a large private correspondence from worried friends no doubt influenced the growing fears for the nation of William C. Rives, perhaps the Upper South's most respected prewar Unionist. From his friend Bedford Brown of North Carolina, Rives heard about the reckless and violent demagogues of the Lower South who promised Virginians office in the Confederate government. Brown and others predicted that if Virginia seceded, civil conflict would develop within the state, thus weakening its ability to resist the North. In his letters to friends, some of them published in the local papers, Rives repeated their reasons for resisting secession. Like so many others who understood commercial and financial matters, Rives insisted his people had little in common with the Lower South. We want economic diversification, they want only agriculture, he exclaimed. The conservative Rives also believed that rebellion elevated mediocre leaders, and those new people were destined to govern the Confederacy. The realist Rives and his friends resisted the abstractions of rebel arguments, the lunacy of unprepared and ordinary leadership creating a Confederacy to fight the Union.

The reluctant Rives also acted on his beliefs as he joined in the call for an Upper South peace conference. In March 1861 he reported despondently the conference's failure. But in those remarks, Rives also revealed additional worries about the coming civil war. In the first place, the reckless South Carolinians had abandoned the Union to make civil war. If they could abandon the Union when things became desperate, would they also desert the Upper South and leave it to fight the war? "Remember," that student of history claimed, "the process of dissolution and division once commenced has no assignable limits—that a new and separate Confederacy, sprung from secession, must soon fall to pieces under the operation of the same disintegrating principle—that endless feuds and strifes will follow." He predicted that the cotton states couldn't defend the Mississippi River valley, and, while the Upper South sacrificed to protect the borders, the southwest, including Louisiana and Texas, would be isolated and lost to the Confederate defense. Then the Lower South, he claimed, would desert the cause and its leaders would flee for the Gulf. An abandoned Upper South, with over a thousand miles of border to protect, would succumb to military dictatorship and a fatal tax system that would sap personal liberty. The result, as Rives understood it, would be the destruction of society, its economy, and its values.

Even after Fort Sumter and Lincoln's call for troops, a worried Rives wrote to George W. Summers that he continued to oppose Virginia's joining the Confederacy. Those rash leaders who created the Confederacy had insisted that secession was the only way to avoid war, and now, he said, they have caused war. This thoughtful student of geographical politics believed it "more incumbant than ever" to stay out of the war, because Virginia would be the victim. On April 19, 1861, he wrote of the Lower South's disgrace, of a suicidal mission of pride, yet he joined Virginia in secession.[32]

The reasons for these Unionist leaders' reluctance to join the Lower South in the new Confederacy surely explains why they eventually became hostile to the Confederate war effort. All of them had become Confederates, and all to some extent eventually abandoned the Confederacy. Yet those men, as Unionists and then Confederates, insisted they had acted only in behalf of the best interests of the slave states. But they did not, as their very anger and worries over what war would cause showed, believe their hostility toward the Confederacy had harmed the Southern people. Thus, their opposition to secession, the formation of the Confederacy, and the coming of civil war go a long way toward understanding the wartime behavior of these Confederates against the Confederacy.

To a person they believed secession and the new Confederacy was bad for business, for their economic and labor interests. The Unionists from the Lower South insisted the costs of war would destroy the Southern economy. Taxation, confiscation, the need to arm and feed the army, all would place demands on a slave-labor-based agrarian economy. Those from the Upper South described their economy as much more diverse than the cotton-dependent Lower South. War would mean that their evolving economic ties with the border and the North would be thwarted by blockades and the costs of running a war. Upper South businessmen would be forced to pay for the war, thus sapping their income. The Lower South would drain personnel and wealth southward. The diversified and mixed slave labor economy in the Upper South, then, would have to sacrifice its own gains from slave labor to the Lower South.

The Upper South Unionists expanded on their economic arguments when they wrote about the radical Lower South leaders who had threatened them if they did not join the Confederacy. Reopening the slave trade would lower the price of Upper South slaves, and perhaps even close the market in slave trade, thus bottling up slavery there. With a growing need for white skilled labor, would this inability to sell slaves south cause labor troubles? Thoughtless leaders of the Lower South attempted to blackmail the Upper South into secession when they threatened to refuse to buy slaves from the Upper South at any price. The sale of slaves to the Lower South had provided funds for economic growth and diversification in the Upper South, and that growth would now be curtailed. Those in the Upper South who looked at the economic differences between the slave societies also wondered whether their true trade interests weren't with Northern industry and the upper Mississippi Valley food-growing population. Some believed a cotton South conspiracy dated back to the Mexican War and the demand to purchase Cuba in order to spread Lower South slavery southward to Latin and South America and away from the Upper South.

Clearly, the secession crisis had revealed many irreconcilable differences in the two Souths' slave economies.

Other antisecession leaders discussed leadership skills and political differences as internal hostilities increased. They asked why the Southern people were disunited at the very time they had to come together. Had the mediocre, radical Lower South leaders exacerbated those internal divisions? To some extent the confrontation over leadership skills supports those today who believe that only poor leadership made war, and that the confrontations were repressible. To listen to the ex-Unionists, their fears over secession were based more on how to protect vital interests than on repressing the conflict. For example, conservatives such as Rives insisted that rebellion caused divisions among the people and worried about the incompetent new class of leaders' inability to unite all slaveholding interersts in those perilous times. Those of a more moderate political persuasion had their own grievances against the talents of radical secessionists. Secessionist leaders, they said, had acted without testing unity in the South. They had made little attempt to unite all the people. Worse still, they had refused to bring their constitutents in on their actions. By opposing a popular vote on their new laws, secessionist leaders had rejected the need to unite all the people in mutual interest and defense. Also, if the leaders could coerce and destroy liberty and the freedom of those who disagreed with them, of the antisecessionists, would those fanatics abuse the rights of the people in the war?

Desperate and mediocre leaders, unsure of their followers, also were underequipped to defend their society. To preserve freedom and their way of life, they would need to require many sacrifices from the citizenry. Confiscation, taxation, brutal destruction of civilian and military personnel, all would sap the freedom and liberty most important to sensitive slaveowners. Confederate leaders undermining the rights of slave owners, the reluctant Confederates alleged, would affect the very cause for which they were fighting. No wonder those politically experienced Unionists, sensitive to the potential of abuse of power, believed the Confederate war itself was destroying their very way of life. Central to that way of life, that which was most threatened, was the very future of slavery itself.

That fear for the future of slavery united reluctant Confederates. Their worries about slave-based values exacerbated their resentments about secession and the formation of the Confederacy. Surely those concerns also influenced their support of the Confederacy during the war. Having taken the Confederacy's measure before the war, when what they had feared came to pass, that slavery itself was threatened, their support would fade. All of them in their prewar dissent had predicted that the Confederacy would harm slave society. They had revealed that as much as they believed tensions over slavery had made for an irrepressible conflict with the North, so too had those tensions created an irrepressible conflict among the slave states over how best to protect their slave economy and the values of slave society. As such, those antisecessionists who joined in the war effort to protect their values of freedom and order in slave society, their very way of life based on slave labor and its control, saw all of it unravel, and they became Confederates against the Confederate war.

3

The Speakers of the State
Legislatures' Failure as
Confederate Leaders

The political leaders of the Confederacy often have been unfavorably described and evaluated as failures. One contemporary analyst of the Confederate political system, Robert Garlick Hill Kean, confided in 1864 to
his *Diary* that the Confederate civilian command suffered from the "absence of a representative man, a Leader." In *The Statesmanship of the Civil
War*, historian Allan Nevins agreed with Kean as he claimed that those
leaders lacked "the power to comprehend exactly the forces that affect the
minds of the people and to discern what they desire and will support."
He also insisted that no Confederate political leader displayed the ability
to plan and to conduct that revolutionary government. In his essay "Died
of Democracy," David Donald attempted to explain such harsh judgments.
Donald speculated that the Confederate leaders could not overcome the
many problems of political democracy. He suggested that the home folks
"insisted upon retaining their democratic liberties in wartime," and that
their political leaders on all levels lacked the talent and perhaps the devotion to persuade them to remain loyal to the Confederate cause.[1] Certainly these judgments on their loyalty and ability have grasped the central
issues of the Confederate local leaders' failure.

Many other works have condemned the Confederate civilian leaders in
the same way. Only a few have praised any of those men. Numerous
studies have been critical of President Jefferson Davis's ability to sustain
civilian morale, and at last count at least six more unfavorable analyses of

his leadership qualities are in process. The Davis cabinet members have been analyzed for their support or opposition to the president, and the verdict on their performances is mixed. "Little Aleck" Stephens has just become the victim of a 600-page, closely reasoned, exhaustive, day-by-day defense of his dissent from the administration. Almost all the governors, especially the bombastic presenters of self, have claimed their modern defenders or detractors necessary to reclaim their wartime accomplishments. A recent excellent comparative collection on the governors' roles in the war concluded that they stridently defended their homeland. Less studied have been the state judges, although a seminal work on their decisions showed that they usually supported the demands of the government.[2] The civilian political leaders' performances on behalf of the Confederate war effort thus appear to have been studied in depth.

But the activities of one group of Confederate state politicians, the state legislative leaders, most particularly the speakers of the state houses or assemblies, has gained little attention. Yet those leaders of the legislatures by mere dint of the powers of their office certainly contributed to the political process of running the Confederacy.[3] The lower houses originated all tax measures and appropriation bills, controlled the direction of internal improvements, regulated banks, and elected and gave instructions to many other political officeholders, including the United States and later the Confederate States senators. Powers to appropriate, exempt, and confiscate meant that the state houses and their leaders also had major wartime governance roles. Most important, as J. Mills Thornton maintained, the legislature "typified the society which elected it."[4]

Perhaps this oversight is connected to confusion about the legislators' actual authority during the Civil War. A few scholars have asserted that wartime powers actually shifted to the state governors, because those executives commanded the state militias and held office when the legislatures were not in session. But since the governors had to await the assembly sessions before they could process any legislation, their jobs too had periods of inactivity. The governors claimed to have struggled continuously with the legislative leaders over control of finances and other matters. In the states of South Carolina and Florida, the secession conventions continued to meet during the war's early stages and thus assumed legislative and executive authority. But the lower houses soon disbanded the conventions and reclaimed their proper duties. Others believe that the central government dominated all branches of state government, and that the legislators simply carried out executive orders. Yet the Confederate Constitution clearly outlined the relationship between central and state governments, and those divisions of authority gave an inordinate amount of power to the state legislatures and thus to the speakers.[5]

County government officials also clashed with the legislators. In those struggles power often slipped to the local leaders. For if the assemblies authorized expenditures, the local officials delivered the goods and services. The county leaders dealt directly with food shortages and other personal problems of the people. If the legislators influenced the key decisions on local military enlistment quotas, and even local defenses, the county officials actually raised the troops. Thus, those disorganized, incompetent, and sometimes crooked local officials at times disrupted the flow of material and personnel. But some legislative leaders believed that they actually worked well with the local power structure.[6] Possibly the legislators' own relationship with their constituents was reflected in those battles with the county functionaries.

The laws that codified state government revealed shared power. Thus, all state leaders had to make compromises. For example, the governors, the upper houses, and the local authorities often challenged the prerogatives of the powerful lower houses.[7] The leaders also had to satisfy an electorate that resisted outside interference and was jealous of its local powers.[8] The legislative leaders themselves were raised and trained in that localistic political environment that questioned all power.[9] At times their commonly based political views would make them appear weak despite their authority and in opposition despite their professed loyalty to the Confederate nation. Historians' questions about legislative power, no doubt, contributed to their verdict on whether those leaders failed during the Civil War.

In the only systematic study of the Confederate state houses, May Spence Ringold claimed that the legislators provided for the folks back home, as they appropriated funds necessary to care for the soldiers' loved ones. She insisted that most of the legislators supported the needs of the national government, although toward the end of the war their leaders defended localistic priorities against the Davis government. Ringold also suggested that the legislative leaders never really gained the experience necessary to deal with wartime financial matters, especially taxation and ·bond issues. Those men just were unable to overcome popular resistance to the draft, to exemptions, and to the government's use of slaves. She stated that by "1863 lack of confidence in legislative capacity to solve wartime problems was widespread and increasing." But Ringold concluded that the legislators failed primarily because "the southern states could only build with straw."[10] In the long run, for her nothing the leadership did could have saved the Confederacy.

Participants during the war years and other scholars have focused their criticism on the legislative leadership's lack of political skills. Reuben Davis, a wartime judge and at one time a member of the Mississippi house, in his memoirs criticized the leaders as inadequate to their tasks. North Carolina politician A.J. Roper, in a letter of 1862 to Governor Zebulon B. Vance, fumed, "don't wait for the legislature, that body indulges in unimportant discussions and delights in delay." Perhaps the best student of the war behind the lines, Charles W. Ramsdell, found legislative leaders ineffectual though earnest. In the introduction to a collection of essays on the Confederate governors, Wilfred B. Yearns stated that the legislative leaders interfered with the governors' duties, and thus sabotaged their states' support for the war. Nash Boney claimed that "Virginia's Confederate legislature was an unimpressive body which seldom responded adequately to the governor's pleas for quick action."[11]

There then seems little reason to question the verdict that legislative leaders, which included the speakers, in large part failed because of their inability both to prescribe adequate legislation to sustain military defense and to persuade the citizenry to sacrifice for the homeland. But save for Donald's brilliant "died of democracy" theme, which concentrates on the voters rather than the leaders, few accounts have discussed why the speakers lacked political skills. Thus, many questions remain about the reasons for leadership failure and resistance to the national government.

Analysis of the careers of the speakers of the Confederate state legislatures may provide some explanations for their failure. This is a difficult task because of the paucity of available information on the lives of the thirty-two men who led their respective assemblies from the outbreak of hostilities until Appomattox Courthouse. Because of the lack of usable data on the careers of the wartime Louisiana speakers, their lives have been excluded from this study.[12] Enough material on the remaining twenty-eight speakers exists to attempt an individual and collective review of their career patterns. Concentration will center on how they prepared for wartime office, their recorded words and deeds during the war, and, in order to assess how their constituents viewed their wartime behavior, the public duties the citizens gave them in the postwar years.[13]

Most of those future speakers would bring years of political preparation to their wartime positions. In what previous capacities had those men served? Thirteen of the twenty-eight at one time had been in the lower houses of their respective legislatures, and four of those had held the speakership. Virginia's Oscar Minor Crutchfield and South Carolina's James Simons, Sr., had spent ten previous years as speakers of their assemblies. A number had served as county judges. Only three had been in the United States Congress. Many had gained election to their states' secession conventions. Only two had attended the Confederate states Constitutional Convention, one of whom was Mississippi's Josiah A.P. Campbell, who drafted part of the Constitution.[14] The pattern of political officeholding, then, seems weighted toward county and district representation, with few of the wartime speakers having had previous national experience.

Prewar interstate or even statewide business careers might have compensated for their lack of political stature. Allan Nevins stated that those civilian leaders who made wartime legislative decisions should have had prior training in financial and corporate management.[15] Of the twenty-eight future speakers, twenty-one had practiced law. Only a few of them had argued before the state courts, since most of them had been small-time lawyers. At least one understood the value of political propaganda, for he had risen in business and in politics as editor of a small town Democratic party newspaper. Two farmed and one for a short time practiced medicine. Three owned and operated large businesses. Florida's Phillip Dell and Thomas Jefferson Eppes directed railroad companies and managed banks in Tallahassee, which gave them experience with loans, taxes, and large payrolls. Virginia's Hugh White Sheffey used his family connections and his Staughton law practice to become a leading Shenandoah Valley banker.[16] Thus, only a few of those future leaders fulfilled Nevins's desire for them to have had prewar business experience outside their local domains.

Although no clear predictor of political or analytical skills, the speakers' level of education reveals something about their political opportunities made through connections as well as their exposure to outside influence. Fourteen of these men were known to have attended college or a university. As did many of his predecessors in the speakership, Robert Boylston went to the home state College of South Carolina, a training ground for public office. The other South Carolina wartime speakers attended their more parochial hometown College of Charleston. After university, the wealthy Washington T. Whitthorne of Tennessee read law in the office of his kinsman James Knox Polk. Walter H. Crenshaw of Alabama went to the state university, where he met a number of bright young men whom he brought to his father's law office, a center of local political activity. Two of the four future North Carolina speakers began their political careers just after they had left the state university, where they had used family connections to make friendships wth other wealthy young men. But those future politicial leaders' college experiences hardly expanded their geographical horizons. Only two traveled outside the South for their education. Sheffey of Virginia attended Yale College and Law School, and the Maryland-born William A. Lake of Mississippi went to Jefferson College in Pennsylvania.[17] It appears, then, that those future speakers' college careers showed the value of local connections and the limitations of parochial schooling.

What of those future speakers who had not attended college? At least three went to primary or "old field" schools near their fathers' farms, and four of them attended preparatory schools. Three of those whose higher education is unknown grew up on plantations, perhaps had home tutors, and eventually took over the family business. One private school graduate, William T. Dortch of North Carolina, came from a small farmer family. His father, realizing that young Dortch would inherit little property, sent him to study law in the office of a prominent judge. As with most of the former college students who studied law, many of those young men who did not go to college read law in a local lawyer's office. Two studied for the bar on their own while working as farmers and teachers.[18] For the noncollege men, then, the lack of higher education seemed no impediment to their local business careers. But their educations hardly spread their horizons beyond the locale in which they had been reared.

As with their educations, the future speakers' mobility patterns reveal their localist upbringing. Of the twenty-eight studied, sixteen served during the war in the legislatures of their native states. Eleven of those sixteen remained throughout their lives in the county in which they had been born. Richard S. Donnell of eastern North Carolina eventually moved one county over because the local Whig majority had declined. Twelve moved either at an early age with their parents or emigrated as adults to states where they rose to the speakership. Especially was this true of migration to the newer slave state southwest, which included the one certain northern-born speaker, as well as at least six others.[19] Thus, the majority of those future leaders learned their politics and gained office within their birth states.

The types of communities in which those men grew up and developed their political values, succeeded financially or maintained their family wealth, and launched their political careers may also help understand what to have expected of them as leaders. Eleven of them lived in rural counties where they either farmed or had small legal practices. Ten came from small towns and belonged to law firms. Only seven lived in large towns where ostensibly they had opportunities for trade, financial, and corporate law practices.[20] Those seven future speakers lived in cities such as Charleston, Huntsville, Murfreesboro (near Nashville), and Tallahassee, environments that could have allowed them to adjust to the new demands placed on legislatures during wartime. But the other twenty-one lived in rural settings or in small towns that may have limited their ability to grow as leaders. In short, they lived and labored much in the same way as those citizens who would send them to public office.

Political attainment, professional careers, educational level, mobility, and even size of community also point to the important issue of class background. A number of scholars have suggested a class basis for leadership disloyalty to the Confederacy.[21] Others, such as Emory Thomas, maintained that the Civil War provided the opportunity for able and ambitious young middle-class men to become leaders.[22] Seven of the future speakers, William T. Dortch, Bradley Bunch, Horace B. Allis, J.F. Lowry, James Scales, M.D.K. Taylor, and Nicholas H. Darnell came either out of the middle classes or from poor farmer backgrounds. All those leaders except Dortch moved to new states in order to enhance their professional and political careers. There is no evidence that any of those future speakers used their class background to rise in office, although both of the Texans certainly prided themselves on being self-made men.[23] Twenty-one came from well-to-do families. Only two future speakers' careers suggest in any way a relationship between class and wartime disloyal or reconstructionist attitudes. If any of them turned against Confederate government politics while in office, one must look elsewhere than their prewar class patterns for the reasons.

Still, other prewar career patterns reveal some of what to expect from the future speakers. Most of those men had been raised in affluent families. Some of them ventured outside their states, perhaps because of ambitious fathers or because of their own political motivations. Many grew up in rural or small town environments. As might be expected, most of them practiced law. Few had gained the skills that came from ownership of large businesses. They rose in public life through family connections, business practice, and party loyalty. Most of them remained cosseted in the political, economic, and social values of their home communities. Loyal to their home places, these local talents would indeed face a new challenge in their wartime legislative careers in which they would encounter statewide and even new national issues.

In addition to their career patterns, the speakers' behavior in office in part might have been related to the stamina and the health that they enjoyed. Although medical records are unavailable, the ages when they attained office could tell something about the wartime speakers' abilities to withstand the pressures of conducting a national war effort. Certainly past generations have placed a different emphasis on what age was considered fit for political office. For example, during the 1850s the Southern house speakers' ages averaged about thirty-eight years when they entered office. Perhaps the duty had been thought most proper for relatively young men still on the rise. But in 1861, most of the Confederate state speakers were in their fifties. Virginia speaker Oscar Minor Crutchfield was sixty-one. The youngest, Mississippi's James P. Scales, became speaker in 1862 at the age of thirty-one.[24] The more advanced ages of most of them suggests a stamina problem and perhaps, more important, a lack of patience with and receptivity to new ideas. But this is speculation, and other factors in their careers, as well as the actual functions of the office, are certainly more crucial to explain their performances.

One such obstacle to speaker success was the lack of time to gain experience in that position. This was because of the historical precedent of turnover in office and the wartime pressures of the dilemma of where their talents could best be utilized. Two of the speakers, one of whom had been in the United States Congress and the other who had served twenty years in public office, died a few months after the war had begun. One of those was Mississippi's William A. Lake, who quarreled with Governor John J. Pettus, resigned his office to join the army, and died as a result of a duel fought in the late spring of 1861. A few, including James Simons of South Carolina, who had been house speaker since 1851, and that enormous legal talent Josiah H. Campbell of Mississippi, left office soon after the fighting had commenced. In all, nineteen served one year or less as speaker, and three of them, including the Republican Unionist Horace B. Allis of Arkansas, served only a few months. Eight held office for two years, and part of that time they appeared distracted by military duties. Only Alabama's Walter H. Crenshaw held the speakership throughout the Civil War.[25]

Fifteen of the speakers resigned from office or refused reelection in order to enter military service. Perhaps the most important was Virginia's James Lawson Kemper, who served in the army and attained the rank of major general in the Army of Northern Virginia. This well-educated lawyer had spent the ten previous years in the state assembly, had helped to lead the state out of the Union, and had held the crucial chairmanship of the state military affairs committee. As speaker he supported the creation of a strong military defense for the Richmond government. Even while speaker, Kemper presided over the board of governors of the Virginia Military Institute and devoted his energies to organize a regiment.[26] This absent leader became a noble warrior, but Virginia's legislature was the poorer.

Two other speakers who left office entered the Confederate Congress, while one became an important state supreme court justice. Georgia's Warren Aiken's departure to Richmond meant that few men of stature in that state remained to cooperate with the Confederate government. Aiken became a staunch Davis administration ally and eventually clashed with Governor Joseph E. Brown and the state legislature because of their noncompliance with national interests. The highly respected Mississippi secession leader, Campbell, also went off to the Confederate Congress, then rose to colonel in the army, and was wounded at Corinth. Governors of Mississippi came to lament the loss of his talents as they attacked later speakers for incompetence and nonsupport of the Confederate war aims.[27]

Another group of speakers' tasks were made more difficult by forced disruption from Yankee invasions of their states. Louisiana's legislature moved so often that today even its journal records are difficult to trace. The northern conquest of parts of Arkansas resulted in the election of two Unionist speakers in that state, neither of whom served the Southern cause. The Mississippi legislature moved often during the last two years of the war. Most upsetting was the demise of Tennessee's legislature in 1862 due to Yankee control of the state. The talented Whitthorne responded to the Northern invasion by resigning his speakership and joining the Confederate army. His replacement, the equally able Edwin A. Keeble, brought excellent legal and rhetorical skills to the speakership. After 1862 he defended Tennessee as an army staff officer.[28]

Thus, turnover in the office as well as the disruption of warfare and invasion exacerbated the tasks of achieving continuity in legislative leadership. Perhaps those speakers who had other important wartime careers would have been strong and able leaders in their respective state legislatures. Certainly, the nine who held office for two or more years had the opportunity to make their presence felt on behalf of a separate Confederate government. Comparison of all the speakers' wartime legislative records provides further explanation for their pattern of failure.

Analysis of their abilities as leaders relates to the powers they had in office. The unwritten informal rules of governance reveal what the legislators expected of the speakers. To govern required personal decorum, knowledge of procedure, and the ability to persuade, both through political manipulation and with rhetorical skills. The prewar assemblies had the reputation for raucous behavior, constant interruptions of the speakers, and the presence of outsiders on the house floor. But the wartime printed proceedings and the few accounts of witnesses described those bodies as orderly and serious in purpose. The traditional closing statements thanked the speakers for their services and always included comments on how well they had kept order and presented themselves to their peers.[29] With such emphasis placed on personal conduct and presence, lack of respect for the speaker's abilities could have affected the activities of the entire legislature.

The speakers' formal duties, which gave them enormous authority, were often printed boldly and forthrightly in the first sections of house journals. The speaker controlled the organization of the house. He decided whom to seat if there were multiple claims to the office, and he could excuse the lengthy absences, which occured quite frequently due to the disruptions of war. The speaker ruled on seating nonmembers on the floor and decided who could address the body. Most important, the speaker appointed all committee members and chairs. Since bills originated in the committees, the speaker's power to name the membership in effect gave him policy control. Chairmen of key committees, such as judiciary and military affairs, often became speakers themselves, which meant that the speaker could select his successor. The speaker controlled debate, because he decided its order and time limits. Because he introduced all petitions and memorials, the speaker could persuade his followers with the powers of his discourse. In most states the speaker voted first, which perhaps influenced the acceptance or rejection of a measure.[30]

The procedures that gave the speaker such powers point to the importance of the opening of the legislative session. The words that legislative leaders used to express loyalty and dedication to the cause meant much to those men who were so taken with the power of the spoken word. But most of the speakers had little talent in that direction, or at least they have not been remembered for such skills. Keeble was an exception. After his close election to the speakership in early 1862, he urged his fellow legislators to support the Confederacy by continued resistance to the Northern army. He affirmed the principles of free speech, free press, and the consent of the governed as the central values for which he was fighting. He proclaimed his own duties to "aid in sustaining our armies in the field, and to expel the dark shadow of want from the hearth of the absent soldiers."[31] Keeble knew that assistance to those behind the lines was crucial to keeping the soldiers in the field.

That Tennessee speaker also understood the importance of symbolic gestures to gain support for his desired bills. Keeble sponsored the measure to create another Confederate congressional district for Tennessee in hopes of strengthening his state's position in Richmond. The limits of his devotion were tested when, during the debates, he was called home to watch his son die. Overcome with grief, he nevertheless returned to the legislature after only five days at home so as to cast his vote for the redistricting bill.[32]

The house records reveal that a number of other speakers achieved some successes through use of their legislative powers. For example, speakers Dell and Eppes, both of whom knew finances, led Florida's legislature to create an adequate currency to fund the war effort. They wrote bond bills and asked for taxes on the profits from those bonds. Alabama's Crenshaw drafted his legislature's impressment bill and conducted it through the house. When confronted with the need to extend Florida's draft ages to 15 and 55, at first Dell rebelled. But at the war's end he asked the legislature to require even older men to take part in local defense. South Carolina speaker James Simons supported calling a special election to admit to the assembly the talented future speaker, Robert B. Boylston. Over the objections of Governor Joseph E. Brown, Georgia's Thomas Hardeman, Jr., spoke out in favor of a repeal of the state's habeas corpus law. Eppes introduced a bill to punish all citizens who planted tobacco rather than the corn so needed for the troops and the ill-fed citizenry. He often fulminated against what he believed were the selfish motives of some of the businessmen. Crenshaw supported confiscation measures but asked for adequate compensation for those who lost their goods to the army. The speaker of the Georgia house at the end of 1864 went so far as to advocate confiscation of the property of deserters who lived near the east Tennessee border.[33] Quite obviously, the speakers seemed caught in a world that required sacrifice for the good of the whole Confederacy and yet could do much personal harm to their constituents.

But even those able leaders' actions seemed more reactive than active. The legislative journals revealed that most of the speakers, despite their enormous authority, appeared to respond to outside pressure rather than to originate measures for the conduct of their states' war effort. Enemy army attacks, the Confederate national government's expressed needs, governors' instructions for policies, state house internal factional politics, and the appeals of their constituents seemed to dictate the speakers' actions. Most of them, apparently, usually supported the legislative initiatives of other leadership groups.

What made those speakers followers rather than leaders? Scales of Mississippi explained that the many ballots required for his election deprived him of a mandate for leadership. Scales implied that the absence of party loyalty meant that he had no constituency in the house to facilitate the passage of legislation. Perhaps David Donald's charge, that few of the party leaders had the ability to exercise control over the many conflicting factions in the Confederacy, obtains also for the state speakers.[34] The majority of wartime speakers had once belonged to the Democratic party and had risen in public life as loyal party followers. But during the war their partisanship gave way to near antiparty animus, probably due to the desire to launch a united struggle in behalf of a brand new nation.

The speakers also registered concern over the contest for power among the branches of the state governments. They often clashed with their states' executive branches. Speaker Lake resigned because of his quarrel with Governor Pettus. Virginia's speakers believed that their governors tried to interfere with the house's financial authority. The Virginia legislators even fought with North Carolina's Governor Vance over the extension of railroads into North Carolina. Georgia speakers and Governor Brown argued over local loyalties and Confederate needs. At one stage of their dispute, Brown accused the speaker of lack of support for national interests. When the speaker asked for copies of all correspondence between the governor and the Richmond government, Brown refused to comply. Speaker Aiken then demanded that the governor give him a report on coastal defenses. Brown accused Aiken of partisan feelings against him, and insisted that the state Constitution gave him the right to refuse information. On another occasion the governor claimed that the house wanted illegal control over state troops so as to turn them over to the Davis government. When speaker Thomas Hardeman offered censure and moved to print Brown's untoward remarks as an appendix to the house journal, the governor exploded. But the governor soon backed off and called for concord and unity between the house and himself. The speaker closed further discussion when he stated that he "would report such action as may be necessary to vindicate the independence, dignity, and privilege of the House."[35]

In the exchanges between the Georgia governor and the speakers much is revealed about those leaders' defense of their wartime authority. The tensions also expose leadership uncertainty over just how to facilitate legislation on behalf of the Confederacy's war effort. The speakers appeared sensitive to local issues and interests perhaps even at the expense of national needs. Were those internal disputes fought over support for the folks at home as well as to protect the interests and feelings of their fellow legislators? A look at their speeches and written communications to the legislatures during the secession movement and during the war captures how the speakers viewed limitations on authority, their ambivalence about their own powers, and even the contradictions in and confusion over their own loyalties to the cause. That the speakers professed loyalty to the Confederacy is clear; that they questioned their new government's efforts is also clear.

In those state legislatures that met to debate secession and in the secession conventions themselves, the speakers often lectured their fellow leaders about loyalty. Taylor of Texas described his support for secession the same way that he would later explain his duties as speaker. Taylor "mourned the loss of equality in the government which was bequeathed to me by a revolutionary ancestry." Just as the war broke out he claimed authority to act "in the name of a free people, whose very liberties are endangered." Speaker Crenshaw drew up the Alabama Declaration of Rights, which the secession convention sent to the legislature. In it he stated, "No human authority ought, in any case whatever, to control or interfere with the rights of conscience." Former speaker Simons sent the South Carolina legislature an impassioned defense of his role in the firing on Fort Sumter. He stated that indeed he had led the house in an action contrary to the desire of the chief justice of the state supreme court. Simons proclaimed, "I will ever claim and exercise, as a freeman of this commonwealth, the privilege of forming my own conclusions, according to my convictions of reason and honor, irrespective of the favors of official power, however exalted."[36] As the Civil War began, these harangues laced with sensitivity over personal honor and opinion from such supposedly powerful men in their states sounded nearly anarchistic.

They used much of the same language throughout the war. When Eppes became speaker at the end of 1862, he promised to commit himself totally to the cause of the Confederacy, which meant to give complete support to the army that would protect an invaded Florida. Eppes nevertheless reminded his peers that at all costs "an idle or careless legislature" must "battle in the cause of liberty and in defense of all that is sacred and dear to freemen." When elevated to the speakership, Alfred P. Aldrich of South Carolina lectured his peers on the delicacy of his task, his determination to hold them to a code of honor, and of his personal duty. He began, "representatives, we are now engaged in a great revolution," but concluded, "we are fighting for our liberty and our civilization." Speaker Nicholos H. Darnell revealed his local attachments when he attacked the Texas legislature for freezing the pay of soldiers from his own county. The speaker of the Mississippi house in 1864 summed up the meaning of all those expressed values when he opposed the Confederate States Congress's suspension of the writ of habeas corpus as dangerous to liberty, because it put civil power under the military and "establishes a precedent of a doubtful and dangerous character."[37]

These conflicting loyalties also appeared in much of the speakers' legislative political activities, which led to charges that they failed to display the proper devotion to the cause of the new nation. But what did those accusations of disloyalty mean? Surely the speakers desired to assist the people behind the lines in order to retain popular support for the Confederacy. Despite their fears of excessive military power over civilian life, the speakers helped to pass bills to aid those in the front lines. Even when they argued over how best to support the cause, they usually claimed to speak in support of a separate nation. Perhaps the types of disloyalty which Georgia Lee Tatum discussed in *Disloyalty in the Confederacy*, still the only full-length monograph on the subject, could focus the meaning of leadership dissent. Tatum identified three categories of disloyalty: those who refused to aid the government and worked against it; the disaffected, who only passively opposed the war effort; and the Unionists, who from the beginning opposed the idea of a separate nation.[38]

A number of speakers at one time or another represented a citizenry that resented, resisted, and refused support to Confederate government activities. Popular allegiance to the Confederate government seemed to decline in Arkansas, Mississippi, North Carolina, and Georgia. Speaker Allis of Arkansas actually led a Northern-controlled house. Both Allis and his successor, J.F. Lowry, actively opposed the Confederate government and supported early reconstruction of their state. Hugh W. Sheffey of Virginia came from a Unionist section of the Shenandoah Valley, and he consistently opposed Confederate States measures. But most of the accused speakers behaved like Richard S. Donnell of North Carolina, whom President Jefferson Davis undeservedly believed opposed the government. Donnell represented the large slaveholding eastern section of the state, which the Yankee army besieged, and he certainly desired an early end to warfare. When it counted, Donnell supported all appropriations for troops, as did most other speakers from communities under Union fire.[39] It appears that many of the speakers who refused to support the central government's wartime initiatives hardly believed themselves disloyal.

Almost all the speakers registered disaffection with the government. To be sure, they were guilty of lack of enthusiasm, or passive support, for the Confederate nation. During the last two years of the war, many speakers displayed impatience with the Richmond authorities, expressed real fears that neither they nor the central government was able to alleviate the suffering of their home constituents, and made errors in judgment in their assistance to the military. Most of those leaders resisted outside force, whether it be from Richmond, the state capital, or Washington. When former Whig Lake fought with Governor Pettus over how best to spend state tax money, he appeared to be an antiwar advocate. Speaker Scales at times vacated his chair out of disgust and frustration. Speaker Hardeman of Georgia named the reconstructionist Linton Stephens as head of the judiciary committee, but Hardeman also supported President Davis's attempt to raise more troops from Georgia. Alabama's Crenshaw often warned of the governor's efforts to control the state house, but he led in the impressment of his fellow planters' goods to feed the troops and the people behind the lines. North Carolina's Donnell, whom President Davis wanted removed from office, opposed his legislative peers' movement for early reconstruction.[40] One asks, what did disaffection from the Confederacy mean?

Tatum's last category of disloyalty suggests that some Southerners opposed a separate Confederacy from the beginning. Was this true of any of the speakers? Arkansas's Allis, who had fought in the Union army, and Lowry, both of whom came from outside the South, obviously never supported the Confederate nation. Perhaps the Virginia Whig speaker Sheffey, who had opposed the secession of his state, might have been a secret Unionist. Because of the activities of Allis, Sheffey, and other Whigs, a number of recent historians have charged that few Whigs or other antisecessionists ever showed enthusiasm for a separate nation. But Thomas P. Alexander and William J. Cooper, two excellent students of Southern politics, dispute this charge.[41] My information on these twenty-eight speakers tends to support them. Eight of the speakers had been Whigs, and five of those men once opposed secession. One former Whig joined the secessionists, and the two who supported cooperation later decided in favor of single-state secession. Aiken of Georgia became a staunch ally of President Davis, Lake died too early for us to know his true feelings, and Crenshaw served as a tower of support for the war effort.[42] That means that twenty-five of the twenty-eight speakers do not deserve the classification Unionist.

Unless further evidence surfaces, for most of the speakers the charges of disloyalty, at least in their own minds, remain on the whole unproved. There is, however, some reason to doubt their undivided devotion to the Confederate nation. The speakers' incompetence with complex tax measures and thus with the ability to fund the war, their inability or unwillingness to work with executives of their states or the nation, national frustrations over the failure of local delivery systems of goods and services to the civilians and the troops in the field near them led some federal and statewide leaders to question their devotion to the cause. The speakers' anger over Richmond's seeming insensitivity to state and local needs and prerogatives at times certainly made them appear unreliable if not disloyal to the cause. Given their prewar career patterns and political values, protection of their personal freedoms and those of their constituents seemed to take precedence over their support for the new nation. At times they appeared willing to sacrifice the whole for the part. Perhaps it was the speakers' fierce defense of community against all outside threats that has been misread as disloyalty.

One further test of speaker disloyalty is how their constituents rewarded or punished them once the war had ended. After the war, Donnell helped to draw up the Black Codes and opposed Governor William W. Holden. Donnell died in 1867, too soon to tell whether the citizens of eastern North Carolina wanted to continue him in public life. As one might have expected, Arkansas's Allis departed the state during Reconstruction. Sheffey of Virginia held a judgeship, but soon moved to West Virginia to declare his loyalty to the Union. Robert B. Gilliam of North Carolina showed his true colors when he joined the Unionist Holden camp, and his neighbors never awarded him postwar elective office. Of the former speakers suspected of Unionist activity, only Arkansas's Lowry held postwar office.[43] Thus, only the most blatant Unionists seemed to have been rejected politically for their wartime activities.

Other patterns of postwar citizen behavior toward the former speakers reinforces what the Confederacy had lost when the best leaders left office during the war. A few of the truly talented wartime leaders who had left state government for military or national political service again ably served their states and sections. Most famous of those were Governor Kemper of Virginia, Chief Justice of the Mississippi Supreme Court Campbell, and federal congressman and United States Senator Whitthorne of Tennessee.[44]

Most of the speakers who had served two or more years during the war found that the local citizenry again required their talents. Of course, some of them died shortly after the war, and a number of others forsook public life to attempt to recoup their wartime financial losses, thus depriving the local citizenry of their skills. Still, John M. Harrell became Arkansas's secretary of state. Mississippi's dignified lawmaker Lock E. Houston served as a state judge, as did Alabama's Crenshaw. South Carolina's Aldrich gained election to the state constitutional convention of 1865, became the principal architect of the Black Codes, lost office through disfranchisement, and later ably served as a state judge. The Texans, Taylor and Darnell, returned to the state legislature, where Taylor held the speakership during the 1870s. Georgia's Hardeman also served as postwar speaker.[45] It seems that these representatives continued to gain favor with their local constituents as their limited talents seemed to suffice for those back home.

The state and county offices with which the postwar voters rewarded those former speakers suggest one important explanation of why they failed as Confederate leaders to give able support to the national government. Their people had returned them to the limited tasks for which those leaders had prepared, and they rewarded them for services rendered to the home front during the war. To be sure, hindrances to successful leadership such as turnover in office, absence of partisan support in the legislature, and tensions with other government authorities made those men appear to be followers rather than leaders. Those issues of power point to a major obstacle to their success. They had learned the ways of political authority in local arenas. No doubt a few rose above their training. Always some do. But the larger number of those local leaders, then, surely suffered the disadvantages of lack of preparation to work adequately with the national Confederate government.

Perhaps even a more important reason for their failure as speakers was the system of political values they had learned during their localist training. Political values are hardly tangible facts. Yet when one looks at those speakers' behavior patterns in office, those values appeared to determine their uses of power, the language they used to describe their duties, and their seeming to be followers rather than leaders. Their values even explain the accusations against them of divided loyalties, if not downright treason, to the national cause. Their localist vision of authority, their desire to concentrate mainly on local issues, and their protection of community interests against national encroachment also are reflected in how they understood the slave states' cause. They would not persuade the people to sacrifice further even if they could and they did not believe in excessive political power. Thus, Donald's "died of democracy" theme, if transferred from the people to the speakers, should then be changed to say that those men died, or failed politically, because of prior loyalties to their localist worldview.

Although these reasons for speaker failure follow from what is known of their career patterns, any final conclusion to the role of local talent and values in the Confederate cause awaits more information about the formative background, the political values, and the wartime activities of those enormously important midlevel facilitators. After all, even in a great war, perhaps all governance is local governance. The strength of a new nation, thus, was dependent upon its smallest and perhaps weakest parts. Again, their lives require more analysis and more information to make these claims. When on May 17, 1864, North Carolina's speaker Donnell presented a memorial before the entire house to former speaker Nathan Neely Fleming, who had died in the Battle of the Wilderness, he proclaimed Fleming to have been a "useful and heroic citizen, whose name will ever be cherished in grateful remembrance by his people." But that simply has not been the case for Fleming or for most of the other wartime speakers, and the evaluation of Confederate state leadership loyalty and abilities, of why they may have been Confederates against the Confederacy, remains the poorer for it.

4

Disloyalty in the Confederate Congress: The Character of Henry Stuart Foote

The role of governance in waging warfare, or the politics of war, usually receives less attention than the actual fighting. This is unfortunate, because government activities contribute to the efforts of the armed forces in the form of procurement of the materials of war, civilian and military morale building, personnel decisions including military appointments and promotions, and war finances. Branches of the government in a democratic modern war, such as the American Civil War, have to find ways to cooperate in order to deliver the goods and services of warfare. The executive department as central governing authority and policymaker interacts with the legislative branches, on both the national and the state levels. Representatives of the peoples' interests, the congresses, pass legislation necessary to facilitate delivery of the necessities of war. If the parts of the government are neglected, too rapidly constructed, weak in leadership, poorly run, or resisted by groups of leaders who claim to reflect the popular will, the impact on the military may be momentous.

In the Confederate States of America the leadership hurriedly formed a government, including a federal congress, along the lines of the old national government. The Confederate Congress met in Richmond throughout the war, often in secret session, to make policy and legislate under the general direction of the commander-in-chief, President Jefferson Davis. Because of the urgent need to support and deliver an often hastily put together war policy, the Confederate Congress gave over many of its prerogatives, including the powers to intitiate legislation, to the president and his central staff. Congress nevertheless had the task of ratifying those government proposals, and at times it amended or rejected them to satisfy particular legislative constituent interests. At times, congressional leaders proposed their own measures. Although the necessities of a defensive war usually kept Congress from using its military oversight powers to question policies and procedures or investigate the army's activities, that function could, when applied, affect the conduct of the war. Regional and personal factions, individual values and characters, all figured into how well and whether congress supported the administration's war policies. The Confederate Congress was, therefore, a political agency where members could do much good or damage to the cause. Personality, ability, or values, in short the character of congressional leaders, all contributed to casting some of them as Confederates against the Confederacy.

Witnesses to Congress's abilities and loyalties awarded its members mixed reviews on their accomplishments. Head of the Confederate States Bureau of War Robert Garlick Hill Kean of Virginia, from his position in the Bureau of War, maintained a close and personal view of the membership and how it operated. He had particular interest in the Congress's appropriation and revenue bills, for he knew that raising funds for the army and its campaigns was vital to the war effort. Confiding to his diary during the March 1863 congressional debates on revenue, Kean criticized its behavior. "Some are said to be uneasy about it," he said, "the split being supposed to be very deep and wide. This is a fresh instance of the *smallness* of this Congress." For Kean, who had himself lost a recent election for Congress, the absence of able leadership meant that Congress often drifted, unable to make clear and supportive decisions on government policy. "They have feared to deal with the question of finance till, leaving it untouched for a *whole year*, the evil is past any remedy they can now apply."[1] In short, that able observer of political action questioned the abilities, and perhaps even the dedication, of those at the very center of the politics and governance of the Confederacy.

Unlike Kean, the always attentive and clever war clerk diarist John B. Jones insisted that an able congress generally supported the executive branch's military policies. He was pleased early on that Congress largely deferred to the president on investigations of military failure, unlike its Northern counterpart. As the war wore on, Jones grew increasingly disturbed over the rise of factions in Congress who seemed to take the parts of certain generals and debated the reasons for military reverses and loss of land. Leaders such as Tennessean Henry S. Foote raised the ire of Jones when Foote condemned the loss of Western territory and demanded a role in making war policies. On the other hand, Jones none too secretly applauded when outspoken congressmen questioned the military judgments of cabinet members such as Judah Benjamin.[2] Mostly, though, the war clerk believed that Congress supported the war, that "a majority seemed to be intimidated at the glitter of bayonets in the streets, wielded by the authority of martial law." Still, he was not surprised in the summer of 1864 to hear rumors of discontent in Congress over presidential policies.[3]

Another knowledgeable if biased contemporary source of Congress's successes, failures, and loyalty was President Jefferson Davis himself. Davis was extremely thin-skinned and too much bothered when congressmen criticized his war policies and personnel decisions. He allowed some of them to color his judgments. He stewed over enemies, real or imagined, and responded to them when he needed to conserve his fragile health to concentrate on the war.[4] By and large, however, he believed Congress loyal to the cause because it generally did what he asked of it. Also, Davis never felt that he had to coerce the members, but instead met privately with its leaders in small groups, where he could persuade them to support most of his policies. On the whole, he regarded that body as a success—but then, Davis regarded loyalty and success as legislative compliance with his design for victory.[5]

Other close observers wondered whether certain congressmen truly supported the cause. They singled out peace activities and resistance to government policies as especially troublesome. By 1864 some critics were questioning both the abilities and the will of a handful of congressional malcontents to sustain the war effort. Edward A. Pollard, in particular, regarded a number of congressmen as hostile to the cause. A Richmond newspaperman and brilliant contemporary historian of the Confederacy, well connected to political sources, Pollard was in an excellent position to evaluate congressional loyalty. Pollard's verdict on Congress, which he probably came to after much discussion with Davis's major critic, Senator Louis Wigfall, was that "the Congress of the Confederate States was a weak, spasmodic body," that capitulated to an egregiously flawed executive will. He wrote that Davis had failed to make adequate war policy, and Congress had gone along. Pollard's views of Congress's lack of talent and support for the cause, its disloyalty, unlike the praise he heaped upon the military, influenced the work of many later commentators on that body.[6]

Members of Congress also commented on the activities of their peers, especially about their abilities and their support for the cause in those desperate times. For example, Senator William A. Graham from North

Carolina believed that Congress did the best it could with what information and talent it had, but that it may not always have had the data necessary to make a considered judgment. Himself a peace advocate, Graham
seemed most critical of his fellow congressmen's unwillingness to take the
initiative to influence executive decisions, especially as their constituents
became more and more critical of the administration's use of the hard
hand of war. According to Graham, "the public men in the service of the
Confederacy are so troubled by the parts they have borne in past events,
and their apprehensions as to a consistent record, that the Government
does not answer the present necessities of the country." Despite his mostly
negative view, Graham praised what he believed had become a beleaguered
body. Given the lack of clarity in the Confederate Constitution about its
official functions, that Congress had kept the president from usurping all
public privilege indeed was an accomplishment, in Graham's view. Especially was Graham pleased that Congress successfully opposed the executive's harsh taxing policies and supported citizen rights.[7] Another
astute member, Hiram Parks Bell from Georgia, commented that wise and
able congressional leaders knew that by 1863 the Confederacy had neither
the personnel nor the funds to fight a successful war, and that members
had begun to discuss in private their plans for a peace initiative to force
the executive's hand.[8] Both congressmen had given high marks to their
peers as leaders, especially in the cause of peace.

The verdict on loyalty, or congressional support for the war effort, of
those who participated in Confederate governance was mixed. By and
large, despite questions of ability, most criticis of the government found
much to praise in the behavior of congressmen. But there are accusations
here and there of lack of devotion or loyalty, or a turning against the
administration. The names of Henry Stuart Foote and Louis Wigfall appear
in the record again and again as opponents of Davis and his policies. Critics
accused some congressmen of desiring a negotiated peace. Others insisted
that the legislators, by resisting executive policies such as confiscation,
suspension of the writ of habeas corpus, the draft, and arming slaves, had
harmed the war effort. Why those congressmen moved into the opposition
appears connected to their worries that the federal government and military reverses had disrupted the lives and the welfare of their constituents
back home. A few even held personal grievances against President Davis.
Surprisingly, eyewitness commentators on their actions made little attempt
to delve into the motivation of the congressional opposition, the disloyal
ones.

Modern historians have built on the judgments of those contemporary

critics to make their own assessments of the abilities and loyalties of the
Confederate Congress. In their analyses, political historians have considered previous government experience, and the attendance and turnover
rates among the congressmen. Comparisons have been made between the
qualities of membership in the optimistic first and wary second congresses.
Some historians have suggested that Congress had little power and too
much turnover in office to sustain an able leadership. Other analysts of
the structure of governance have concluded that the members of Congress
lacked the administrative talent to influence the war's outcome.[9] Thus
issues of the qualities and abilities of leadership, as well as the structure
and process of governing, have influenced scholars' views of the ways in
which, but not whether, congressmen supported the cause.

A few historians have looked in detail at voting patterns to assess the
members' contributions to the war effort. One study of Congress's voting
shows that the second congress modified, occasionally refuted, and at
times rejected presidential policy. As Wilfred B. Yearns says, "while orig-
inating few major policies, it probably meddled too much with those of
the administration."[10] Still, in contrast to what some of Congress's contemporaries asserted, Yearns believes that Congress generally was hardworking
and loyal to the cause. A more systematic study of congressional voting
patterns suggests that Congress passed much of the president's agenda,
and refused, despite having a growing peace minority, to give in to Union
demands for unconditional surrender. On the other hand, Congress "refused to give Jefferson Davis the instruments of war that he considered
necessary," such as unrestricted power to suspend habeas corpus and complete control over taxation policy.[11] Alexander and Beringer assert nevertheless that most congressmen believed themselves to be loyal
Confederates, devoted to the cause, if not always to the administration,
and able supporters of the war effort. If Congress at times questioned the
chief executive's policies and procedures to accomplish victory, Alexander
and Beringer conclude that most supported their new nation. The viability
of an opposition, let alone what motivated it, rarely concerned those authors.

Works on the institutional structure and detailed voting patterns of the
Confederate Congress have shown that hasty construction of a new and
supposedly revolutionary government, turnover in office, and a lack of
clarity of legislative functions and oversight proved an obstacle to effi-
ciency. Lacking a patronage system, historians conclude, Congress was
unable to maneuver internally to negotiate policies. Without organized
political opponents—though certainly some kind of an opposition devel-

oped in the second congress—no possibility of a loyal presidential party existed to deliver the necessities of war.[12] But these analyses of congressional behavior only partly contribute to understanding the behavior of the Confederate Congress. They neither focus on an opposition nor explain the motivation of those who turned against the Confederacy.

If most lawmakers considered themselves loyalists, a significant minority subverted the cause even if they did not believe they had fully explained their own opposition. Congressmen fought among themselves about their loyalty, both verbally and physically. But to uncover an organized opposition to the administration and to its cause—a bloc of dissident Confederate congressmen—is most difficult. Perhaps congressmen were too independent for that. Talk of peace indeed surfaced often, but few Confederate congressmen actually publicly joined a peace movement. If peace organizations existed in some states, and they did, especially in North Carolina, only a few congressmen took the leadership in those movements. Fewer still, even if some defended civil rights for all Southerners, gave any support to the South's outspoken Unionists.[13] In short, disloyal Confederate congressmen rarely organized in opposition and seemed quite careful how they exercised their dissent. This makes it even more difficult to explain why they turned in opposition.

Why organized opposition rarely occured is revealed in the words and deeds of William R. Smith of Alabama. A prewar Unionist who intrigued against wartime radicals in his state, Smith nevertheless became a member of the Confederate Congress. He spoke often, as did a number of others, of his opposition, but he did not publically attempt to persuade others to his position. Smith eventually opposed the war and supported the cause of peace, but he was most careful how he presented himself to his peers. If he appeared or sounded too defeatist, Smith knew he would face charges of treason or worse, cowardice. At times he even feared for his life. Desperate colleagues threatened to harm him. So he tempered his criticism, often kept quiet even when he did not want to, and eventually slipped away from Richmond. Only later, in the shelter of postwar Washington, did he acknowledge the pressures he had been under as an opponent and explain why he had become a Confederate against the Confederacy.[14]

One able congressman, the fearless and reckless Henry Stuart Foote, who represented Nashville, Tennessee, in both congresses, seemed unbothered by what his colleagues thought about his views or what they might do to him. Foote had no compunction, even when unity was most necessary, to speak out and declare the president a tyrant and his fellow congressmen spineless and lacking ability. He brawled on the floor of the

Congress figuratively and literally. His talents, veracity, and loyalty were questioned, as some of his colleagues scrutinized his every response to the war effort. Other congressmen derided the bills he placed before them. Not a few suggested that nuisance had replaced substance. Foote also railed against those who attacked his wisdom and his loyalty, and came close to challenging the most outspoken of them. The prickly Foote had given his fellow congressmen reason indeed to wonder why he had become so hostile to Confederate war policies.

How does one explain the actions of this Confederate congressman against the Confederacy? Modern historians, among them William J. Cooper, the latest biographer of Jefferson Davis, believe Foote practiced the politics of liberty. Conscription, suspension of the writ of habeas corpus, and overt executive powers were to Foote attacks on the fundamental rights and liberties "of all people in slave society." Others historians, such as Alexander and Beringer, suggest that Foote's opposition was like that of a number of prewar national Whigs who, in war, reverted to form. Because he changed sides so often in his political career, there is a charitable view that he emulated the "character of a Trimmer," switching sides to do the best for his country. Contemporaries somewhat bitterly implied that he was consumed with ambition. Still others wondered whether Foote rejected the Confederacy because he was possessed or demented.[15]

Whatever the reasons for Foote's disloyalty, certainly no other Confederate congressman attacked the president's veracity and policies in such public and personal ways. No other so openly and vociferously opposed the Confederate cause of independence. Few had the political talents he displayed in his opposition. In fact, Foote became the symbol, if not the leader, of a congressional faction hostile toward a failing executive government's policy, and perhaps even one that rejected the Confederacy itself. Certainly those actions he took against Confederate policies in part explain his reasons. Radical defender of liberty, committed Unionist or at least separatist, blindly ambitious, or merely driven to dementia, all require review to understand Foote's motivation, and perhaps by extension the controlled yet active disloyal congressmen who sought to save Southern life and values by making peace. Fortunately, Foote made a public written record of his activities during the war, had a long prewar political writing career, and during Reconstruction explained himself in detail. To his words we must turn to explain his deeds.

Who was this man who so often seemed to put his foot in his mouth? What were the principles and values in his character that led him into opposition? To understand requires a look at his career experience and its setting, and how he expressed his values. Short, rotund, balding, distinctly unprepossessing, by the beginning of the war nearing his mid-fifties, Foote nevertheless had the energy, the wit, and the intelligence to rise to a leadership position in the Congress of that new Confederate nation. Although he spoke with a shrill and high-pitched voice, he had great skills as a stump speaker and a debater in those times when possessing verbal dexterity was a way to success. Foote had been known to fly off the handle, suspend all attempts at tact, and attack his opponents at their weakest point, their personal pride. Pride itself also marked the man as, like many of his peers, he took offense perhaps too quickly. During the course of his long life in public service, he challenged others at will, fought four duels, and created many enemies, some of whom would have killed him if given the chance. For all that, no one of his contemporaries, not even those who believed him crazy, doubted his intelligence, his skills, his willpower, or his character.

Born in 1804 in Fauquier County, Virginia, into a successful planter family, Foote maintained a lifelong love of that too-proud state. He graduated in 1819 from the Presbyterian bastion, Washington College (after the war renamed Washington and Lee), near the head of his class. Ambitious to rise in Virginia society, he read law in Richmond and joined the bar in 1823, even before he had turned twenty-one. Unable to gain favor in Richmond society and its emerging Whig supremacy, like many a young man of promise he lit out for the raucous new southwest. Settling first in Alabama, he went to Mississippi in 1830, where he established successful law practices, first in Vicksburg and later in Jackson. Foote owned a Democratic party newspaper, which no doubt gained him the favor of local politicos, including the powerful Joseph Davis and his brother Jefferson. In 1854 he moved to California. He practiced law and dabbled in real estate there, but he failed to rise in public life. On the eve of secession Foote returned to the southwest, made a successful marriage, and practiced law in Nashville, Tennessee. He left middle Tennessee in 1862 for Richmond to serve in the new Confederate Congress. Near the war's end, Foote fled from the South, first to Washington, D.C., and then to Europe. During Reconstruction he resided in Washington. Never again would he settle permanently in his beloved South.[16]

During a long career in public life Foote developed political skills that should have placed him in the forefront of Confederate government life. As a young man in Mississippi Foote entered Democratic politics, served in the state legislature, and became a presidential elector in 1840 and 1844. A staunch expansionist, Foote favored the Mexican War. In 1847 the legislature of Mississippi sent him to the United States Senate, where he supported the war policies of President James K. Polk. That winter of 1847, in a dispute over popular sovereignty, he fought verbally and physically with fellow Mississippi senator Jefferson Davis. He accused Davis of being a secessionist, but in 1849 he trafficked with his hero John C. Calhoun's Southern rights group and applauded Calhoun's radical Southern Address. In 1850 Foote again reversed himself and called Calhoun anti-Union. The Nationalist and Unionist Whigs of Mississippi then nominated Foote for governor in 1851, and he again quarreled with Jefferson Davis, this time accusing him of advocating immediate secession. In a bruising election contest, Foote defeated Davis, thus silencing the Mississippi secession movement for a while. He resigned from the state senate and gave up membership in the Democratic party. His close friend, the lawyer and judge Reuben Davis, insisted that from that hour Foote "accomplished nothing." When Democrats regained power in Mississippi in 1852, the governor's political career there was over. Foote moved to California out of political frustration. In 1858 he came back to Mississippi, again found political advance closed to him, and went to Tennessee. An outspoken Unionist, he supported Stephen A. Douglas for president in 1860. At first a close ally of the Tennessee Unionist John Bell, Foote changed sides again and supported the secession of Tennessee. In 1861 the citizens of Nashville elected hm to the Confederate Congress, where at first he staunchly supported the war effort, especially in the defense of the Upper South, and rose in positions of importance. Elected to the second Confederate Congress by voters in exile from Nashville, Foote turned into an outspoken opponent of the Davis government's war policies and became a peace advocate.[17]

Many of Foote's contemporaries charged off his wartime behavior as madness, a person who held grudges, the most lasting and dangerous being against Jefferson Davis. A closer look at that fractious relationship with Davis shows that it began in verbal dissonance that eventually led to violence. Earlier, in the wild world of southwestern politics, Foote had honed an abrasive and sarcastic debating style. In 1844, during a debate over presidental electors, Foote so humiliated an opponent that the man refused to appear with him again in public. He also traveled with Jefferson Davis that year, and the two young Democrats became friends as well as competitors. Even at that time Davis had questioned Foote's excessive use of verbal ridicule. Foote also used sarcasm as a political tactic in the United States Senate and constantly squabbled with fellow lawmakers. In that fractious winter of 1847, Foote and Davis resided in the same rooming house and often dined together. Their caustic dispute one morning after breakfast led to vicious words and an exchange of fisticuffs. Foote insisted that he gave the first blow, and Davis became furious. Davis immediately challenged Foote to a duel, no doubt because his pride had been wounded when Foote asserted he had struck first. Cooler heads kept matters from getting worse, but the men parted bitter enemies. Two years later, in Davis's presence, Foote again said he had delivered the first blow. Only Albert G. Brown's cool behavior kept Davis from again challenging his former friend. When they debated in the race for governor, "Foote indicted Davis as a disunionist while Davis damned Foote as a submissionist." Reuben Davis, a friend of both men, said that ever since 1847 "party rancour had flared into personal hatred, which no after time or circumstance could mitigate."[18]

Their battles of words continued into the war itself. Foote often availed himself of sarcasm and ridicule in characterizing the president's war plans. Davis in turn grew so hot about Foote's insinuations that at times he lost his composure. Certainly, the tale of who struck first gets to the heart of their obsession with personal pride and honor. Those feelings also may have affected the abilities, actions, and values displayed among the often fractious Confederate leaders' attempts to unite over the war.

Another dangerous side of Foote, his enormous ability and learning, affected the way others regarded him. Reuben Davis called him "one of the first men of his time." He was impressed with Foote's excellent education, erudition, and continued learning. Foote, said Davis, had studied the "history of nations," and understood "the structure and theory of different governments." But Foote's brilliance often surfaced as a cockiness others regarded as unseemly behavior for a political leader. It was important in those times to know a great deal about the nature of governance, but not always to show off as Foote did. Reuben Davis also saw in his character a refusal "to deliberate," a man "full of impulse," "relying upon his ability to mould the thought of men, he believed he could accomplish any purpose." Or as a modern historian, impressed no doubt with Foote's skills, said: "Foote was a one-man committee on the conduct of the war, repeatedly urging an offensive war, demanding military information and battle reports . . . investigating defeats, and ordering no less than thirty inquiries."[19] Indeed, that Confederate congressman, who had already written a two-volume study of the Mexican War and would write two more books after the Civil War, not only irritated other leaders with his speaking skills but also may have understood too much about the history of nations at war for his own good.

Foote employed his learning, and his oratorical and writing skills, as a leader of what passed for congressional opposition to the administration and the Confederate cause. Louis Wigfall too came to hate Davis with a passion as strong as Foote's and led the Senate antigovernment forces, but Wigfall's public (if not private) pronouncements were more guarded than the Tennessean's. A number of others in the second congress turned antiadministration. William A. Graham and other North Carolinians desired peace, and they often voted against policies and programs for the continuance of the war. William C. Rives and even Robert M.T. Hunter of Virginia pushed the peace movement. Few of those men, however, formed an allegiance with Foote, even if they at times agreed with him. Most cabinet members hated him. Only a small number of the most outspoken generals, such as Joseph Johnston and P.G.T. Beauregard, remained his allies throughout the war. Eventually a majority of Confederate congressmen voted to expel Foote from that body.

Foote's decline and fall, some would say, began early in the war. Full of himself after being elected chairman of the Committee on Foreign Relations, so the argument goes, his ambitions, his dislike of Davis, and his belief in his superior manner got the better of him. He early attempted to influence foreign policy, clashed with Secretary of State Robert M.T. Hunter, and resisted the president's foreign-trade policies. Foote formed the opinion in early meetings with Secretary of the Treasury Christopher G. Memminger that the latter did not know how to keep up trade with Europe or how to use the diplomacy of cotton for funding the war. In addition to his squabbles over foreign affairs, Foote quarreled with members of Congress about government spending. On the floor of Congress, Foote also criticized the president for failing to advance on Washington after the victory at First Manassas. Some members thought he sought personal political gain when he called for less caution and more military audacity. War clerk Jones said Foote had little use for the war cabinet. The congressman clashed with Secretary of War Judah P. Benjamin in early 1862 over Roanoke Island and called for Benjamin's dismissal. A few congressmen insisted that Foote wanted the office for himself.[20] The Tennessean actually felt the administration too defensive-minded and unable to protect its own land, unwelcoming of his ideas, and unwilling to advance his ambitions.

This belligerence over the conduct of the war from a man who eventually turned to peace may be explained when one looks at whom he represented. Middle Tennessee was vulnerable to invasion from the beginning of the war. An amateur student of warfare, Foote knew that if

Kentucky's neutrality turned to Federal support, that state would become a launching pad for an invasion of the upper southwest. Foote's offensive war strategy and his friendship with Johnston and Beauregard appear based on worry that Davis would not defend Nashville. For those reasons, Foote favored those generals who hated Davis and wanted to aid Tennessee. Even when he attacked the policies of Secretary of War George W. Randolph, Foote did so because he believed that Randolph opposed a major war commitment in the west. Virginia, his home state, Foote loved. But he did not love it at the expense of his adopted home. Therefore, finding ways to acquire the necessary funding, raising an army large enough to fight on two fronts, even if at first it meant violating neutral rights, all were acceptable and necessary in Foote's mind to win the war. Those who called him a localist for defending his own region are correct. But his outlook at that time also was national in scope, as even in 1862 he understood that to lose the west, especially the Mississippi River, meant Confederate defeat.[21] On that issue at least, Foote's hostility to the government is explainable. He had argued to keep from losing any more western territory, because it would harm the new nation, and he lost that battle.

After Nashville fell to the Federals, Foote appeared to change in his support for the war. He became an administration opponent, at least in that he questioned the cost of the policies needed to carry on a successful war effort. He kept up his ties with the people out west, supported western-oriented generals, and, as Connelly and Jones point out, became a leader of the congressional western bloc.[22] But Foote also had come to doubt the Confederacy's future. Certainly, when he ran for reelection in 1863, it was as an administration opponent. But what kind of opponent was he? He continued to lampoon the president's policies, he criticized cabinet member's actions, and he opposed commandeering civilian goods to wage the war. Victory, he protested to those who questioned his loyalty, still was uppermost. But how to achieve that victory, how the war was to be waged, that was another story.

By 1863, Foote had grown concerned about congressional prerogatives and the costs of war. Already in January of that year he had repudiated central executive control of Congress and insisted that Congress had become a mere rarifying agent for the administration. Foote and some of his allies rejected the President's call for military exemptions and claimed that Congress had the knowledge and the loyalty to determine for itself who should serve. He supported the twenty-slave exemption, and explained why. He wondered whether planters who produced food for the war and controlled slave labor back home were fighting the war in their own way. Besides, if they remained at home and kept slaves from running off or running amuck, that eased the fears of the people. Even though he knew that troops were needed for a proposed western campaign, he now combined control of slaves with the language of personal liberty to question the draft. Allocation of men and materiel for Foote had become tied to the question of a home defense. Even if additional troops were required for the depleted forces of the hated Braxton Bragg's western army, Foote refused to waste young men. Besides, Bragg was a pet of the president's and no true defender of the west.[23]

Foote insisted that, despite the failure of certain generals, he continued to support a vigorous war effort, and he swore to fight on to victory at all costs. At the same time, he vowed to continue to criticize administration incompetence. In December 1863, around the time of his reelection, he railed against what he called executive failures. He attacked Commissary General Lucius Northrop, another close friend of President Davis, for being unable to feed the troops. Of course, Foote's real target was Davis himself. In January 1864 Foote proposed that the commissary general be removed, and insisted Northrop continued in office only because he had the allegiance of the president. Foote managed to convince only twenty of his colleagues to go along. More devastating for administration morale was that Foote solicited a popular letter-writing campaign against the executive branch. Many of those letters that listed grievances against executive office incompetence influenced Congress's growing negative relations with the president. Northrop, as well as other incompetent cabinet members and petty bureaucrats, was removed from office, but too late to reverse the pattern of public prejudice against a failed administration. Foote's constant drum roll of presidential incompetence, according to the rebel war clerk, especially after he had called for a dictator to replace the president, "has produced some sensation in the city, and may produce more." But the members of Congress, or at least many of them, soon grew tired of Foote's attacks, and Jones predicted that "it is possible the president will regain his control."[24]

Did Foote's persistent attack on administration incompetence bear any fruit? Cooper claims, as do many other historians, that the touchy and prickly president expended entirely too much effort responding to the Tennessee congressman's queries, ad hominem arguments, and criticism of his personnel and policies. The president continually discussed personnel matters with his aides and plotted how best to counter Foote. When he did speak out, Davis showed Congress only weakness and rash behavior unbecoming to his office.[25] No doubt, even if he claimed not to have become an opponent, Foote contributed to Congress's growing increasingly wary over the administration's inability to conduct the war. Foote even took credit for the removal in late 1864 of Secretary of War James Seddon, ironically one of the few cabinet members who favored a western military initiative. Foote's call for wholesale resignations, according to J.B. Jones, had resulted in the loss of many able executives. Just how much that congressman aggravated Davis is best seen in the ex-president's own history of the Confederate defeat. In that work of a highly personal and defensive nature Foote is not mentioned even once.[26]

Another act of antiadministration behavior, one that reveals much about Foote's hostility to wartime policies, concerned the issue of arming slaves. Only recently, in the work of William Freehling, has the dilemma in this debate been shown to have exposed the very soul of the Confederacy. The long argument in Congress over that proposed government policy reveals, in short, the contradictions in slave state society itself. Ironically, the administration's most hostile critics in Congress and the states, the radical win-at-any-cost leaders and those who covertly worked for peace, led the opposition against arming the slaves, because they claimed that would have freed the slaves.[27]

The subject became so touchy for Southern unity that, when military officials in late 1861 first proposed arming slaves, President Davis sought to silence discussion on it. Over the years, and especially in 1864, congressmen had heard from generals that the Confederacy was desperate for troops of any kind. By the end of 1864, the president felt he had to propose congressional action, and he asked Henry C. Chambers and Ethelbert Barksdale of Mississippi to offer a bill to arm the slaves. Opposition surfaced immediately. From North Carolina, peace advocate William W. Holden rallied his forces against the proposal. In Richmond, Senator William A. Graham blamed Judah P. Benjamin for persuading Davis to act. Peace leaders Graham, Robert P. Dick from the North Carolina legislature, and Thomas Gholson of Virginia united to insist that the war was being fought to protect slavery, yet Davis now wanted to free the slaves. They concluded that a separate peace was the only way to save slavery. Hardliners who hated Davis, under the leadership of Wigfall, Governor Joseph E. Brown of Georgia, Robert B. Rhett, and even Robert M.T. Hunter all spoke against the bill. Who will pay for the freed slaves? they asked first. Then, as the debate turned into personal attacks, the radicals insisted that the only reason they had supported separate action in the first place was to save slavery from the radical Republicans. Now, in order to win the war, the government planned to abolish Southern society. This they would not accept.

Foote, who wanted to unite the peace and war antiadministration forces, joined in the debate. He used irony and cruel personal attacks to undermine the slave-arming forces. But Foote also plotted to embarrass the administration. He proposed in a bill that "no important movement looking to the emancipation of the slaves of the South . . . should be taken by this Government without the unanimous consent of the people (of the) States in convention assembled." His measure lost, but it had gained much support. The act to arm the slaves passed both houses on March 13, 1865, with the stipulation that any emancipation stemming from arming the slaves must be decided by each state alone.[28] The historian W.B. Yearns said the debate revealed the major internal flaw in the South itself. He stated, "the fallacy in the whole argument was that . . . Congress itself was not ready to arm the slaves until the very last days of the Confederacy."[29] Indeed, as Foote well understood, the act of arming the slaves was a proposal of Confederates who had turned against the goals of the Confederacy.

At the same time that Foote participated in those wrenching discussions about slavery, he also took the lead in the movement for peace. Secretly, an unofficial peace contingent had formed around Foote and others as early as September 1862. In a private congressional session Foote and Hines Holt of Georgia had moved to send a peace commission to Washington, but their motion had been tabled 59 to 26. Those 26 members of the first legislature could be seen as a loosely united peace bloc. By the end of 1863 an undisciplined but outspoken movement for a separate peace had grown in Congress. Yearns said that discontent at losing battle after battle, resistance to the extreme behavior of a government lashing out at everyone to defend itself and continue the war, and hopes of a Northern peace movement motivated some in Congress to speak out for peace negotiations. The Georgia congressman Hiram P. Bell wrote in his journal that in the second congress "another class of wise, practical, conservative men," who knew that the Confederacy had neither the men nor the funds to win the war, "favored an effort at negotiation." Thomas Adkins, John Echols, George Lester, and Bell "were quietly active" in Congress, and "it was soon discovered that many members favored it."[30] But the congressional peace movement failed, in part because it never organized opinion back home, it feared recrimination as opponents talked of peace as dishonor, and its leaders could not agree on what shape separate negotiations should take.

This defeat, however, did not deter Foote as he continued to speak out for peace, at first through working with others such as Graham, and failing, and later in his own disruptive, and yet thoughtful, way. In January 1863 Foote had spoken in favor of a new Confederate nation to include the northwestern proslavery states of Indiana, Illinois, and Ohio. But he assured his colleagues that he had no plan for reconstructing the former Union or in creating a third way, that he wanted only an honorable peace to assure slavery's protection. In June 1864 he changed his tune, and along with James L. Orr of South Carolina, he proposed that a peace commission be sent to Washington. In December 1864, he brought two resolutions to the House for discussion. In his first measure he sought to assure allies he did not want individual states to sue for peace, but that states could confer together on peace. His second measure called for the Confederate States to meet in convention "touching the present condition of the country, and offering such advisory suggestions to said Confederate Government as might be calculated to prove . . . conducive to the establishment of an early and honorable peace." Although one congressman said it would get nowhere, and indeed Foote's resolution was laid on the table, thirteen members voted to discuss it in full. In early January 1865 Foote pressured members of his Foreign Relations Committee to call for negotiations with the North. After the Hampton Roads peace conference failed, Foote went into a frenzy, blaming Davis for undermining the peace process. He vowed to make a dramatic gesture to force peace on the failing Confederacy.[31]

Dramatic it was, for Foote asked the Tennessee congressional delegation to approve his travel North to seek peace. On January 5, 1865, rumors spread that Foote was behind the enemy lines. On January 13, President Davis announced that after returning south, Foote had been arrested near Fredericksburg, Virginia. As war clerk Jones said, the South is burning and Davis announces "a triumph over a political or personal enemy." Jones and others said let him go. On January 17, Congress ordered Foote released from custody. In an affidavit he presented to Congress, Foote said he was not a reconstructionist, but that he had sought peace to save slavery. On January 19, Foote made a speech in Congress, "a savage one." Then a Missouri member offered a resolution to expel him. It failed, but others talked of censure. Foote again crossed the Potomac. On February 6, he was in a Washington prison, having had no luck gaining an audience with U.S. President Abraham Lincoln. Vice President–elect and fellow Tennessean Andrew Johnson argued that Foote should be delivered behind the Confederate lines, but not be allowed to go to Nashville for fear he would cause mischief. The Confederate House on February 27 expelled

Foote from Congress.[32] Foote had joined Williamson R.R. Cobb of Alabama as one of only two Confederate congressmen expelled from that body. The Tennessean seemed hardly to care, as he was on a ship to Europe. Too hot for either the North or the South, U.S. Secretary of State William H. Seward sent him out of the way. Foote's career as a Confederate leader was in shambles.

To explain what had motivated this one man anti-Confederate wrecking crew, Foote had published a message meant for Congress in December 17, 1864. Foote possibly had met with Vice President Alexander H. Stephens in mid-November to discuss peace and his proposed document. In that work Foote had devised a "catalogue of the ills of the Confederacy." He insisted all the Confederate failures had stemmed from the poor leadership decisions of the president. The Davis cabinet had mismanaged financial matters and had failed to secure aid and recognition from foreign governments. Also, Davis had interfered constantly in military affairs, especially in his battles with the able Joseph E. Johnston. Finally, Foote turned to what Davis had done to Congress. Through abuse of executive powers, the president forced Congress to pass legislation fatal to state sovereignty and freedom. Because the president had forced suspension of the writ of habeas corpus, free deliberation and free speech had been lost. Thus, Foote's prewar hatred and jealousy of Davis had wound its way into his maverick wartime congressional behavior. Foote's hatred of Davis had turned him into a radical states'-righter who sacrificed the Confederate cause to protect his ideals.[33] Indeed, Foote became one of the great Confederates who had come to oppose the Confederacy. In fairness, let it be said that perhaps there is more to explain his behavior than personal hatred and localist ideals.

Foote later reflected on his own wartime activites. U.S. President Andrew Johnson had forced him into exile in Canada, and Foote there wrote a personal version of the *War of the Rebellion*. Later, in 1874, while practicing law and writing for local newspapers in Washington, he wrote his own life and times, *Casket of Reminiscences*. Because he was a brilliant and facile writer, one who used his pen for self-aggrandizement, historians have doubted that Foote's postwar works contained much truth on why he had turned on the Confederacy, if indeed he had. Daniel Crofts, quite suspiciously, suggests that Foote's postwar writings only served as a way to get into the good graces of the Union government. In short, Crofts and others believe Foote probably lied when he claimed he had turned against the Confederacy, and thus his argument for why he did so is specious.[34] But Foote has a larger paper trail than his postwar revisions of his life. In the 1840s, he published extensively on Texas and western expansion. Before the war, he had written much about his Southern Unionism. Those works, along with a sympathetic appraisal of the veracity of his postwar self-portraits and personal analysis, taken together with what has been shown of his actual wartime behavior, may help to explain why this Confederate turned against the Confederacy.

Although Foote's prewar career had many changes as he went from committed Unionist to secessionist in 1861, mostly Foote had spoken and written as an expansionist slave-owning nationalist. Characteristically, as a citizen in the greater Mississippi Valley trading system, Foote favored Gulf Coast expansion, and that is why he had been drawn to Texas and to its struggle for independence. Though he borrowed from earlier histories of Mexico in writing *Texas and the Texans*, published in 1841, he had made a valuable study of the nature of southwest governance and economic development. Foote knew he wrote for an intolerant, ambitious, and rambunctious audience of democratic Americans ever suspicious of politicians and keenly jealous of their freedom. Jealousy and envy, he knew, often undermined what was best for the country. But his story is a political tract written to encourage southwestern expansion through the annexation of Texas. He constructed the tale of a beleaguered band of successful democratic Americans who resisted the Mexican dictator Santa Anna's desire to take away their freedom. "In . . . Texas alone," he proclaimed, "were men to be formed bold enough to take a decided stand against the monster of Centralism." He portrayed his Texans as "resolved to do battle in behalf of *state sovereignty* and civil . . . freedom."[35] Those very ideas of individual freedom no doubt would guide him in his Civil War behavior.

Aside from his discussion of political values in *Texas and the Texans*, Foote also showed why southwesterners might find that land appealing, and thus want to acquire it. First, this paradise was "uncommonly healthy," unlike some of the swampland and sand spits of the lower Gulf Coast. Slaves enjoy good health there, flourish, and work well. "Unrivaled" as planter country, large quantities of cotton and sugar could easily be grown in that rich soil and winterless climate. Best of all, ready game, fish, and soil for food crops "enable the planter to appropriate nearly all his labours to the growth of cotton and other staples for foreign markets." Timber, gold and silver, salt mines, and coal mines abounded. Then, there was the future trade that he foresaw in this book that rapidly became a travel guide to a Mississippi River and Gulf Coast trading bonanza. He projected for his avid readers an internal trade with Mexico, the continued growth of the river town of St. Louis, and the development of Houston, Texas's largest city. Good coastal ports and a level land surface for constructing railroads meant economic ties from the inland to the coast for the entire southwest. Foote exulted that "the increase of the Anglo-Saxon population, the state of society, its progress in the arts and improvements of civilized life in Texas" would aid the entire slave-based region.[36] The expansionist Democrat with Whig market expansionist proclivities clearly showed his economic hand.

What indeed had Foote revealed about himself with this vision of a southwestern utopia? Would this vision have some influence on his future behavior? I think so. Trade becomes crucial to his scenario. Trade south to Mexico, he envisioned, would link a slaveholder region all the way up the Mississippi to St. Louis. As a Confederate congressman, he had been an ardent defender of Tennessee and the southwest. When he saw the Confederacy losing its future, he supported a separate peace and the formation of a western Mississippi River nation. In addition, the slave culture that had given him a career and personal gain would not be bottled up along the Gulf Coast and Mississippi delta, but would expand into a separate western nation. The way to restore the Union would in Foote's eyes be linked to slave expansion.

Therefore, if any one, supposed friend or foe, attempted to disrupt this vision, Foote would explode. That is why in the second volume of *Texas and the Texans* he struck out against enemies who wanted to prevent the annexation of Texas. Those who opposed annexation he exclaimed "thus indirectly assailed" the system of domestic slavery in the South and "obviated the danger apprehended of the Southern and Western states of the Union, ultimately gaining an influence among fellow adventurous states, which might interfere with the existing ascendancy of the Northern and Eastern members of the Confederacy [using the term in 1841 to refer to the United States]." Thus the archenemy became John Quincy Adams, opponent of western growth, opponent of Mississippi and its role in that hoped-for future. Foote lampooned the failed ex-president as a tool of eastern business and political interests out to stifle the dynamic development of the Gulf and western states.[37]

Three other of Foote's major speeches, all printed as pamphlets, given during the crucial years of 1849 and 1850, when he broke with the Mississippi Democratic party and stood firmly with the Union, or at least a united southwest, reveal much about his future Civil War behavior. In a eulogy on his slave and western state hero, former president James K. Polk, Foote spoke of how Polk had been consistent in his opinions and conduct. Polk, he said, was a committed Jeffersonian democratic expansionist, known for his vision of a growing slave society in which all people would participate. Polk cherished state authority as the oldest aspect of government organization, and especially saw it as strong when border states banded together. Factions to him proved unprincipled, but also un-American. Polk also supported free trade as the best hope for the country's continued economic growth. In a Fourth of July speech on patriotism, delivered at the base of the Washington Monument, Foote added to his previous position on western growth. For him, George Washington had been the great hero of the American past because he had resisted partisanship and had spoken for a united and growing nation. Of course, that was the time Foote left the Democratic party and became the leader of Mississippi's Whigs. So he could rise above partisanship, attack the particularism and divisiveness of Jefferson Davis, and attempt to unite the slave states in their quest for expansion of slavery.

Later that year Foote traveled to Philadelphia, where, on December 30, he delivered a major address, *A Lecture on the Value of the American Union.* Relying on his enormous storehouse of American history, and applying his personal understanding of governance, Foote spoke of the dark and dangerous days of 1787 when "there were as now, many persons, of no inconsiderable influence, who were openly in favor of dissolving the Union." Madison's perceptive *Federalist* number 14, on the issue of governance, Foote said guided his own political understanding. Again questioning faction, he called on the country to accept concession and compromise. That was why, in his hostility to Mississippi's secessionists of 1850, Foote so wanted to compromise over expansion and why he supported the Compromise of 1850. Quoting from the works of his nationalist hero, Daniel Webster, the Mississippi senator showed the advantages of Union. Prophetically, he stated that war over expansion would be war in the border states and along the Mississippi, and the hated east would pick up the fallen pieces. Foote praised President Millard Fillmore for his support of compromise. But then, looking out on his Philadelphia audience, he said intently, "it will not do to tamper, as some of us have heretofore madly done, with this irritating and perilous question of slavery."[38]

Irritating and perilous indeed if slavery were unable to expand westward. The irritant also was that radicals like Jefferson Davis took advantage of the situation and divided the slave-owning people who wanted to protect their interests. Foote insisted that most Southerners had been calm and collected in defense of their rights and thus opposed precipitate actions. Rather, it was easterners who had stirred up the division, and the southwest would be the victim. In 1860, when Foote, recently returned from California, settled in Tennessee, he had hoped for a unified west behind Stephen A. Douglas and the Democrats. Although an ally of Tennessee's John Bell, Foote chided Bell for joining the hated easterners. Foote turned to secession, a move that he would come to lament and even deny. At the time, however, he claimed to support secession because he was a southwesterner determined to protect slave expansionists' interests.[39] For a time he believed a Southern Confederacy could guarantee the protection of an expansionist slave society. But only for a time.

After the war, in two major books, *The War of the Rebellion* and *Casket of Reminiscences*, Foote built on the thoughts in his earlier works to explain his wartime behavior. Like many others of the time who wrote of their war experiences, Foote certainly appears self-serving. No doubt Foote hoped to curry favor with the winners. But he also sought to understand for himself why the Confederacy had failed its people so hopelessly. A careful reading of these so-called apologies reveals self-discovery in the semi-chastened Henry S. Foote. Both books are built around a historical reconstruction of events. In neither does Foote apologize for his attacks on personal enemies. In the books, he explains why a Confederate turned on the Confederacy.[40]

To understand how the slave states seceded, in *The War of the Rebellion* Foote reconstructed the sectional conflict. At the center of his argument was the proposition that abolitionists, his most hated enemies, had thwarted the expansion of slavery. Foote quoted from a speech he had made in Nashville in July 1860, in which he had begun to doubt that southwestern slavery could survive in the Union. In the North and South he saw that "anarchy, licentiousness, and lawless violence are everywhere displaying themselves." When Southern leaders rejected any hope for compromise in early 1861, Foote felt he had to go along with his state. He had not been a leader in the secession movement, but he was an early revisionist in his view that secession and war were repressible. For him a blundering generation of weak political leaders had replaced the giants Henry Clay, John Calhoun, and Daniel Webster. To make his point, Foote declared that if Calhoun had been alive, the moderates would have rallied around him to avoid war. Foote had argued that weak leaders could not protect the interests of their people, and that deviant elements had stampeded those leaders into action.[41]

Of course Foote was revising history, and he was the typical Trimmer in politics, as he claimed to have risen above party to protect the nation.

Once allowed back in the country, he settled in Washington, and perhaps in the capital city he gained new perspective on the war. Others, of a less charitable mind, would say that a Washington law practice made for a political conversion. Certainly he angered some former friends when he declared that secession had been unwise. Even Lincoln, in Foote's new thinking, had been a moderate. Fort Sumter had been a miscalculation, a disaster. The war had been a failure for the South, he proclaimed. So, in reconstruction he turned to Andrew Johnson. Then he switched to join Grant and the Republican party. President Hayes named him superintendent of the United States Mint in New Orleans, a post he held from 1878 to 1880. At last, Foote held the position from which to protect his beloved Mississippi delta southwest.[42]

But Foote was not content in those books just to declare he had been wrong on secession. He also revealed why he had turned against the Confederacy but not the South. In *Casket of Reminiscences* he elaborated on the poor leadership theme. The greatest leadership flaw had been the inefficient, radical, partisan, thoughtless Jefferson Davis. Reasons for Confederate failure could be explained in the major appointments Davis made to his cabinet, in his poor judgment on personnel. The proof was in the executive department's actions, and that is why Foote claims he separated from the government. Other problems with the leadership he found in the very formation and later functioning of the Confederacy. Ever the student of governance, Foote analyzed the Montgomery convention to show a failed revolutionary constitution, a legal system flawed from the beginning. This, he said, led to inadequate protection of the rights of states and individuals. In addition, the leaders had failed to unite the people, and to get them to sacrifice would necessitate violations of human rights. Ever the revisionist, belatedly he discovered merit in the actions of Tennessee Unionists, especially William G. Brownlow, a man he came to admire. In defense of the Southern Unionists whom he never actually joined, Foote said that early in the war he had cautioned the Confederacy against violating the rights of the people of eastern Tennessee. He continued in that personal revisionist vein as, like Davis and Stephens, he wrote of the dangers of war to the rights of states. However, Foote blamed the ex-president for undermining the very values of the Southern people.[43]

But there was more to Foote's charge against a failed institutional and leadership system, more than its violation of state rights. The turning point of his own conversion to peace was when the Confederacy lost Tennessee and the Mississippi River to the Yankees. His vision of a successful slave society had been connected to western expansion and the material growth that came from it. He had joined the Confederacy to protect this western slave society. With the west lost, why should he oppose a separate peace movement that might regain the west at least for his kind of Southerner? In the reprint in *Casket of Reminiscences* of parts of his pamphlet in which he explained to his constituents in 1865 just why he had gone north to make peace, he said President Davis had sold out the west.[44] Then he explained what the South and its western expansion truly had meant to him, and thus why he had turned against the Confederacy, which could not protect the southwest. For Foote, the southwest held the future of southern slavery; losing it meant the end of slavery.[45]

That central focus on the protection of slavery, its meaning for society, and its influence on individual rights may appear strange given the Tenneessean's postwar revisionism. After the war, Foote questioned continuing slavery. He said that in his peace message to Lincoln he had offered to end slavery by 1900.[46]

Given his behavior during the war, and his prewar view of the slave states, the only explanation for this reevaluation was ambition, or perhaps frustration over the multiple meanings of slavery. Perhaps his own personal relation to slavery explains the actions and the values of one who blustered and postured his way through life, who nearly caused his own death because of the kind of honor that would insist that he had struck the first blow with Davis. When Foote said that central authority and leadership incompetence failed the Southern people, he really was talking about fear of being enslaved, at least figuratively. To succumb to the northeast meant the end of slavery, and that would make the Southern people slaves. But the way the South fought the Civil War had resulted in loss of personal liberties, perhaps even to enslavement to the Confederacy. The subtitle of *The War of the Rebellion* was aptly given as *Scylla and Charybdis*. Slavery for Foote had been a victim of resisting the Union. His way out of the contradiction was to be a Confederate who opposed the Confederacy. Certainly any judgment on the Confederate Congress's accomplishments and loyalties must consider this dilemma of its most infamous, most outspoken radical leader, who understood why Congress seemed "unable to come to clear and supportive conclusions" on continuing the cause. At least this was so in the character of one Confederate congressman, who perhaps resembled others less voluble who turned on the Confederacy.

5

The Contributions of the Southern Episcopal Church to Confederate Unity and Morale

Church leaders and popular religious values had large roles in the American Civil War era. The people's faith no doubt led some to rebel and others to resist rebellion. Clergy leaders prayed for peace, encouraged the war efforts, and even participated in the war itself. Civilian and military leaders alike expressed how their faith led them on to greater exertions on behalf of their cause. Ordinary citizens prayed for the courage to persevere in that desperate war. Because of the relation of religious belief to morale, historians have studied many of the evangelical and fundamentalist churches' roles in the lives of the Confederate people. Had their God deserted them because they were wrong in their cause? Certainly their failing morale, scholars say, made a crisis in confidence. But study of religious values in the Confederacy for the most part has ignored church institutional behavior and governing policies. This is because most of the mainline Protestant churches in the South lacked an institutional order or a system of church polity. However, for one denomination, the Episcopal Church, the crisis in faith that led to faltering morale was as much connected to hierarchical doctrine as to fundamental beliefs. Both church order and belief should be looked at to understand how Episcopal Church leaders contributed to the Confederacy, and to turning Confederates against the Confederacy.

The Episcopal Church's hierarchical organization and evangelical moral fervor influenced some of the Confederacy's essential personnel, both in their public and in their private lives. The Southern Episcopal Church leaders, clergy and military, had important roles in the Confederate nation's Civil War. When the war came, Episcopal bishops and clergy met in convention, officially seceded from the national church, and created the Confederate States Protestant Episcopal Church. As members of an institutionally organized and hierarchical church, the clergy and the bishops left a documented record of their vital activities on behalf of Southern society during that momentous period. Those leaders' wartime attitudes and behavior reflected both the unity and the divisions within the Confederacy itself.

The wartime activities of two presiding bishops and two Confederate generals and a few other bishops have been used to analyze the contribution of the Episcopal Church to the Confederate nation. Those four are Bishop William A. Meade of Virginia, who served as the first presiding bishop of the Confederate States Protestant Episcopal Church; Bishop Stephen Elliott of Georgia, who succeeded him in 1862 and held office throughout the remainder of the Civil War; Louisiana Bishop Leonidas K. Polk, educated at West Point and The Virginia Theological Seminary in Alexandria, Virginia, who became a lieutenant general in the Army of Tennessee; and West Point–trained Brigadier General William Nelson Pendleton, rector of the Episcopal Church in Lexington, Virginia, who served as Robert E. Lee's chief of artillery in the Army of Northern Virginia.[1] The wartime activities of these religious and military Confederate leaders and their supporters, when related to church doctrine on hierarchy and liturgy, reveal connections between faith and morale, authority and acquiescence, and their meaning for allegiance to the Confederate war effort. All these church leaders supported the Confederacy, but in different ways and for different reasons during the war, some of them became less than wholeheartedly loyal to the Confederacy.

Just what kind of church did those leaders belong to? Unlike the other American Protestant denominations, the post–American Revolution Episcopal Church had lost many members due to its long and cherished ties with England, its resistance at the time to the growth of evangelical religious practices, and its hierarchical structure in a new nation quite hostile to obtrusive authority. The Episcopal Church had been unable to compete with the proliferation of postwar Protestant denominations, especially the Methodists, to whom the church had lost many members. Constant movement of the American people westward also took members from an Episcopal Church committed to the eastern seaboard. When part of the church divested itself of its Anglican authoritarian and hierarchal ties in the wake of the Revolution and supported a reformed and evangelical liturgy, a few Southern and middle state leaders and congregations insisted it had become too Protestant. In short, both supporters of evangelical Protestantism and of high Anglicanism held their own grievances against the struggling Episcopal Church.[2]

Even before its post-Revolution decline, the church had founded an evangelical, quasi-Methodist branch, especially in Virginia, to compete with the growth of fundamentalist Protestantism. Revered Devereaux Jarrett of Virginia had attacked paternalism, hierarchy, and communion-centered liturgy, and had proposed an evangelical, anti-institutional, sermon-centered faith. The historian Rhys Isaac said Jarrett and his up-country Virginia followers rejected the low-country coastal Episcopal elites' snobbish, hedonistic, ultra-materialistic display of drinking, horse racing, and card playing. Some historians believe the rise of this religious populism resulted from the new work ethic of a market-driven, capitalist society, and that the Episcopal leaders, lay and clerical, divided over this public display of material energy.[3] Whatever the reasons for such reactions to old Episcopal elite ways, the church's authority in the postwar had crumbled under assault from the up country.

Young Father William Meade of Virginia entered the priesthood at just that low period of the church's history. Determined to revive his church, he set out to find ways to make it acceptable to Southerners in the new nation. Full of evangelical fervor, like his hero Jarrett, he opposed status and authority and decried sinful displays of wealth. A student of Methodism, he devised evangelical liturgy. After years of experience riding the circuit among Virginia's spreading churches, he became assistant bishop of Virginia. Meade won fame for his hellfire sermons and his stirring essays on the church's history, and he used those talents to revive the church's position in his native state. Even his appointments to the clergy had to pass a rigorous test of evangelical fervor. He named the young priest William Nelson Pendleton as headmaster of the revived low church Boy's School in Alexandria, Virginia, to lure some of the state's brightest minds into the priesthood. Meeting in 1823 in historic Christ Church, Alexandria, with other like-minded priests, Meade and selected clergy founded The Protestant Episcopal Seminary in Alexandria. Set on the fabled hill across the Potomac from Washington City, the seminary was to become a bastion of low church training. Meade expected his homegrown and trained clergy to settle the upper southwest and spread the word of a reformed Protestant faith. The bishop stressed among his young priests faith in what he called low churchmanship, meaning anti-institutional church order and evangelical liturgy. As bishop in his own right after 1841, the charismatic leader took pride in the renewed strength of the church, at least in his part of the South.[4]

But while Meade promoted his reformist church, another controversy led other Southern churchmen to fear further disruption in their church. During the 1840s, clergy of the English Oxford Movement wanted to return the Church of England to a hierarchical order similar to that of the Roman Catholic faith.[5] Many worried Southern low churchmen believed that the gains they had made in membership might be lost to the revival of devotion to hierarchical authority and the return to a eucharist-centered faith as opposed to an evangelical, word-of-God church. When Bishop Levi Silliman Ives of North Carolina in the middle 1840s converted to the Roman Catholic Church, Virginia leaders felt that their worst fears had come true. Ives had conducted a preparatory school in North Carolina for planters' sons, and panic spread among that state's clergy who believed that the bishop had proselytized the youth for Rome. Ives vacated his see and moved north, but the damage had been done.[6]

Others wanted an Anglican rebirth in the United States, the tradition of Anglo-Catholicism or high church Episcopalianism, which had spread through England among those who did not go over to Rome. The General Theological Seminary in New York began to train priests in the high church mode. Southwesterners had resisted any outside authority for fear of interference in their way of life, but laity and clergy in the more densely populated and wealthier parts of the southeast joined the high church movement. After all, in a conservative slaveholder hierarchical world, many longed to restore their church's lost authority in Southern society. A few Southern bishops, including Ives's successor in North Carolina, Bishop Thomas Atkinson, and Bishop James H. Otey of Tennessee, considered themselves more hierarchical than anti-institutional. Both bishops believed in the authority of the *Book of Common Prayer*, the doctrine of apostolic succession, and the idea of a bishop-controlled diocese. They rejected low church evangelicalism and what they regarded as excessive reform of the church. Those high church leaders brought a number of younger priests into their fold as they called for a united church to transcend statewide diocesan boundaries.[7]

To convert other Southerners, the high churchmen planned a new seminary more sympathetic to their views than Bishop Meade's Virginia Theological Seminary. In that endeavor the high churchmen gained support from the Southern bishops who called for a "middle way" between Evangelism and Romanism. Those "middle way" bishops and priests and their lay followers, like the low church leaders, had long advocated doctrinal reforms, but they also held to many historical hierarchical traditions, and thus came under the influence of the Oxford Movement. Georgia's Bishop Stephen Elliott, from an old established South Carolina family, and Louisiana and the southwest's Bishop Leonidas Polk, from a wealthy North Carolina family, led this new movement. Tall and charismatic, and a persuasive church leader, Polk became the dominant vision behind the proposed University of the South and the new seminary, at Sewanee, Tennessee. Unfortunately, the Civil War interrupted plans for the school, and its start-up would have to await the return of peace. Still, middle way forces had united with the high churchmen to resist what they sometimes called the chaos of unstructured evangelical teachings. Thus, the middle and high church contingent took as its mission the unity of all branches of the church.[8]

By the Civil War, then, at least three antebellum Episcopal Church groups had emerged in the slave states. They consisted of the large, evangelical low church of Virginia's Bishop Meade; the small, but influential, authoritarian high church of Bishops Atkinson and Otey; and the middle way church of Bishops Elliott and Polk. Their squabbles over seminary education had exposed real differences over hierarchical authority, diocesan autonomy, and sermon-centered versus communion-centered liturgy. Those divisions within the antebellum Episcopal Church leaders, which were not found to the same extent among the other mainline Protestant denominations, would inform their support of Southern secession, the formation of a Southern Confederacy, the creation of a Confederate States Protestant Episcopal Church, clergy and lay support for the Confederacy's war effort itself, and even how they handled the war's end.

How did those three Episcopal Church factions' leaders respond to the secession movement in the South? As might be suspected, from the crisis's beginning, the outspoken, dynamic leaders of the middle way, Bishops Polk and Elliott, advocated united Southern secession. They stressed the need for a unified front against the North. Other leaders of the middle way, including Bishop Gregg of Texas, joined Polk and Elliott. Perhaps they believed that secession and service to their new country gave them opportunities to build their middle way hierarchical church among those in the slave states who believed in their form of conservative control. But their actions frightened a number of bishops who feared the consequences of secession. Bishop Meade and other low church Episcopalians, perhaps wary of threats to their autonomy from any body of power, including a new nation, at first resisted talk of secession. Bishops Atkinson and Otey of the hierarchical contingent also initially argued against secession, perhaps because they viewed secession as a revolution that would upset the South's social order.[9]

After Fort Sumter, the two groups of Episcopal leaders who had resisted both individual state secession and the formation of a new nation gave their support to the Confederacy. For old Bishop Meade of Virginia, the low church's most famous leader, the North had become a threat to the South's way of life and to the church's rights and independence. He put the full weight of his reputation in support of the cause and used his many talents of public preaching and writing to persuade others to join the Confederacy. On May 8, 1861, Meade, who had once believed slavery immoral, preached a sermon in which he asked the Lord to support the cause of the new Confederacy. But in that sermon he also struggled with what might possibly be a problem for the newly founded Confederacy. For Meade had spoken eloquently of the importance of the rights of his beloved Virginia in the new and untested Confederacy.[10] The hierarchical authority in the high church, Bishops Atkinson and Otey, also linked their church's fate with that of the Confederacy. Otey exclaimed that "the cause of the south was just, and that God will favor and defend us." Atkinson preached on the themes of a defensive and just war. He wanted to protect all the Southern people from "those who fought from carelessness of duty, from confusion and fear, from mutiny and disorder, . . . and from forgetfulness of Thee." A careful listener to his sermon also might have heard the warning that the orderly new Confederacy had as its primary task the protection of the people and their way of life,[11] but what if the Confederacy was unable to protect that social order?

When the war broke out, Bishop Polk, of the sensible and conciliatory middle way, called for a general convention of all the Southern Episcopal diocesans for the purpose of creating a separate Confederate States Protestant Episcopal Church. A few of the Southern bishops at first refused to heed the call, as they did not welcome the request for a separate church. The low church contingent feared a new, untested authority; the high church leaders worried about the end of a known hierarchical relationship. Their substantive disagreements with Polk again reflected deep divisions among the church's leaders and even their lay followers.

Although hardly a gifted student of church polity, never having been one to study his church with care, Polk nevertheless argued for a separate church on the basis of instititional obligation to the Confederate nation. Soon to be preoccupied with military duties, while he was organizing the church leaders Polk had offered his services to his old friend and classmate

Jefferson Davis, but he continued to exercise some leadership in the new church. At the gathering that set up the Southern church, in conversations with his fellow bishops, Polk insisted that the freedom of consent that had formed the revived church after the American Revolution also justified the Southern Church's right of separation from the national Church. This spokesman for the middle way declared his belief in the church's ideal of intense nationalism similar to the ideal of its relationship with the mother Church of England.[12] The president of the House of Deputies, Reverend Christian Hanckle of South Carolina, reiterated Polk's views with fervor. He stated, "We are doing no more than our forefathers did, when they organized our Church in the United States."[13] Bishop Elliott, Polk's ally, who at first feared the Louisianan soon to be a general had gone too far too fast, in short order came round to the need for a separate church. Elliot had linked the church's survival in the South to its loyalty to the Confederate cause. An old Whig, he had once feared state interference in church activities, but he also believed that the church owed responsibility to what he called the "civil will," and that meant to the unified new Confederate nation.[14]

The high churchmen, because of their allegiance to a national and ordered hierarchy, at first refused even to attend the convention and only later reluctantly acquiesced in the formation of a separate Episcopal Church. Their idea of the proposed new church, however, differed considerably from that of their friends of the middle way. At the convention, after they finally came round for fear of being left out, the high church leaders moved that the new Southern Episcopal Church be named the Confederate States Reformed Catholic Church. Of course they got nowhere, either with Polk or the low churchmen. More important for the future of a unified Confederacy, Atkinson made it clear to all present that his primary allegiance was to the church. He decidedly opposed Bishop Polk's linkage of the church to the new Confederate States but instead supported the concept of Southern dioceses' subservance to a centralized church authority. Bishop Otey also insisted that the new church stand above any civil authority. Atkinson and Otey appeared in their words and actions to support the new nation in order to enhance the Church's central powers in the South.[15] High churchmen, therefore, showed more concern with the state of the church than with the Confederate States.

Low churchmen, under Meade's mentorship, also in the beginning disagreed with the need for a separate Confederate States Protestant Episcopal Church. Unlike the high churchmen, Meade insisted that he opposed the "consolidation of power in any central representative body." Yet he eventually agreed to endorse a separate church. But Meade, like most of his fellow low churchmen, wanted to protect the church from the new Confederate States. Most important, he truly feared excessive power of a central ecclesiastical authority.[16] Obviously, his actions were consistent with his many years of battling to restore the Southern Episcopal Church to prominence through linkage with the evangelical and anti-institutional beliefs of his fellow Virginians.

These heated differences among the three groups of Episcopal bishops and their trusted clergy advisers over secession and a centralized national church shouldn't have hindered their religious faith-based activities on behalf of the spiritual needs of the Confederate nation, including their home flock and the boys in gray. They did not at first. The Episcopal bishops and most of the clergy called for civilian sacrifices and preached on popular support of the war effort. The Confederacy enlisted a number of Episcopal chaplains, many of whom sacrificed their obligations to the people back home, and a few even their lives, in order to bolster the morale and calm the fears of the unruly young soldiers. Some of those chaplains actually fought in the war. In addition, the church published diocesan newspapers, owned a wartime publishing house that issued religious tracts for the troops and for people back home, and distributed a *Confederate States Book of Common Prayer*. Conversions, baptisms, and confirmations of the troops and even of major military and civilian leaders no doubt contributed much to the symbols of faith in action so necessary to popular morale. In their revivals and prayer services for the troops, and even the requisite ritual celebrations of funerals—those of J.J. Pettigrew and Leonidas Polk come to mind as the most extravagant—the Episcopal clergy also supported the propagandistic images used to build up morale for the cause.[17] Of course, the rituals and the pageantry of church activities were part of Episcopal tradition.

Closer look at the wartime activities of the bishops themselves, most particularly the low churchman Bishop Meade and the middle way Bishop Elliott, reveals how their doctrinal beliefs influenced the ways they sustained morale among civilians, soldiers, and leaders. Meade did not live to see the war's effect on his Virginia, but his successor carried on the struggle in his own way. The hierarchical Bishop Otey died before he could see the war's result for his church, but he had seen enough to worry. Atkinson supported the war effort in North Carolina, but his actions during the war were less important than his handling of the movement for peace and the restoration of the church. Comparison of the ways the clergy-generals, Polk and Pendleton, supported the military cause shows that doctrinal differences affected even those two leaders' devotion to the war effort.

The Confederacy's first presiding bishop, Meade of Virginia, held dual loyalties to the Confederacy and to his beloved people of Virginia. His prewar activities on behalf of religious reforms had combined state chauvinism with a desire to rebuild the church as protestant.[18] Thus one is hardly surprised to hear in an address on June 13, 1861, to the congregation at Millwood, Virginia, Meade's desire to protect both the people of Virginia and the Confederacy at any cost. He exclaimed that the Lord sanctioned only a defensive war for the people and their church. At the same time, Meade, ever the cautious student of the past, understood that during the American Revolution the church had nearly been destroyed because the people regarded it as unpatriotic.[19] That low church bishop's state chauvinism and religious fundamentalism had converged in a special kind of limited support for the Confederacy.

To the end of his life the old bishop continued his efforts to support both the church and the military cause in Virginia. To Virginians Meade became and remains a legendary figure of fidelity and determination. His loyalty gained much notoriety because lay female leaders (like Judith W. McGuire, wife of a faculty member at Meade's seminary and a fugitive from her home who wrote at length of the powers of her faith) nearly deified him. McGuire also described how her evangelical faith had been a great comfort in the time of troubles, at least while Virginians were able to defend themselves. Meade's image among Virginians was enhanced by his famous deathbed encounter with General Robert E. Lee. The story goes that, as the gray-haired general bowed his head before the dying old cleric who had taught him his catechism, the bishop was heard to say, "don't shed tears for me Robert. Do so for Virginia." The bishop's final words to the general blessed Lee's sacrifices on behalf of his native state.[20] Perhaps the general too well followed the admonition of his old rector.

Meade's successor as bishop, John Johns, also supported with vigor his mentor's allegiances to Virginia. At first Johns used the enemy's desecration of Episcopal churches in northern and western Virginia to stir his fellow Episcopalians to resist the Yankee war of aggression. He surely created in his sermons symbolic images of great sacrifice as well as God's support for the cause, both necessary to keep up the morale of the Southern people. Johns's movingly descriptive sermon on the accomplishments of the wounded General Richard S. Ewell, when he confirmed that general at the plush upper-class St. Paul's in Richmond, received the applause of Mrs. McGuire. Johns often talked to and exchanged correspondence with General William S. Pendleton, and he used that general's uplifting messages in his sermons. Constantly in his early wartime sermons the bishop harped on the necessity of personal sacrifice and the home defense of the people of Virginia.[21]

Soon, however, another tone sounded in this low church bishop's voice of encouragement to his flock. His unpleasant forced uprooting from one church to another as he fled before the invading men in blue, his sorrow over the hungry and homeless, his recognition of a growing defeatist attitude among the people, and his pity for the many wounded Virginia boys took its toll on his own confidence in the Confederate cause. Bishop Johns soon complained about the number of military defeats, which he described as messages from heaven.[22] By mid-1863, he preached openly and often on the moral defects of his own people. Mrs. McGuire repeated these comments as she too asked whether such an unworthy people deserved punishment from God. Perhaps this low church Calvinist had come to regard defeat as a sign of the loss of God's benevolence for Virginians and himself. Perhaps too Johns's faith included his own peculiar form of state chauvinism as he rebelled against a Confederate government that had inflicted such horrible losses on Virginians. At the war's end, Bishop Johns served as the spiritual leader only of Virginia's failed cause.[23]

If both Meade's and Johns's religious values and doctrines influenced their failing wartime loyalties, could the same have been true for the high church bishops? Atkinson and Otey also had urged chaplains to preach to an unruly army, and they prayed openly and in private for civilians and military leaders alike. But few of the high church warriors for God gave continuous service to the Confederate cause. They never in fact really joined with gusto the movement for a Confederate nation, nor had they attempted to sustain popular and military morale. Atkinson's biographer says of him that "of all of the Southern Bishops he was the least embarrassed or trammelled by the results of the War."[24] Bishop Atkinson's lackadaisical support for the Confederacy no doubt was connected to the conflicts in North Carolina over support for the war and the rise of a peace movement there. But Atkinson's actions may also have been motivated by his high church hierarchical beliefs. In his early prayers for the new nation, he supported the government and the war effort. There is little evidence, however, of much continued support. He seemed to have placed the church's survival in the United States above that of his commitment to the Confederacy. As institutional authority and support for an organized system of faith and governance diminished, Atkinson had little hope for his church in a ragged and disorganized Confederate nation.

If high and low church Episcopalians' doctrines influenced their support for the Confederate nation, what in the beliefs of the middle way Episcopal leaders determined their allegiance to the Confederate cause? The prewar career of Bishop Elliott of Georgia in large part explains his enthusiasm for the Confederate war effort. Spreading a message that neither praised too much church order nor advocated fundamentalism, he had hoped to enlarge the church in Georgia and to build it in the southwest. His activities on behalf of the Confederacy no doubt were connected to his desire to see the growing church have a role in a separate Southern nation. Elliott believed more than the high church forces did in a hierarchical church that could benefit from a strong central authority such as that of the Confederacy. But he also supported free will and defended individual choice, perhaps because he knew all too well the human frailty of his flock, meaning a susceptibility to fundamentalism. Still, he remained for them throughout the war a steadfast example of national unity, devotion to a central church, and an advocate of collective moral uplift.[25]

Early in the war, Bishop Elliott advocated the adoption of a new prayer book so as to influence and sustain national values. He believed that the *Confederate States Book of Common Prayer* restored "many of the omissions which had been made in the ritual of the Church of England," and he wanted "to carry back our Book to a more primitive standard." In a number of articles written for the *Church Intelligencer*, he described the importance of the cause and the duties of the people to the Confederacy. Elliott practiced his beliefs as he sent many young priests off to the war as chaplains. He urged them to deliver sermons in support of President Davis's military policies. During the Atlanta campaign, which so sapped the will of many Georgians, Elliott joined the warrior-bishop Leonidas Polk in baptizing and confirming Generals Joseph E. Johnston, John Bell Hood, and William J. Hardee, all fighting in the west. He knew that the ritual of baptism linked civilians to the cause and built up their morale. Perhaps Elliott's finest wartime moment came when, in mid-1864, he eulogized his late colleague Leonidas Polk as a staunch nationalist and a martyr to the vengeance of Northern fanaticism, and he urged on the Southern people to continued resistance to avenge the fallen hero. Unfortunately, neither Governor Joseph E. Brown nor Vice President Alexander Stephens, two Georgians with little enthusiasm for further sacrifices, seemed to hear him. Even so, as the war wound down, Elliott continued to pray for the Confederacy's success.[26]

If Bishop Elliott's devotion to the "middle way" in part explains his wartime loyalties, the warrior-bishop Leonidas Polk's military performance also reveals how that church doctrine contributed to his desire to support the Confederate nation. Polk's prewar activities on behalf of the church also tell much about how he would fight the war. His support for a seminary in the South's heartland on that mountaintop in south-central Tennessee, his desire to convert the southwest to Episcopalianism, his immediate enthusiasm for secession and a new Confederacy, and his leadership in making a Southern Episcopal Church showed his longtime Southern nationalist fervor. Lost to the church leadership during the war and hardly a great warrior, nevertheless Bishop Polk's wartime religious and military life demonstrated the relationship between his beliefs and his deeds.[27]

When the war began, the West Point–educated Polk, a former classmate of President Jefferson Davis, accepted a summons to Richmond to meet with his commander-in-chief. Desirous of giving spiritual aid to the new country, and curious to see the fighting for himself, the bishop hurried to the Virginia front. He visited with old friends there who had become important Confederate officers, went to the First Manassas battlefield, and then met his destiny at the president's mansion. Davis offered him the post of brigadier general in the western theater. Perhaps Davis himself well understood the symbolic importance of having a great man of the cloth in military uniform. Certainly the president had little reason to respect his old classmate's military abilities, and so he must have believed that Polk's appointment to the west, where he had served the church so well, would aid popular support for a united effort there. Whatever the president's reasoning, the bishop accepted the appointment from his old friend.

Both the Episcopal clergy and the church's laity commented on Bishop Polk's joining the army. Their opinions reveal something about the relationship of the Episcopal Church to the new Confederate government. While in Virginia, Polk took the opportunity to visit his mentor Bishop Meade to receive his blessing. Less than enthusiastically Meade said to the new general that both his education and his character pointed toward acceptance of the new post, so he "would not condemn it." High churchman Bishop Otey of Tennessee explained his own reluctant blessing of Polk's decision in a letter to Bishop Meade. "I am satisfied that Bishop Polk is where he is by God's will, and not by his own," he exclaimed. But Otey wondered whether Polk had chosen the correct devotion. Bishop Elliott regarded the appointment simply as good for the entire South. The *Church Intelligencer* covered in much depth the bishop's decision and registered in its letters column civilian opinion. Could a priest be a warrior? one layman wondered. Another admired the bishop's patriotism. On the whole, the letters and editorials in that influential Southern church news-paper revealed that Episcopalians supported Polk's unprecedented action because it was good for the South.[28]

But why did Bishop Polk accept military duty? Bishop Meade believed Polk had joined the army to support the home guard protecting the Mississippi River and the people in his own diocese of Louisiana.[29] Polk explained his decision to replace his gown with a sword and to become a warrior for church and state a bit differently. To President Davis the bishop wrote that Tennessee governor Isham G. Harris wanted him for the local defenses, that his New Orleans clergy had requested his presence in the military, and that he desired to serve under his old friend Albert Sidney Johnston. But the bishop also mentioned the defense of the South's heart-land, the Confederacy's center, as most important to national war aims. Two modern military historians, Thomas L. Connelly and Archer Jones, excellent students of the mistakes in the western theater, understood what the bishop had meant when they stated that "despite spotty field performances and a reputation for troublemaking in the army, Polk was a far deeper strategic thinker than historians have credited him with being."[30] They insist that Polk had put aside his robes and donned the gray uniform in order to serve the vital center of the new nation.

Much of what was important in Polk's strategic thinking and his service as a Confederate national religious symbol has been obscured by the verdict that he was a foolhardy fighter and a most political general. His failures in battle reveal him to have been a soldier too long removed from military service. He must bear the blame for the disaster at Belmont, Kentucky, for poor construction and defense of Fort Henry on the Tennessee River, for possible disobedience of superiors at Perryville, Kentucky, for egregious and costly delays at Murfreesboro in September 1863, and for his overly complicated and unworkable plans to break the Federal concentration around Chattanooga, Tennessee. His political intrigues, always he said in pursuit of the greater good, confirm that the bishop knew that church-manship may only have been politics by another name. His feigned attempts at resignation from office because of his antipathy toward General Pierre G.T. Beauregard seem at best unseemly. As to Polk's leadership in the generals' conspiracy to remove Braxton Bragg from command of the Army of Tennessee, many believed that Polk had placed ambition over military victory.[31] To be fair to Polk, he sacrificed much in support of the entire Confederate nation.

Even Polk's role in the anti-Bragg conspiracy, certainly one of the most sordid if necessary political actions during the Civil War, captures the

warrior-bishop's zealous Confederate nationalism. That Bragg had preferred charges against the bishop certainly influenced Polk's strident response. But Polk also had sent letters to President Davis about Bragg
behind his superior's back. Polk presumed perhaps too much on his old
friendship with the president. Still, he told the president rightly that
Bragg's actions had contributed to loss of civilian morale in Kentucky and
eastern Tennessee and had led to mass desertion in the army. Polk insisted
that Bragg had failed to construct a loyal and coordinated command system. In short, Polk's enormous sense of faith in the cause and desire to
bolster soldier and civilian morale meant for him that Bragg must be replaced because he simply had been unable to lead in the defense of eastern
Tennessee and had destroyed civilian confidence in the Confederacy.[32]

Despite the truth and passion in the bishop-general's arguments, President Davis kept Bragg in command. But the president insisted that Bragg's
charges against Polk had to be dropped and rewarded his loyal friend with
an important command in Mississippi. As commander of the Department
of Mississippi, the warrior-bishop again succeeded in raising civilian morale, and he persuaded a number of army deserters to leave their home
communities, where they had fomented unrest, and return to the front
lines. Polk also bolstered the morale of his troops with his message that
the fanatical puritan Yankees planned to destroy Southern institutional
and social order (read as slavery). He held many religious services for the
troops and officiated at public baptisms of members of his officer corps.
Thus Polk had united fear of loss of slavery with the moral cause of the
Confederate war. Young officer Henry W. Watterston, later to beome the
famous editor of the *Louisville Courier Journal*, revealed how the troops
and officers viewed their commander's strident preaching and military
bravery. He declared that the bishop "inspired everyone as he seemed to
be able to pass along a line of fire like the children through the fiery
furnace, untouched."[33]

Unfortunately for Confederate morale, the bishop-warrior made one too
many forays near the Union lines, perhaps one too many tests of faith,
and at last met the fate of many of the ordinary soldiers for whom he had
prayed. Even in death Polk's image of sacrifice became useful to the Confederate cause. As he viewed the body of the dead warrior-bishop, General
Joseph E. Johnston was overheard to say that "the Christian patriot, soldier, has neither lived nor died in vain." The funeral took place at the
largest Episcopal Church in Atlanta, with Bishops Henry Quintard and
Stephen Elliott and multitudes of wailing laity in attendance. The bishops

had dressed the body in Confederate gray, put his sword by the coffin, and conspicuously placed a cross of white roses to rest nearby. Those military-religious symbols no doubt were meant to display Polk's unwavering devotion to the Confederate cause. The funeral procession carried the body past lines of troops, all with bowed heads. Later in Tennessee, where Polk's remains had been taken for burial, Bishop Thomas Wilmer, Polk's successor in Louisiana, preached that the general's example of fidelity to the Southern nation had helped to unite a resurgent southwestern church.[34] Polk's greatest epitaph thus linked the national with the spiritual.

Bishop Polk's Confederate military actions and faith in the cause revealed the support of a middle way churchman for a united Confederate war effort. The activities of another priest-general, William Nelson Pendleton, by contrast captures the soldierly behavior of one of Bishop Meade's greatest low churchmen, like his mentor a problematic Confederate. A longtime priest of the diocese of Virginia, Pendleton descended from two illustrious old Virginia families. Before the war Pendleton had held plum diocesan assignments, as headmaster of the elite Boy's School in Alexandria, and later as rector of the prestigious church in Lexington, Virginia, where he influenced the young elite cadets at the Virginia Military Institute. Pressed into wartime military service because of his West Point education, at the time Pendleton held grave reservations about military duty, if not also about his hopes for a Southernwide Confederacy.[35] Perhaps those conflicting actions and thoughts, and service with reservations, stemmed from Pendleton's anti-hierarchical, state particularistic views.

Low church Pendleton was. Opposed to drink, gambling, and dancing he belonged to the Calvinist, localist, anti-institutionalist branch of the Episcopal Church. He had entered the ministry during a period of spiritual and evangelical awakening in Virginia under the leadership of Bishop Meade. At the Boy's School, Pendleton had uncovered a Tractarian (Oxford Movement) plot and had enlisted the faculty from the Theological Seminary to quash that high church movement in Virginia. While residing in Maryland during the 1850s he had accused his bishop of being too partial to Rome. In Lexington he instructed his young son Sandie on the duties of a low churchman. A student at Presbyterian Washington College, Sandie had won a speech prize for his oration on the first families of Virginia. Sandie had spoken glowingly of his own family's colonial Virginia heritage, its connections with the Lees, and its devotion to the Episcopal Church. William had urged Sandie to praise Virginia, but he had cautioned him against too much comment on the Anglicanism of his eighteenth-century forebears. The elder Pendleton long had labored to bring Presbyterians around to his church's evangelical ways, and he did not want those fundamentalists reminded of the Episcopal Church's earlier mistakes.[36]

After the war broke out, William Pendleton's loyalty to Virginia and his hopes for the church there meant he had to accept, whatever his worries, a commission in the provisional army of Virginia. Just a few hours after he had received a post in the Rockbridge artillery, he set down in his diary his reasons for shedding the cloth to fight. Pendleton wrote that a "defensive war cannot on gospel grounds, it seems to me, be condemned." In that diary entry he also described his beloved state, his sense of honor and independence, and his place in the home guard to defend Virginia against "a most unChristian" Northern society. In May 1861 he wrote to a Northern friend that Bishop William Meade had encouraged him to fight in the defense of Virginia.[37] But his evangelical and state particularist reasoning actually caused harm to his support for national Confederate war policy.

In the beginning Pendleton, whom Joseph E. Johnston called a Christian soldier, did fight for his state and pray for the survival of his church. He rose in rank to become Lee's chief of artillery in the Army of Northern Virginia and in that capacity participated in many engagements in his native state. Pendleton also served informally as an army chaplain; he built chapels in his camps and often led troops in prayer. He begged local congregations for blankets and housing for the soldiers. Pendleton often spoke with General Lee about troop morale and the ability to sustain a united war effort in defense of his native state. He even believed that he had assisted in his commander-in-chief's own prayer life and stiffened his will. Both generals certainly told their troops that to defend the sacred ground of Virginia was to join in God's just war. To the Sixty-seventh Annual Diocesan Convention of Virginia Pendleton explained his loyalties and his activities on behalf of his state and his faith. He exclaimed to the delegates that "divine Providence has entrusted to me an additional talent, the responsibility for using aright what I deeply feel." He went on, "that large numbers attend where a general officer prays and preaches is something, yet how much more important that he has the spirit of Christ."[38] Surely, Pendleton meant that the church had a responsibility to keep up the spirits and the morale of the Virginia people.

That military officer indeed gave heroic Christian service to his native state throughout much of the war. But he belonged to the mainstream Southern evangelical Episcopal Church, and his attitude toward the war was influenced by that localist and Calvinist faith. In May 1864, after dark days had come to Virginia, Pendleton blurted out "the Judge of all the earth will do right" by the cause of all Virginians.[39] When news arrived of the death of his beloved son Sandie, Pendleton stoically said that it was God's will. As battle after battle was either lost or drawn, as more and more of Virginia fell under Yankee control, he called for prayers from the men for intervention from heaven. But soon Pendleton, like Mrs. McGuire and others, was saying that God appeared to have had another purpose for Virginians than mere military victory. On Christmas Day 1864, he prayed for the Lord to "visit" the enemy for such abominable destruction of Virginia's Episcopal churches. Even at the very end of the war he believed that the cause for which he had labored had been just, but he also stated that "the Lord has allowed us to be overwhelmed so that we must cease to be such comparative idolators in our estimate of Virginia." He concluded, "as God allowed us to be overwhelmed, I accept."[40]

Unlike Polk and Elliott, or for that matter, Atkinson and Otey, Meade and Pendleton had preached a fatalistic vision of the South's future. Pendleton said, albeit cautiously, he had truly done his duty. Perhaps somehow he had come to understand that his particularist support for Virginia over the united Confederacy might have damaged the war effort. One wonders whether he also grasped that his evangelical beliefs and those of many other Virginians, as well as those in the rest of the slave states, had contributed to a localist military thinking and to his own and others loss of morale. Had his religious beliefs in the fundamentalist view of the literalness of the Lord's will indeed influenced the morale of himself, his troops, and the civilian population? Had his loss of faith in the cause turned that loyal Confederate against the Confederacy?

Perhaps another way to view the relationship between national fidelity and faithfulness is to see how those church leaders who survived put their church and section back together after the war. If the military general Pendleton seemed to understand the Confederacy's defeat, what would be that evangelical priest's and other Episcopal Church leaders' postwar attitudes toward the national Episcopal Church, and indirectly, toward reconstructing the nation? How, indeed, did leaders of the three branches of the Southern Episcopal Church approach reconciliation with and restoration of the national Church? Reconciliation surely recapitulates what has been discovered about their different actions during the war.

As the Confederacy collapsed, and indeed even before the body had grown cold, some church leaders made plans to return to the national fold. Bishop Atkinson of North Carolina moved to reunite with the national Episcopal Church and the nation even before the war had ended.

Historians might say that his actions merely reflected North Carolina's lackluster support for the Confederacy. But they have not looked at that Carolinian's beliefs. Bishop Atkinson belonged to the hierarchical wing of his church. For him the established church always had been more important than either the Confederacy or its Southern Episcopal Church, which he had joined only reluctantly. His faith probably made it easier for him as early as 1864 to desert the Southern church and nation. Low church Bishop Johns of Virginia also moved quickly to restore ties with the national Episcopal Church. But Johns stated clearly that it was the diocese of Virginia, free and independent, evangelical and methodist, which returned to the national church and national union. General William N. Pendleton agreed with his bishop. Bishop Stephen Elliott of Georgia, he of the middle way, hesitated over reunion with the national church. Only after the war had ended was he finally convinced that the South and the Confederate States Protestant Episcopal Church must reunite with the national church. In short, the very same interests in the South that had made Elliott and Polk such nationalists led the Georgia prelate to delay and then reluctantly rejoin the national church.[41]

But time and inattention has confused the story of a divided wartime Episcopal Church and of those Confederates in it who in their own ways came to oppose the Confederacy. Only work of those historians who recently have related Southern faith to wartime morale has revived issues of internal divisions in that horrible brothers' war. Reverend William Nelson Pendleton's postwar career shows how much historians have left to do to overcome the legends of Confederate loyalty, even of institutional unity in the cause. His postwar personal trials and tribulations became part of the legend of the lost cause. As soon as the war ended, Pendleton baptized his grandson, bitterly calling him the heir to his nearly destroyed Virginia clan. Later this evangelist mounted the pulpit to proclaim the greatness of the Confederate national cause. He preached all over the state on his favorite topic: how a united South under the military leadership of Robert E. Lee had sacrificed much to fight for its rights. Because of their enormous faith, went Pendleton's revisionist view, the people had shown the courage to stick together to the end.[42]

One wonders just what the former warrior-priest had needed to excise from his past to survive in the world of the new South. What is certain is that for generations Pendleton's historical revisionism has helped to muddy those deep and divisive currents of the Confederate past. The wartime contributions of the Confederate States Protestant Episcopal Church leaders, and of evangelical church leaders so vulnerable to self-loathing because of God's desertion, of church Confederates against the Confederacy, need to be washed clean. Until then, their voices will remain drowned in a sea of false modern Southern nationalists, and particularist monolithic mythmakers.

6

"Personal Remarks Are Hazardous on a Crowded Riverboat": Mary Boykin Chesnut and the Gossip on Confederate Divisiveness

The women of the South during the Civil War, as many historians have shown, made many public and private contributions to the Confederate war effort. In the early days of the war they applauded as their young sons, husbands, and other loved ones joined the army. Women of the upper and middle classes sewed clothes for the troops and provided relief for the poorer people at home. Some even more adventurous women, or those better placed, served in hospitals as nurses and orderlies, and a few of them became hospital managers. Others with political contacts took jobs in government offices in Richmond and elsewhere, especially as inflation and war debt necessitated that they earn an income. Privately and not so privately women's letters urged on the efforts of those they loved. Women even petitioned high officials to aid the troops and lobbied against and for government policies. Others kept private accounts of their own activities that reveal their rich and varied wartime activities in support of the cause. Especially during the early days of the war, then, in many ways women gave devoted and nearly united support to the Confederacy.[1]

Before long, however, the war had begun to wear down many women in mind, spirit, and body. They lost many loved ones. Some of them had to disrupt their lives and move often to avoid the Yankee invaders that the army could not keep out. Others faced hardships behind the lines because they could not control the slaves or could not obtain support from the government to control them. Still others, even among the upper classes, went without because the government was unable to feed them. Because of these hardships, a number of those upper- and middle-class women turned against the war, or at least those who conducted the South's defenses. They criticized in public and private the Confederate government's war. They called for their men to desert the army, to come home to protect them. In short, the women became a material and morale problem for the Confederate military effort.[2] Whether they believed they had remained true to the cause or not, and many did believe so, some women actually became Confederates against the Confederacy. To understand why women turned against the war requires a careful look at their negative activities. More often than not, because they had little in the way of what was considered normal powers, their actions took the form of words rather than deeds.

Still, a number of women acted out their political dissent from the dominant Confederate government. Women's political disruptions, well known today and even during the war despite attempts then and after to mitigate their significance, took many forms. Most visible were the wartime so-called bread riots in at least twelve of the Confederacy's cities and towns. Although scholars have had difficulty finding motivation for those acts other than dissatisfaction with the government's food distribution system, the most salient fact is that most of the demonstrators and rioters were women.

The most careful, if lifeless, account of those riots is Michael B. Chesson's study of Richmond's on April 2, 1863.[3] That work links events in Richmond with other women-led riots around the same time in Atlanta; Salisbury, North Carolina; Mobile; Raleigh; and near Petersburg, Virginia. Richmond's women rioters, estimated to be over 1,000 from the city and the surrounding countryside, looted stores and shops throughout the downtown section. Their targets appeared to be merchant profiteers, those who speculated in food and clothing and charged excessively high interest rates on loans. Some of the women interviewed insisted that such businessmen were disloyal to the South. Civic and Confederate leaders failed in their attempts to quell the disorder and protect the storekeepers. They knew that the militia and the army would refuse to fire on unarmed women, especially since many of the soldiers were the husbands of the rioters. The riot spun its course, as President Jefferson Davis was said to have calmed the worst of the demonstrators. Other riots continued into the spring of 1863 and on through the fall of 1864. Some leaders said that the women's actions played into the hands of Northern propagandists who had used them to reveal decline in popular morale. That did not faze the women.

Respectable women, though some Confederate officials claimed otherwise, had taken matters into their own hands. Some of the upper- and middle-class women who worked for the government recorded the events in their diaries, and in their postwar memoirs they actually praised the audacity of the rioters.[4]

Yet another, more brutal, kind of riotous women's political activity took the form of armed resistance to Confederate officials. Women joined male resisters and army deserters in sabotaging various supply areas and building fortifications. The mountain regions of western North Carolina and eastern Tennessee and the northern border of Texas were sites of pitched battles. Soldiers and local guerrilla brigands, and what passed for sheriff's officers, fired on the resisters, male and female alike. Women and young boys died alongside ex-soldier and deserter fellow protesters. In both regions women were hanged, having been charged, often without trials, with treason against the Confederacy. Even the actual trials were mere shams. Those women had carried their opposition to the Confederacy to armed resistance.[5]

Less physically violent, because women rarely had the opportunity to express armed dissent, were the writings of those who had found fault with the Confederacy. As has already been pointed out, resistance also took the form of letters to the front urging soldiers to come home. Likewise, women's petitions and missives to government officials reveal the written word as weapons of political dissent. Less visible and more personal were the diaries and published postwar memoirs in which women recorded their own feelings. Those efforts registered the declining morale of the people as the rapidly failing Confederate government and military seemed unable to halt the Yankee assault on the South. At times these efforts capture much more than stories of the individual diarist's failure of morale, as the women diarists often recorded what others in their circle felt about the war effort. The spread of rumors, the overheard comments of the males, powerful politicos, and worried civilians alike became grist for the mills of a widespread female politics of resistance. In those writings are clues to why so many women who claimed to support the war in fact undermined it and thus became themselves Confederates against the Confederacy. Moreover, these works tell the story of a number of leaders' opposition to the Confederacy and the consequences of those divisions.

One of the best known and most loyal of Confederate women who published her wartime diary was Judith W. McGuire, wife of an Episcopal priest and seminary professor from Alexandria, Virginia. She recorded many of her experiences as a refugee caught behind Union lines in western

Virginia. McGuire also, as a sojourner in wartime Richmond, described at length leaders' comments on failed governmental policies and personnel. McGuire, who unfairly considered herself a mediocre writer, published her diary shortly after the war. She claimed to have recreated a "true record" of personal hardship. McGuire insisted she had written as a loyal Confederate, supportive of the war and of all Southern institutions.[6]

Despite her efforts at personal propaganda and perhaps subterfuge, McGuire actually reveals to the reader a sad story of a Confederacy in part destroyed by the politics of rumor and gossip about internal divisions among the leaders that had undermined civilian morale, including her own. A faithful low-church Episcopalian, when times grew grave, Judith relied on her beliefs to keep her going. Of course, as loss after loss in battle, as churches burned, as women were forced to flee before the Yankee hordes, McGuire began to feel that God had a purpose in destroying the South. She shared with friends the messages she heard in sermons and told them that the priests had begun to lose hope. Those same friends whose faith she so wanted to revive also damaged McGuire's personal support for the cause as they talked to her of rumors of Yankee invasion and Confederate leadership incompetence. McGuire herself wanted to record the civil history of Virginia as a great and good struggle against evil, but she also included the actions of failed officials in her account. She wrote that certain Confederates claimed great military victories, but as a friend said, "victory never seems to do much good." When rumors of the great hero Thomas J. Jackson's death proved true, she concluded that Virginia no longer could be defended. All hope passed as she heard of Atlanta's fall and her friends blamed President Davis. Then she said "I will no longer make myself uneasy about what I hear"—but she did. Too much truth, McGuire knew, was dangerous to Richmond's leaders, as "such harmful prophecies" upset her increasingly. Then, as William T. Sherman marched through Georgia, she damned Governor Joseph Brown and Vice President Alexander Stephens, saying the Confederacy bore "the bitter fruits" of their treason. At St. Paul's in Richmond after the government had fled south, she applauded her rector, who refused to pray for President Abraham Lincoln. But McGuire also declined to pray for President Jefferson Davis. As a woman with little power other than to spread words of hope or despair, she captured her own usefulness when she allowed "almost every woman of the South, or at least Virginia, will have her tale to tell when this 'cruel war is over.' "[7]

Few writers of any kind told their story as well as Judith McGuire, but others certainly revealed what rumors had done to Confederate women.

Kate Stone of northeastern Louisiana also kept a bitter journal about being forced to flee her home and go to Texas out of fear of Yankee and slave marauders. She resented that her "part in war is to watch and wait," but, like McGuire, Stone hung on every rumor, every piece of gossip, that spread through the Gulf Coast. Rumors of lost battles in Virginia, of slaves running away up there, only lowered her hopes of defense at home. Rich young men who stayed home to control the slaves she heard the venomous locals call cowards. When Stone required news to know what actions to take herself, she could not get it. Finally, from Tyler, Texas, in early 1865, she and other refugees learned that the Confederate peace commissioners had failed in their mission. Although she was told that Lee had surrendered, Stone continued to hope for troops to rally in the Lower South. But she understood the impossibility of that, so she maligned the peace commissioners for failing to make a bargain to keep slavery. Stone insisted in her narration of the many rumors of failure that the rumors had in no way undermined her confidence in the government or kept her from being a Confederate, but quite clearly her own morale had collapsed.[8]

Another who recollected her life during the war was Jesse Harrison, wife of President Davis's personal secretary. Because of her husband Burton's close proximity to the seat of power, she had the unique opportunity to hear firsthand many rumors of division among the Confederate leaders themselves. In her *Recollections*, Mrs. Harrison wrote of the harm rumors and gossip had done to the Confederate effort. It was all she could bear to hear of the "heartbreaking story of the final days before Appomattox," said that loyal female Confederate. But at times Harrison herself was unenthusiastic about her divisive government. Of course she supported the president, and, after she heard Davis had removed the incompetent General Johnston from Atlanta, she applauded. She also dropped a bomb of a rumor: "People we met said outspokenly that the Executive's animus against Johnston was based upon a petty feud between their wives." Their wives' constant gossip, she claimed, ruined the Confederacy's hopes. This accusation Harrison had learned firsthand from Mary Chesnut, whom she regarded as a surrogate mother and a "comrade."[9] As a part of Chesnut's circle of bright young women, Harrison certainly had overheard many rumors about divisions in the Confederacy. Indeed, of all those Southern women who wrote of leadership behavior, Mary Boykin Chesnut emerges as the most important purveyor of the political gossip of Confederates who opposed the Confederacy.

Mary Chesnut's *Diary from Dixie* indeed is the finest and most explicitly political memoir by any Confederate woman.[10] During the war only a few friends saw the diary or journals because Chesnut feared she had rendered personalities too explosively. Kept while she sojourned in Montgomery, Richmond, Camden, Columbia, and parts of lower North Carolina, because of always traveling and never settling, Mary seemed upset with what she was recording. Travels and personal worries no doubt contributed to the gaps she left in her journals, especially during the crucial period from the fall of 1862 through the fall of 1864. She did, however, reconstruct lost periods later in memoir form. Never published during her lifetime, reworked over the years after the war as she gained confidence in setting a scene, recording dialogue among the leaders, and revisiting what she had overheard, by the 1880s she had turned her diaries and journals into a brilliant memoir.

Historians have rightly worried whether Chesnut had changed many wartime stories to fit her own mood during the dark days of the emerging New South. But the most recent analysts of her work insist that she reconstructed accurately much of what she had lived through during the war.[11] For the purposes of this study, her journals, diary, and later memoir tell brilliantly how Confederates turned against one another, even if Chesnut may have embellished what she was told or had overheard. Other diarists and memoirists close enough to events to overhear and participate in personal political gossip and intrigue corroborate what she put down. Because of where she lived and the company she kept, and her skills at understanding exactly what she had heard, Chesnut in her work revealed internal division and the decline in leadership and civilian morale connected to this division and even contributed as a sharer, exchanger, and conduit to the climate of division.[12] Hers is a major commentary on Confederates against the Confederacy.

Just who was this brilliant political and society diarist, what had prepared her to understand male weakness and pride, why had she set down what she heard, and what does she tell history about Confederate leaders' growing dissatisfaction with the cause? Born into a low-country family of planter wealth and political experience, Mary Miller had all the educational advantages allowed to a young woman of her class in society. Educated largely at home by private tutors and in a fashionable Charleston school for young women, and quick to learn, she developed into a great reader and apt conversationalist. Mary read widely all her life; especially did she absorb the fiction of manners and rumor of Trollope and Thackery, and she delved with care into historical writing. Her father held office as governor of South Carolina, served in the United States Senate, and became an ardent Nullifier. Young Mary thus grew up in the presence of men of political substance and had the learning, experience, and opportunity to grasp the meaning of their exchanges, for she often assisted her father in entertaining the great Southern men of public affairs.[13]

Mary Miller married an ambitious South Carolina political leader, James Chesnut, and spent much energy in the furtherance of his career. Although she endured the curse of childlessness—in the Old South a woman always was faulted as the barren one who had not fulfilled her function in life— Mary's place in South Carolina society nevertheless was secure. Her status and her skills were of great use to James. Like a few other brilliant women who could not themselves hold public office, she did political chores, including writing letters, drafting speeches, and hosting functions for the best and the brightest in the state. Her biographer Elizabeth Muhlenfeld suggests that Mary's "own sense of worth became increasingly identified with his success." When James served in the state legislature, Mary became his personal secretary. In 1858 the legislature sent James to the United States Senate, and Mary went along as his assistant. In Washington she made the acquaintance of other powerful political and military wives, such as Charlotte Wigfall, Virginia Clay, and Mary Lee. Although there is some question about how close, Mary also became a friend of Varina Howell Davis, wife of the future president of the Confederacy. Certainly, both Mary and Varina had political curiosity and ably assisted in the social politics so necessary to success in Washington, a city consumed with public affairs. Like those other women, Mary supported Southern secession, and her husband's career on behalf of the Confederacy would open many doors for her political charms.[14]

During the war Mary constantly had the ears of, often overheard the conversations of, and even became the confidant of political wives and, more important, their Confederate husbands. Although considered unattractive physically, and therefore supposedly no threat to other women, powerful men flocked to her gatherings, warm to her solicitude for the cares of office, and often confided in her. Other women joined Mary because they too could have access to the best and the brightest. Mary also lived in many places of importance where the great leaders did business. When James became a member of the Confederate provisional Congress, she traveled with him to Montgomery to observe the chaotic birth of the new republic. She went also to Richmond and rekindled her friendships with Varina Davis, Charlotte Wigfall, and Virgina Clay, although she often would squabble with Charlotte Wigfall. In Richmond, early in the war, she lived near the Confederate White House and was in daily attendance on the Davis family. When James went to Columbia, South Carolina, to become military attaché to the governor, she dutifully followed, taking a part of her female political entourage along. In Columbia, she became fast friends with Louisa McCord, certainly one of the ablest political minds of the Old South, male or female. Though Mary lived with her shrill, critical, Unionist in-laws, she received at their home important political rumor-carrying friends, such as John R. Thompson, former editor of the *Southern Literary Messenger*. James next became a military aide to President Davis in Richmond, and they resided there from the middle of 1862 until the middle of 1864. At the war's end she lived in comparative squalor near Camden, South Carolina, where she observed the final unraveling of the Confederate leadership.[15]

Why did that keen observer record so much of that political rumor and gossip? Obviously, one major reason was to gain the information necessary to further James's career. As political and military aide to President Davis, knowledge of what other leaders did and thought was of importance to him. On occasion, frustration over Mary's role in gathering political gossip, and perhaps purveying it too, spilled over and James chastized her. But mostly he shared with her what he had heard in high places, and she with him, and they no doubt discussed the meaning of what they had heard. "Rumors were rampant," she exclaimed, "and everyone spent the days running from one meeting to the next, then visiting everyone else to hash over the latest gossip."[16] Her biographer says that, in addition to assisting James, her years of political experience, her love of political drama, and her natural literary bent meant that Mary desired to record what information she gathered so that she could weave a tale of Confederate heroics. "In the revised Civil War journal," says Elizabeth Muhlenfeld, Mary "takes real events and persons and . . . gives them life and places them in a complex, multidimensional society." Mary also had other and perhaps more personal reasons for recording the political gossip of Confederate leaders. She herself appeared frustrated that her only weapon was rumor and gossip, and she said often that if only she had been a man she could have participated in events and perhaps helped to quell the divisiveness among the leadership. Certainly she remained loyal to the cause and she showed much anger over the dissent she recorded, for she saw it wrecking the Confederacy. Perhaps she couldn't help herself, as Cassandralike she determined to describe how Confederates turned against the Confederacy.[17]

Describe she did. At first, in the early days of keeping her diary, Chesnut recorded a harmony of purpose among Confederates. Of course, even then she was wary, for she feared the strength of the Union, the illpreparedness of the Confederacy, half-heartedness among certain Virginians, and the ominous potential of a race war. But early military successes and the seeming unity of purpose for a time stilled those fears. When President Davis in private conversation with her said only fools doubt the Yankees' courage and willingness to fight, Mary believed she was listening to a great leader who had united the South with his realism and would prevail. She made a pact with other wives of key officials to support the men in every way possible and vowed to help keep up the leaders' morale. Wary at first over some early reports of military setback in western Virginia, she later rejoiced in the victory at First Manassas. But shortly this perceptive woman recorded how Northern incursions undermined morale and turned leaders one against another. Still, her refrain became stay firm, "it will take a little time." So she warned others that "quarreling among ourselves makes me faint with fear." Soon, indeed, Mary began to regard herself as a Cassandralike person, recording arguments and divisions and wondering just what harm they were doing. As she plunged into setting down growing resentment among the leaders, she warned all who would listen, woe be it on us if we are not serious in the beginning.[18]

Because of her connection to members of the Confederate Congress in Montgomery and later in Richmond, Chesnut early saw what she regarded as a lack of seriousness and a divisiveness that boded no good. She wondered why members in Montgomery seemed to distrust one another, why they accused others of favoring reconstruction if they questioned policies at the beginning. She exploded with anger when a member accused the president of reconstructionism. Rumors of government inaction, and of a Congress filled with disloyal leaders, passed often in the corridors of power in Montgomery. James tried to counter those rumors and assure Mary that there was adequate preparation for a vigorous new government. Mary knew differently. She met with political wives whose stories convinced her that members of Congress had become discouraged even before the permanent government had been formed. Her former guardian, the old curmudgeon Judge Thomas J. Withers of South Carolina, also in Montgomery during that spring, supplemented what the women had told her. He regaled her with tales of old and lasting grudges against the president nursed by such leaders as Lawrence M. Keitt and the Rhett family that would "injure our cause." When James went to Charleston to take part in the events surrounding Fort Sumter, Mary went along. He assured her again that the onset of war would unite all factions in Congress. Unsure of that, she recorded that Upper South secessionists had taken too long to join the Confederacy, and she wondered how much to expect from those states' congressional contingent. Later, events in Richmond, to which the Chesnuts had traveled for the opening of government, fed her fears that proud Virginians loved their own state better than they loved the Confederacy.[19]

From May until September 1861, Mary and James lived in a Richmond hotel, while James completed his service in the provisional Congress. Mary became the center of a group of bright women, ambitious for their husbands' congressional careers. Among the most important were Charlotte Wigfall, wife of Texas senator Louis T. Wigfall, and Virginia Clay, wife of Alabama's Clement Clay. Charlotte Maria Cross, born in Providence, Rhode Island, to a wealthy family, had married Wigfall and become a devoted Southerner. Virginia Clay, who herself carefully recorded political gossip, had years of political experience in Alabama and Washington, and she knew how to wring information from the men and how to spread it effectively. At parties, luncheons, and evening teas, those friends entertained the Richmond power brokers. It was at one of those gatherings that an incautious Charlotte Wigfall informed Mary that her husband intended to make an enemy of his old friend Jefferson Davis.[20] In fact, Wigfall had already begun his vicious attacks in Congress on the president's policies. By August 1861 a loose group of opponents had formed in Congress, and Mary became privy to much of the venom spread against the president. Of course, she supported the president and reported what she heard to Varina, which may have led to a temporary rift between herself and Mrs. Davis.[21]

In September 1861, perhaps tired of Richmond intrigue or hoping for reelection to the Confederate Senate, James Chesnut took Mary home to Camden to politic. He failed to gain support from the legislature, in part, thought Mary, because James seemed too loyal to President Davis. James took a position as military aide to the governor of South Carolina, and in January 1862 they moved to Columbia, where Mary became the fast friend of Louisa McCord, a wealthy widow and a gifted political observer. There, too, Judge Thomas J. Withers often appeared at Mary's gatherings, where so much information was exchanged about goings-on in Columbia, Charleston, and Richmond. More particularly, Mary heard about activities in the Confederate Congress, and she passed on what she knew to her husband as well as discussed matters with Louisa McCord.[22]

In March 1862 the pipeline of rumors from Richmond about attacks on the president again picked up. Mary claimed to have heard constant bickering from members, and she recorded a story told to her about Henry Stuart Foote of Tennessee. It seems that Foote barely avoided a duel because another member took umbrage at his comments on the failings of the president. Mary also heard that Foote had criticized government policy, and that he had said that no one in beleaguered Mississippi was willing to sacrifice cotton profits for the Confederacy. Appalled, she knew that Foote had struck at a weakness in an unraveling policy, and that congressional members registered the feelings of their constituents in their Richmond debates. It was the major event of April 1862, however, the fall of New Orleans and its fallout in Congress, that most worried Mary about the Confederacy's future. In Columbia, people told her that the country was now divided in half, that Texas and Arkansas had been lost to the Confederacy. She reported that many congressmen had called for an investigation of presidential defense policies. Squabbles broke out on the floor of Congress, and Mary understood that congressmen had charged one another with neglect of their constituents. Some members, she heard, even sent secret information to the Richmond press that contributed to newspaper attacks on government policies.[23]

Both Chesnuts, alive to events in Congress, seemed to grow weary of provincial life, for they sought ways to return to the action in Richmond. Perhaps they hoped to use their connections to defuse congressional attacks on the administration. The ever-loyal James took a position as military aide to the president, and in December 1862 they hurried back to the Confederacy's capital. This time they rented a house near the Confederate White House, and Mary became the confidant of Varina. Many visitors came and went in the home of this gracious hostess, and of course, with James now so close to the president, there was much gossip about congressional activities. They remained in Richmond until May 1864, but Mary discontinued her journal. Still, she must have kept enough notes of what she heard to reconstruct them later in her memoir.

Louis and Charlotte Wigfall, despite Mary's support for the president, came often to visit and brought a number of congressional allies. Wigfall reported to her that Robert Toombs of Georgia had become a troubled failed general, but that Congress did not have the strength to stop his criticism of the president. Wigfall also told her with much glee how congressmen hated Secretary of State Judah Benjamin, especially because that Louisianan had become so close to Davis that he even wrote the president's messages to Congress. Mary got back at Wigfall when she asked him how he could defend General P.G.T. Beauregard's actions when many in South Carolina believed him unable to defend Charleston. In December 1863, at a gathering with her husband, Secretary of War James A. Seddon, and Wigfall, where hatred of Davis was tempered only by accompanying venom against weak and vacillating members of Congress, Mary set down her comments about congressmen who opposed key personnel matters.

They told her that two powerful members, James Orr of South Carolina and Benjamin H. Hill of Georgia, had revealed their lack of patriotism when they opposed the substitution bill. Seddon said that keeping planters home to control unruly slaves was more important than sending them to fight. Mary agreed.[24]

It was Wigfall who relayed to her what perhaps elicited Mary's most troublesome verdict about Congress. One September day in 1863, Wigfall told her the story of Quartermaster General Abraham Myers's fate. Toombs had called Myers an incompetent, and the president planned to remove Myers. Under the leadership of William P. Miles of Charleston and Wigfall, congressmen fought to save Myers. They insisted on a full congressional debate on personnel policy, of course to thwart the president's will. Myers was saved for the time being.[25] Mary now knew that some members of Congress were committed to undermining the president's powers.

She also recorded information from debates in Congress on the future of the Confederacy itself. In January 1864 she learned that Congressman William W. Boyce of South Carolina, a personal friend of the Chesnuts, had begun a movement with John Ashmore and L.M. Keitt to force the Congress to begin peace proceedings.[26] Of course, nothing came of that action, but others there began to talk openly of a failed country that must make the best peace it could. Disgusted with Congress, and fearing for Mary's security, in May 1864 James sent her home to South Carolina.[27] It would be a time of running from danger, anger over peace proposals, and other frustrations for Mary. Even in exile she continued to damn Congress for its flagging support of the administration.

Congress's political actions consumed most of Mary's writings and became a most disturbing account of Confederates against the Confederacy. Mixed in with that political gossip were many other stories about executive government actions, often reported gleefully to her by close friends such as Secretary of the Navy Stephen Mallory and former Undersecretary of State William H. Trescot. Both men had worked with her husband, and both had great respect for Mary's abilities as well as her charms. Indeed, Mary dazzled them with her bright and perceptive comments and also her flirtatiousness. For Secretary Mallory, Mary early had been a pipeline to the president for appointments, both in Montgomery and Richmond. Rumor had it that Varina believed Mallory an unreliable Confederate and unfaithful to his wife, but that Mary had persuaded her to gain the president's support for the secretary. A frequent visitor to her gatherings in Columbia, Trescot loved to exchange stories with Mary of political intrigue in the Richmond cabinet. Trescot, a man of enormous learning, became greatly attracted to Mary, and James seemed jealous of him. But Mary admired his writings on diplomatic history, read them carefully, and seemed to encourage his attentions. Both Mallory and Trescot's gossip provided her with much information on events in the Confederate government.[28]

Trescot corresponded with friends in government and shared their comments on events and rumors in Richmond. Mary said to friends, he tells me everything. Indeed, Trescot gave her much inside information about intrigue over cabinet shuffling. Mary also discussed with Mallory the president's appointment of the known Unionist Thomas H. Watts of Alabama to the cabinet as attorney general. Watts would become a liability, she claimed. Still, Mary defended the president and believed rightly that he controlled his cabinet of mediocrities to the extent that they at least followed his policies. At the same time, she knew subcabinet appointees often undermined those policies. She especially resented infamous rebel war clerk John B. Jones's habit of spreading rumors about Benjamin and others to the press and to Congress to use against the government. Mary, however, did not hesitate to talk about these personnel issues and to record what others had said about lack of talent in the cabinet.[29]

Toward the end of 1864, while in South Carolina, Mary kept in touch with government affairs through the wife of Burton Harrison, secretary to the president. Harrison's young wife also kept a journal based on her husband's comments and the conversations she had with many admirers, who gave her much inside information. This gossip she shared with Mary. Mary understood from her that the government was unable to present a united front to the Southern people. Squabbling among bureaucrats she believed most damaging. Harrison reported to her that the *Richmond Examiner* editors so hated the president that the cabinet vowed to unite behind him. Alas, it was too late. In October 1864 Mary heard from General William Preston, her young friend Sallie's father, that Burton Harrison said Richmond could not be defended. Then her cousin, the Union sympathizer Edward Boykin, informed her that squabbles and inefficiency in the cabinet had worked "like a dryrot in the army." In November 1864 Varina Davis wrote that scandals were rife in the government, and that the thieves who had refused to stand by her husband were themselves falling out. Confiding that crescendo of dire information she had heard and overheard to her journal in April 1865, Mary said that Varina merely had recapitulated what she, Mary, knew already about the government. The divided Confederate executive government, Mary wailed, never had a war plan, and that ruined us.[30]

Yet another group of Confederate leaders, the generals, appeared frequently in Mary's journals and memoir; the generals had concerned her
from the beginning because of their bickering among themselves and with
civilian leaders. Mary adds little to the tales historians have taken from the
generals' memoirs. Most historians know about the struggles for preferment in both the Union and the Confederate army. Still, the angle from
which this bright civilian woman angrily recorded those battles among the
generals shows just how much they must have demoralized Southern people in the know. Again, from those she entertained, Mary heard about the
problems in the high military command. She recorded her own feelings
about them, many of whom, such as John Bell Hood and Joseph E. Johnston, she knew personally if not intimately. Of course, James's being a
military aide in Columbia and then Richmond added to Mary's store of
political gossip of military preferment and turnover.

Everyone of Mary Chesnut's set had heard, she reported, about the
quarrels between President Davis and Generals Johnston and Beauregard.
She commented at length on what others had told her about the results
of that bickering. Neither officer enjoyed the president's confidence, she
knew, and she also understood that those personal divisions upset other
high-ranking officers. Of Johnston's view of Davis she said, "he hates not
wisely but too well." This feud Mary also connected to James Longstreet's
ambitions for high command, which led him, she believed, to undermine
Braxton Bragg. From James, who had gone west in December 1863 to
investigate the decline in morale among Bragg's general staff, she learned
that Bragg had been as much sinned against as sinned. She took some
delight when James told Wigfall, a Johnston supporter, that Johnston himself had advised the president to retain Bragg in command. Of course Mary
knew how congressmen and generals had joined hands to demean the
president, and she worried that the politics of war had disrupted military
policies. When an old family friend visiting in Columbia, the Texas lawyer
Henry Brewster, told her in June 1864 of the squabbles between Davis
and Johnston over Atlanta, Mary said that she was not surprised. Brewster
stated that Johnston had refused to tell anyone of his plans for that town's
defense, because he feared Davis's lackey generals would betray him. Mary
also knew firsthand the wounds to General John Bell Hood's vanity and
pride from a failed love affair with "Buck" Preston, and she worried about
the affect that this would have on his generalship. In her memoir she wrote
that reports about Hood being drunk at Nashville were off the mark, unless
he was drunk from personal failure with the opposite sex. Personal and
private views of a female observer perhaps, but Mary was correct when

she depicted the results for the Confederacy of that general's human frail-
ties.[31]

Events of the central command system, including the Congress, the
executive government, and the generals occupied much of Mary's political
gossip. But her connections to the home front, both as an observer from
Richmond and from the heart of South Carolina, revealed to her how anti–
federal government intrigue had sapped the will and affected the unity
among Confederate civilians. Her sources appeared at her parties and other
gatherings and talked openly about problems in the hinterland. Travelers
through Camden, Columbia, and Charleston, such as wealthy Florida
planter Edward Haile, often brought news. Also she entertained powerful
South Carolinians, like the wealthy planter John De Saussure. Often she
shared information with Louisa McCord, a person of conservative values
and calm exterior. But her major allies, or enemies, or at least purveyors
of quality gossip, again were Judge Withers and William H. Trescot. What
she learned added, no doubt, to her fears of influential private citizens'
unwillingness to tolerate failure in the high command. They had turned
hostile and no longer would make sacrifices for the cause.

It was Haile who reported to Mary that the Richmond government offered little or no assistance to the states and indeed meant only to take
from them to pursue a selfish war effort. This, she observed, had led the
Rhett family as early as October 1861 to condemn the president's policies.
Mary believed that constant attack on Davis from the Rhetts undermined
the popular will. Certainly this was confirmed for her in November 1861,
when Camden planter De Saussure told her bluntly that if South Carolina
were lost, he simply would go over to the Yankees in order to save his
cotton and slaves. De Saussure and his family were old friends of the
Chesnuts, and his comments obviously shook her own resolve. If Carolinians who had so much to lose joined the enemy, what, she wondered,
would others less fortunate do? This was followed with Trescot's almost
gleeful information that in South Carolina she would find the Confederacy
in disintegration. Old colleagues such as Congressman Lawrence M. Keitt,
he said, had left Richmond in fury over President Davis's war policies. Ker
Boyce, who served in Congress throughout the war, had written to friends,
including Trescot, that he had no faith in Davis. Finally, she learned that
James Henry Hammond, grown old and skeptical, hated Davis's attempts
to dictate agricultural production in South Carolina.[32] Is there any question, she stated, that those men in public life stirred up resentment against
Richmond among the people back home?

Back in Camden at her Chesnut in-laws, Mary uncovered a den of

Unionists. To add to Mary's worries, Judge Withers, whom she called "the comfortable cynic," told her that many commercial leaders hated both the Union and the Confederacy. Then, after James lost his bid for election to the permanent congress to James L. Orr, she asserted that the state legislature preferred a Unionist to a sturdy administration supporter. As she followed James to Columbia at the year's end, to his position as military aide to the governor, she discovered for herself the soft support for the Confederacy there. At a party in March 1862, she heard that pro-Confederate governor Francis W. Pickens was in virtual war with the assembly to persuade it to acquiesce in federal government requests. To make matters worse, the press attacked the governor as too much a Jefferson Davis man. No wonder she reacted with anger at the assertion of her old friend, sometime suitor, and intellectual peer, Trescot, that he had no good information to report. Trescot felt himself passed over, his own talents wasted in a problematic cause. When he mused about fleeing to Mexico ahead of certain defeat, she refused to listen further.[33]

Mary spent much of June 1862 in the company of two bright Carolina women, Caroline Preston and the widow Louisa McCord. Both women despaired in their own way as they talked incessantly to Mary about what they had overheard in Carolina. When Caroline and Mary took to whispering their discontent, Mary reported Louisa's anger at them. McCord told her to speak out, speak for the country; "the real ammunition of our war is faith in ourselves, and enthusiasm in our cause." For herself, McCord dropped her subscriptions to the Rhetts' *Mercury* and the Columbia papers because they played into the hands of the Yankees. She reported to Mary that those papers had published maps of the Charleston defenses. Worse, McCord believed that businessmen, or usurers, in the guise of blockade runners, exploited the wartime situation by inflating prices on needed goods. Then those Carolina profiteers made fun of volunteers by suggesting that those who joined the army were fools. No wonder Mary was happy to leave grumbling and traitorous South Carolina for what she hoped was loyal Richmond. At least for a time, aside from the exchange of letters, such disturbing events at home passed from Mary's written worries.[34]

Mrs. Chesnut had to flee Richmond in May 1864, since James believed the capital was under threat from General Ulysses S. Grant's invasion. For the remainder of the war she was on the run, hearing and recording what former Confederate supporters in North and South Carolina were saying about the country's collapse. Again she met with and traded political gossip in Trescot's company. He warned her that faulty government policy, this time the bill to arm slaves, had forced South Carolina's leaders to talk of secession from the Confederacy. Of course, the Rhetts led the charge in editorial after editorial in the *Mercury*, which Mary read perhaps too carefully. Franklin Moses, later a Republican, Trescot himself, and others talked to her about reconstruction. To save slavery, Mary recorded with anger, those men would destroy the Confederacy. Because Columbia had come under siege, Mary had to go to North Carolina, where she heard friends in Charlotte also support reconstruction. For her those people had always opposed the Confederacy. The last straw of the perfidy of state disloyalty for her came in March 1865, when former governor Francis W. Pickens and Senator James Orr organized a secession movement in South Carolina against the central government.[35]

This talk of reunion reverberated through Mary's journals and memoirs, as she seemed obsessed with a fifth column inside the Confederacy, as well as with Southerners who had gone north to plea for peace. As early as April 1861, Wigfall had reported to her that a few political leaders even questioned whether President Davis was a secret reconstructionist. Radicals pointed out colleagues as Unionists, and charges flew thick against those who even questioned the staying power of the Confederacy. In her many travels, Mary heard these accusations and repeated them. Charleston lawyer George S. Bryan she regarded as a committed Unionist. In April 1862, the ever-faithful Trescot told her that Bryan, Judge John B. O'Neall, Benjamin F. Perry, and James L. Petigru had made a pact to return South Carolina to the Union. The accusations were only partially true. Nevertheless, rumors made those men suspect in some eyes. In May 1862, Mary heard that the Alabama leader and friend of the Clays, Jeremiah Clemens, had gone into the Union lines. In fury Mary wished good riddance to all that kind. That way she and her supporters could be "free of half-hearted, outspoken abusers of our Confederate government." In February 1865 she held long talks with St. Julian Ravenel and his wife Harriott, close friends from South Carolina, who had fled to North Carolina. Ravenel told her that he never had supported the Confederacy because he had no faith that it could succeed. He seemed to delight in reporting to her the traitorousness of Wigfall when that congressman moved that President Davis resign.[36] One wonders whether in her gloom and sorrow Mary herself had come to question the loyalty to the Confederacy, even of Wigfall.

In addition to being upset over rampant Unionism in the South, Mary reflected on just what the various peace initiatives had done to the will of leaders and people alike. As the war rushed to its conclusion, an undernourished refugee journal keeper lashed out at the peace advocates. Franklin Moses, Willaim H. Trescot, and William Whaley, she learned, had tried to influence the recent election for governor of South Carolina with demands that the candidates all join with the peace advocates. Even earlier, in January 1864, James had brought home bad news that North Carolina's leaders talked of a separate peace. Of course, in both South and North Carolina in 1864, rumors abounded of peace movements. At gatherings in Columbia, Mary heard that vice president Stephens and Judge John Campbell were part of the mission to seek peace. She insisted that those two leaders had never believed in secession.[37] One wonders who of Mary's friends, save Mrs. McCord, joined her in rejecting any movement toward peace and swore to fight on to the bitter end.

As she praised herself and Louisa for their fidelity, she also had little good to say about the supposed steadfastness of the women of the Confederacy, or at least the class of women that she knew. Not only did the women hear and repeat the doom and gloom of division, but among themselves they also talked about what the war had done to them. When Mrs. Wigfall revealed her hatred of Varina Davis, Mary cautioned her that the wives' battles could affect the husbands. For Wigfall to tell the women that Varina was coarse and uncouth accomplished nothing good, since "quarreling among ourselves makes me faint with fear." In addition to the dangers of personal animosity, over and over Mary listened to women grieve over the loss of loved ones. A friend told her that anxiety over what might happen was more than women could endure. Mary herself recorded death after death of friends and their sons and began to wonder, "are women losing the capacity to weep?" Then there also were the rumors of dangers to women behind the lines. Above all, they worried about slave insurrections. It is well known that Mary wrote about the famous murder of Mrs. Witherspoon in her own bed by slaves. It is less well known that she set down many other episodes and rumors about slave insurrections in her journals and memoir. For example, Minnie Frierson, the wife of a Sumter District planter, told her about hanging of slaves in Mississippi and Louisiana for attempted insurrection. Of course, most of those stories were about events far away from the storytellers. Then, in Columbia in August 1864, another refugee, Eliza Pinckney Rutledge, spoke of women's fears of the government arming the slaves. To add to Mary's distress, the Confederate government's proposed policy had frightened the wives beyond any measure.[38]

Those worries about family safety and race fear, along with scandal, mutual recriminations, and other talk, Mary knew, undermined the will of the women and thus of the cause. Despite her own claims that she resisted these fears and remained loyal, Mary herself at times cracked. In September 1864 she went to hear the famous Presbyterian divine, Benjamin M. Palmer, himself a refugee from New Orleans, deliver a sermon in Columbia. Palmer joylessly preached of despair and martyrdom. Mary allowed: "He spoke of the times of our agony." Of course, she had broken. By February 1865 Job had become her "comforter." Women's plight, she wailed, was to make endless chatter, mindless gossip.[39] She was whimpering.

To add to her personal woes, Mary's political gossiping at times found her in deep trouble with James. Though devoted to his career and to him in her fashion, at times she used her charms to gather information that he found damaging. Perhaps her coquettishness, along with his own real worries of the dangers of spreading gossip, set James off. On May 17, 1862, at their home in Columbia, he exploded. Supposedly, the ambitious Dr. Robert W. Gibbes, who wanted to be named surgeon general of the Confederacy, heard through Mary that James had scoffed at some policy of the state's governor and council. Mary recorded that James told Gibbes that "he was never to mention my name under any possible circumstance." James also fumed that others had used Mary's gossip to injure his career. Of course, she wrote that James was kind in his admonitions, that he believed Gibbes had fabricated the story, but still she knew what political gossip could do. On December 5, 1863, in beleaguered Richmond, James once again attacked his wife. Wigfall, a too-frequent guest, often quarreled with James over President Davis's policies. On that occasion, Wigfall alleged that Davis should be hanged. James sought to quiet him. Then James called Mary out of the living room and, in private, violently attacked her verbally. Wigfall's actions and words were all Mary's fault, he shouted. With your gossip you stirred him up. James then alerted her that Judge Campbell and his wife, no friends of the president, were coming to visit. Mary must watch herself. She was to be quiet and discreet. In her private memoir Mary wrote: "personal remarks are hazardous on a crowded riverboat."[40] Indeed, they were for all concerned.

That image she used of the riverboat is a verdict on Mary's own actions as well as on what the rumor mill had done to Confederates. Gossip and rumor were dangerous. They revealed the existence of disruptive factions in the Congress and stirred up national political leaders to unify against government policies. They damaged the functions of federal government personnel. Jealousy and intrigue emerged as leaders jockeyed for preferment, and some sought personal confidentialities with the president. The turnover in the Confederate cabinet cannot be put down to gossip alone, but the vicious rumors of impending change revealed a true division over policies and how to carry them out. Likewise, one expects even wartime commanders practiced what they had learned in the peacetime army, that the way up in rank required political intrigue and the denigration of other talents. Surely Lincoln's search for a general to lead in the east revealed how gossip and innuendo destroyed Federal careers. The Confederacy had less room, however, for officers to wiggle. So the squabbles over the ambitious Beauregard and Johnston often placed those needed talented officers on the shelf. The rumors about Bragg led to destroyed or damaged careers of important generals. The gossip mill that elevated and then helped to destroy Hood meant that many men died. State leaders spread rumors of federal government excesses and noncooperation among the officials throughout the Confederacy. Can one doubt that Governor Joseph E. Brown's personal exchanges with Vice President Stephens helped to destroy that leader in Richmond? Rumor and gossip hurt leadership, but it also revealed a deeply divided leadership.

Division over policy decisions among the leaders surfaced in the gossip of politics. So also did friction result from personal animosities, some left over from peacetime struggles, some because of the character and the values of Southern slaveholders. Gossip about individuals cut to the quick and weakened many leaders. Nothing seemed to divide those leaders more than personal remarks about loyalty, about devotion to the cause. Suspicions over whether they gave their all made some leaders drop out and affected the morale of others. A few fled the South for their lives because they had been deemed unfaithful. Known Unionists at times were linked with Confederates who had questioned policies and actions, to the detriment of the loyal skeptics. Some of even the most loyal were unjustly lost to the cause because of rumors of untrustworthiness. Peace movements, some of them legitimate attempts to save what was left of Southern society and culture, all became tainted with the brush of disloyalty. To talk of a negotiated peace in a country coming apart, unable to defend itself, the leaders insisted, undermined popular morale. Indeed, the citizenry, or at least the articulate ones without power, also heard the rumors and gossip of leadership failure, leadership struggles, and disloyalty and were influenced by them. Certainly Mary's own fidelity often had been tested in that society so prone to rumors about disagreement, disruption, and failure. Her own work, better perhaps than any other in the Confederacy, revealed that divisions led to a decline in morale.

Mary Chesnut's revelations also captured the extent of the damage of rumor and gossip to the cause. She and her loyal friends talked often about the hatred against President Davis. To attack Davis merely because of personality differences, she insisted, had divided Confederate against Confederate. While in Richmond and back in Carolina Mary also recorded how an invaded and thus beleaguered territory had fueled the gossip-mongers.

Virginians and others in the Upper South divided in part because they saw their land invested and devastated and a Confederate government unable to stop it. Hostilities toward the Confederacy emanated from the Rhett family and South Carolina elite planters, business leaders, and government officials, James told Mary, because they felt that the Davis government had failed to protect them at Charleston harbor and later from General William T. Sherman's army. Also, Northern penetration and occupation of the Confederacy's heartland led many to blame Davis for losing their land. Of course, many leaders from the occupied territory were the Confederacy's most loyal; but others, like Foote, turned on the government. Women and other noncombatants caught in the swirl of occupation were excessive in their fear of slave uprisings. The government and the army were seen as unable to stop internal racial insurrection and, worse, the growing worries of supposed insurrection incurred from rumors and gossip. Mary thus had described the war weariness of the people who blamed leadership flaws for fears of invasion and occupation. Perhaps above anything else, Chesnut's gossip about divisions among the leaders accurately depicted a society that, in order to survive, had turned against itself.

Knowing the harm rumor and gossip had done to the Confederacy, why did Mary Chesnut set down this messy story of internal division? As late as 1876, her old friend, the portly and aging Robert M.T. Hunter of Virginia, himself perhaps one of dubious wartime fidelity, suggested that the moment was inpropitious to publish a memoir taken from her most personal, private journals. She, he said, may have been too close to the sources, may have known too much about the Confederacy's problems. Did the warts, he wondered, need to be exposed? In other words, in this time when Southerners had come together on the memory of a glorious and united cause, could any good come from talking about wartime disunity? Historical truth, he suggested, must give way to present need. Then, in 1884, perhaps because she thought division should be understood as a cause of defeat, Mary turned her notes, journals, and diaries into a great memoir.

Had she embellished her material? No doubt she had. Did she rearrange some incidents for literary effect? Surely she did. Still, do these literary devices take away from what she had lived through and recorded? Certainly not. Her understanding of history and her talents for personal politics had led her to write down the life of a "disrupted society," of "chaos itself." In 1884 her old friend, worthy foe, and former suitor, William H. Trescot, insisting on his devotion to the old cause, suggested that she publish what she had been told and had overheard. As usual, she hardly needed his advice. She wanted to remember, to set down, to chronicle the internal divisions that she believed had done such damage to the Confederacy. Trescot did, however, comment on what he hoped her work would accomplish. "If you would add your own recollections of the inside history," that diplomatic historian said, "I think you would throw as much light upon our troubles as the history of the battles—private or public—of a dozen generals."[41] Correct he was. Even more accurately than Edward A. Pollard, the historian gossip, and John B. Jones, the rebel war clerk or bureaucrat rumormonger, Mary Boykin Chesnut had overheard a Confederate leadership divided against itself. This woman, frustrated over having no other weapon with which to fight, had indeed understood that "personal remarks are hazardous on a crowded riverboat." She had shown brilliantly one role of Confederate women in the tragic tale of Confederates against the Confederacy.

7

⚜

A Consideration of the Causes and Effects of Slave States' Leaders' Disloyalty to the Confederacy

Many leaders from the slave states made enormous contributions and major sacrifices for the Confederacy. Up to the war's very end, most leaders continued to support resistance to the Yankee invasion. If not always happy with the plans and procedures of the Confederate government, most of them were determined to protect their way of life as they understood it. Certainly the activities of those leaders on behalf of their society, if deemed by some as disloyal to the United States, have gone down in history as a noble defense of their new homeland. No part of this tale of Confederates who did not always support the activities of the Confederacy is meant in any way to demean the actions of those who did support them or believed they had.

A number of leaders from the slaveholding states, however, in many ways opposed the policies of the new Confederate nation and thus undermined the war effort. From the beginning of the secession crisis some Southern Unionists opposed the formation of the Confederacy and labored to restore the lost Union. (This group of loyalists or Southern Tories is the subject of a separate study and here will receive only a cursory view.)[1] Another group had been conditional Secessionists; some of them had professed desire for slave state cooperation before they would join in secession, and some refused to vote for secession. When the war began, or after the firing on Fort Sumter, many of those conditionalists joined the Confederate cause.[2] The third group, Secessionists from the beginning, professed devotion to the Confederate war effort throughout the long years of turmoil and travail. In many ways the actions of some of those most devoted to the war undermined the Confederate central government's objectives, which were to achieve a separate nation. Uncovering the disloyal Confederates' actions and why they became opponents are the subjects for discussion in this concluding essay on Confederates against the Confederacy.

To be sure, historians have long known about and discussed pockets of disloyalty and internal resistance to the Confederacy.[3] Early efforts studied the rise of yeoman discontent and the areas in the mountain regions where there were few slaves. Recent works on yeoman resistance, which amounted to a war within a war, and on the slave rebellions that came close to race war, most brilliantly that of William W. Freehling, have uncovered much about those groups.[4] The most thoughtful and informed scholarly study of Old South and Confederate leadership discontent is Carl Degler's *Other South*, published in 1974. Building on the earlier work of Frank L. Owsley, Georgia Lee Tatum, and others, Degler, in his two chapters on Southerners during the Civil War, has uncovered a viable group of sometime dissenters. Recently, scholars have looked at those leaders who supposedly supported the Confederacy but became disenchanted with the governmental and military policies of President Jefferson Davis.[5] Their focus, however, has been on the failings of Davis, both in plans for defense and in the inability to rally the Southern people during times of adversity, a focus that has ignored those who turned on the Confederacy. Others have analyzed the "will to fight" theme and have questioned the staying power of a leadership rapidly demoralized by military losses.[6] This study in civilian leadership opposition builds on the earlier work of Degler and others who have begun to look more carefully at the Confederates against the Confederacy.

One disloyal group consisted of persistent Unionists from the border slave states that did not secede. Technically never a part of the Confederacy, those states nevertheless had representation in the Confederate Congress, military, and federal executive. John C. Breckinridge, descendent of a great Virginia family and major leader from Kentucky, gave great comfort to the cause and consternation to the Union when he joined the Confederate army. Many border state leaders, on the other hand, resisted the separatist activities of the new Confederate nation and damaged it considerably. Freehling recently has shown that border slave states' support for the Union deprived the Confederacy of much-needed manpower, business and financial resources, and geographical protection. By manpower he meant not only the foot soldiers, but also industrial and farm labor that could have been of much use to finance and supply the Confederate army. In addition, the border slave states of Maryland, Kentucky, and Missouri could have served as a buffer to protect the capital in Richmond and the rich lands of the Tennessee Valley. The Ohio River, Freehling points out, thus could have been an obstacle for the Union war effort.[7] All the same, Freehling, despite his rich contribution to the story of dissent, pays scant attention to the leadership classes of those border slave states, the political and business talent pool lost to the Confederacy and gained for the Union.

Most of those border state leaders who remained loyal to the Union supported slavery but rejected the Confederacy's assertion that it could defend slavery militarily. Such loyalist border leaders as John C. Crittenden and Lazarus W. Powell reminded slave state Unionists that they represented the true interests of the slaveocracy. A number of loyalists from border states, by the same token, conflicted with the Federal government's antislavery policies. Border state leaders in high places in the administration and United States Congress, as well as important people back home, refused to persuade their constituents to end slavery. A number of them, however, eventually understood that to win the war slavery must be abolished. Friends of the Union they were, but their primary allegiance was to the border and its way of life.[8] Therefore, study of the Southern Unionists' wartime activities must consider their racist and proslavery position.

Those two major political figures, Crittenden and Powell, represented the border slave states against the Confederacy. Before the war those two slaveholders had ably defended Southern causes in Washington. When secession threatened the Union, both men sought compromise rather than radical actions. Crittenden, highly regarded as a national leader, became a symbol of border slave state moderation as he sought compromise on the divisive issue of protection for the extension of slavery into the territories. Once the war started, he continued to represent Kentucky in the Federal congress. He supported Union war measures, the invasion of the Confederacy, and Kentucky slaveowning interests until his death in 1863. Lazarus Powell remained in the United States Senate even though he at first opposed military appropriations for the invasion and conquest of the Confederacy. He knew that Kentucky would become a battleground during the war. Northern Republicans, even though they needed support of the loyal border leaders, did not hesitate to criticize them. Radical Republicans heaped opprobrium on Powell because he protected Kentucky's Jewish population from Grant's accusations that they traded with the enemy, denounced the cruel treatment of Confederate prisoners of war, and rejected the Thirteenth Amendment. As a result, some Northern congress-men attempted to remove him from office. Still, the loyal Powell raised troops for the Union effort and pronounced that loyal Kentucky had "fur-nished her quota of men to the armies of the government, and her sons had lain down their lives fighting for the integrity of the Union." In his last speech before Congress, an old, tired, and disappointed Crittenden discussed his and Powell's contributions to the Union and opposition to the Confederacy. He declared: "I have endeavored, consistently, to do whatever I could for the suppression of the rebellion."[9]

Countless other political leaders from the border slave states who sup-ported slavery and opposed the Confederacy offered immeasurable assis-tance to the restoration of the Union. For example, in Missouri and Maryland members of the prestigious Blair family influenced the wartime policies of the Lincoln administration. One of the Blairs served in the cabinet, and others rallied border Republicans to the cause. They walked a careful path on the abolition question. Missouri governor Hamilton R. Gamble, who led that state's immigrant Unionist population, defended slavery. By 1863 Gamble realized that the "material interests of Missouri would be promoted, and her resources . . . rapidly developed by the sub-stitution of free labor for slave labor." No doubt he understood that the state's German and Irish population gained from free labor competition. On the other hand, Gamble insisted that loyal Missourians be compen-sated for giving up their slaves. He also organized a number of workers and planters into a loyal militia to root out Confederate guerrillas and make the state safe for freedom. Certainly, if leaders such as Gamble and the Blairs had joined the Confederacy, many of their supporters would have followed them.

If political officeholders from the border slave states made contributions to reunion, equally important were civilian business leaders who labored on behalf of the Union. The loss of such talent to the Confederate war effort was immense. One such Unionist was Kentucky's James Gutherie, a lawyer, railroad promoter, and former United States secretary of the treasury. Gutherie had a brilliant mind for finances and was an expert on government bank regulations and how to avoid indebtedness. Adept at marketing bonds, he secured loans for the United States government useful to the war. The work of Confederate financiers and government experts like Christopher G. Memminger paled in comparison with Gutherie's ac-complishments. Gutherie also raised funds to build a railroad in Kentucky useful to the Union army's Southern invasion. His Louisville and Nashville Railroad transported troops and supplies into the heart of the Confederate southwest and "was one of the deciding factors in the conquest of that region." Gutherie supported the Union, he said, because a united nation served the best interests of Kentuckians and his many investments in the deep South.[10]

Another important border slave state leader who remained faithful to the Union was the Old School Presbyterian divine, Robert J. Breckinridge, cousin to the Confederate John C. Breckinridge. Unlike Powell, Critten-den, or Gutherie, he had questioned the good of slavery for the long-term interests of the great American border. Breckinridge, out of frustration over the radicalism of both sides, had called for a border state confederacy to organize against both the cotton slave states and the northeastern indus-trialists. Fortunately for the Union effort, during the secession crisis he advocated that Kentuckians remain in the Union. Not only had the Con-federacy lost a morale-building man of the cloth, but the Union had gained a social and spiritual propagandist who encouraged others to make sac-rifices to put the nation back together again. Breckinridge's wartime mag-azine, the *Danville Review*, published in Cincinnati, circulated in both the border and the lower southwest slave states and fomented disaffection within the Confederacy. In the *Review* Breckinridge used his biting and sarcastic pen to accuse the Confederacy of destroying its own people. He pointed out that the Confederacy could not win the war and that its efforts merely disrupted the way of life of good citizens. In the pages of his magazine and in the pulpit, Breckinridge had called for resistance, deser-tion, insurrection.[11]

This group of political, business, and church leaders from the border slave states, thus, ably assisted in preserving the region for the Union. Perhaps that area was lost to the Confederacy from the beginning, but the failed attempts to undermine the authority of the Unionist leaders there no doubt cost the Confederate government immensely in time, effort, funds, and pride.

Of equal and perhaps greater harm to the Confederacy were Southern Unionist supporters of the Federal army's early penetration into the upper South's seceded states, which contained strong pockets of disloyal South-erners. In the mountains of western North Carolina and eastern Tennessee, where Federal troops had difficulty finding the best means of egress, pro-Union guerrillas kept the Confederacy at bay. Even along the Federal-occupied Atlantic coast in eastern Virginia and North Carolina, Unionist-led farmers and slaves caused the Confederacy no end of worry. The Union army presence or threat of invasion had allowed those leaders to rise against the Confederacy.[12] Even when the Confederate guerrillas and rouge cavalry succeeded in regaining some of that territory, as Wayne Durrill has shown so graphically, to suppress the Unionists required manpower and matériel much needed elsewhere.

The principal architect from Washington who planned and organized those penetrations was United States Army Chief of Staff Winfield Scott, a native Virginian. Where he chose to invade and how he gained his information of Unionist or soft Secessionist support requires careful study. To understand Scott's thinking might help us to grasp the depth of disloyalty to the Confederacy. Just look at the results of the Federal army's capture of the Norfolk region as one example of Scott's planning. No doubt he had talked with the Union congressman from Norfolk, Joseph Segar, a slaveowner and successful businessman who had risked his life to oppose secession in Virginia. Likewise, United States Senator John S. Carlile, a western Virginia slaveowner who had voted against secession and remained in the wartime Union Congress, may have consulted with Scott on the importance of the mountainous western Virginia region for the protection of border cities and Union railroads. Carlile at first had supported the movement for a separate state of West Virginia, then turned against it, and finally saw the usefulness of a new state for the Union war effort. Both those Virginia Unionist leaders certainly helped Scott undermine the Confederate position in their areas so vital to the defense of Richmond.[13]

The same is so for eastern Tennessee and the Nashville basin, once the Federal army had freed Unionist leaders to take action. Many of the businessmen in those areas probably had traded with both sides during the war, but a number of them became useful to the Union army of occupation. Unionist leaders who had been forced to flee their homes also returned to positions of leadership. The two most important of these were William G. Brownlow, who returned to Knoxville, and Nashville-based Andrew Johnson, who became military governor of Tennessee.[14] Their activities generally are known, and they properly belong to my larger study of Southern loyalists, but their contributions to upset the Confederate war effort require some mention here.

Much has been written about Andrew Johnson's life because of his infamous behavior as president of the United States during the early years of Reconstruction. During the dark days of the war, however, Johnson ably served his country as senator, anti-Confederate political propagandist, and as war governor. He was famous enough to be chosen in 1864 as Abraham Lincoln's running mate. To the Confederates he was an eastern Tennessee demagogue, a traitor to the cause. Why was he so despised in the Confederacy? Early in the war, Johnson had implored Winfield Scott to liberate the many Tennessee Unionists. He also traveled west on the northern lecture circuit on behalf of the Union cause. In his speeches of 1861, especially those delivered in Kentucky, Indiana, and Ohio, he accused Tennessee Secessionist governor Isham G. Harris of violence and oppression against the state's Unionists. Johnson pounded away at what he called a Confederate conspiracy to undermine "laboring interests" and threaten the lives of Southern nonslaveholders loyal to the Union. For spreading such anti-Confederate propaganda, the slaveholder elite branded him an "enemy alien" to be shot on sight.[15]

Back in Washington during the winter 1861–1862 congressional session, Johnson lobbied the powerful Joint Committee on the Conduct of the War to invade Tennessee. Lincoln appointed him military governor of the newly liberated Tennessee, and Johnson set up office in Federal-occupied Nashville. In one of his first actions, he gained the release of Tennessee Confederate soldiers from Federal prisons in return for their support of the Union cause and defense of their homeland against a Confederate reinvasion. That a number did join his home guard perhaps reveals the softness of small farmer loyalty to the Confederacy. With the assistance of allies in Washington, such as Tennessee political leader Emerson Etheridge, he persuaded local business leaders to provision the occupying Union army. Johnson also was a heavy-handed partisan, and he failed early to persuade Tennesseans to give up slavery. Always ambivalent on slavery, Johnson eventually regarded the abolition of slavery as a war tool and probably as his way to rise in national political importance. He also failed to curtail smugglers and Confederate spies, and so Nashville and the vicinity never became a safe haven for wartime loyalists. All the same, along with his new comrade in arms, his former enemy "Parson" Brownlow, Johnson neutralized middle Tennessee and turned its commercial power to the use of the Union's invasion into the lower South.[16]

Like Johnson, Brownlow had fled north for fear of his life. He too went on the northern lecture circuit, and he published accounts of his experiences. He regaled Northerners with tales of his life in a Confederate prison and called himself a martyr to free speech and freedom of mobility. He attacked the Confederacy as an ill-conceived, poorly organized, brutal government determined to root out, arrest, and even murder those who supported the Union. In recounting the adventures of narrow escapes, bridge burnings, and the sacking of villages, Brownlow showed that many Unionists lived in east Tennessee. He encouraged assistance from the border states of Kentucky, Ohio, Indiana, Illinois, and Missouri to liberate his homeland. In those speeches he defended slave society, which he would not do once he had returned home, and he told Northerners that he believed that Southern interests could better be preserved in the Union.

Through his writings and speeches delivered to eager Northern audiences, Brownlow became a popular Southern loyalist in the Union and hated in the Confederacy. An enterprising Indianapolis publicist printed his biography, copies of which circulated through the North, in border towns, and even into the heart of the Confederacy. His role as a martyr became useful to Northern political propaganda. The Beadle Dime Series in late 1862 printed a volume, *Parson Brownlow, and the Unionists of East Tennessee.* The book became a bestseller in the North and certainly contributed to building support among those who wanted to defeat the Confederacy.[17] Brownlow sent many copies of the book to the Upper South to foment unrest there.

Once the Federal army had moved into his homeland, Brownlow triumphantly reopened his Knoxville newspaper to the cheers of his neighbors. He then collaborated with his former enemy Andrew Johnson in making Tennessee a commercial, political, and propagandistic center for the Union war effort.

Unionist pockets also existed in the Lower South. In northern Mississippi and Alabama, leaders who had refused to support the secession governments secretly advocated reunion. In Texas, especially among hill country Germans and along the border with the Indian territory, lived a number of Unionists. Likewise, on the Gulf Coast and in the lower Mississippi River towns, business and political leaders secretly supported early reconstruction. After New Orleans had fallen to Admiral David Farragut in April 1862, Unionist supporters in the Gulf region resurfaced. By and large most loyalists in the deep South kept silent, because the Federal army liberated them only during the last stages of the war. Nevertheless, a few important leaders spoke out against the Confederacy.

Mississippi farmer-politician John W. Wood had opposed secession in the state convention even though radicals threatened his life. After middle Tennessee fell to the Union, Wood's enforced quiet gave way to an outburst against the Confederate government and Jefferson Davis's treatment of Unionists and others in northern Mississippi. He sent a manuscript to Memphis that he dedicated to "Faithful Union Men of Mississippi." In the pamphlet *Union and Secession in Mississippi*, which circulated widely on the Gulf Coast, Wood wrote, "to aid in affecting a re-union in feeling and sentiment between the masses of the people of the United States, for social and commercial advantages, as the only basis of a Union worth preserving." He described how misguided Secessionist leaders, who wrongly believed that they had preserved the interests of slave society, had forced their fellow Mississippians to join the Southern Confederacy. Rather than protecting the slave states' interests, according to Wood, the Confederacy actually had caused hyperinflation, closed hotels and farms, bankrupted merchants, and set evil tax collectors on innocent citizens. Wood stridently called for a free state of Attala, where Unionist feelings prevailed. He insisted that his "sentiment has been bold and outspoken, despite the taunts and threats of the party in power."[18] Trapped in the deep South, Wood could contribute only his pen to the Union cause.

Especially important to Lower South Unionists was Andrew Jackson Hamilton, a Texan who had served in the Federal Congress on the eve of secession and had led the Unionists in his home state. He, too, fled his home for fear of his life. Hamilton escaped through Mexico to the North and later went to New Orleans. He traveled to New York and New England, at the request of Unionist societies, and spoke before large audiences about Union loyalists in the Lower South and in Texas. He urged northeasterners to continue the fight, to support the invasion of the Lower South, and to liberate the Unionists there. Hamilton lobbied Northern politicians, gained an audience with the president, and obtained the post of Texas governor in exile. From New Orleans he launched a propaganda war into Texas, in which he called for an uprising against the Confederacy. Although he returned to Texas for a short time in 1863, Hamilton never managed to persuade the Federal government to liberate his state, and as a result he had no role in wartime public life back home.[19]

Those loyalist leaders the Confederates called Tories had supported the Union from the outset, and they had important roles in the Federal war effort. The Tories' or loyalists' values and actions revealed deep divisions within the slave states. Some of them allied with antisecessionists and committed Secessionists who had turned on the Confederacy, either actively or in their private sentiments. Tories have received little attention from historians, but I do not want to confuse the Tories' efforts with Confederates who turned against the Confederacy, and so this part of the story has been held to a minimum. It is the actions and beliefs of the Confederates against the Confederacy, the central focus of this piece and volume, to which we now turn.

In the lower South, antisecessionists like Alexander Stephens and James Lusk Alcorn, when they had lost the battle for the Union, joined in the final vote for secession. Some of them hoped even after the creation of a Lower South Confederacy that the North would accept compromise on the extension of slavery into the west in order to restore the Union. To the original Secessionists such people were untrustworthy reconstruction-ists. The moderates, then, had to prove their loyalty by speaking out in favor of a permanent new republic. None of that changed the fact that the Confederacy had begun with distrust among its leaders, as original Seces-sionists worried about the antisecessionists who had joined the fray.

In the Upper South, a number of leaders who feared the consequences of secession for their region, men like William C. Rives of Virginia and William A. Graham of North Carolina, supported the Crittenden amend-ment and attended the peace conventions. They resisted pressure from their own states' Secessionists and from Lower South emissaries sent to persuade, cajole, and even threaten them into joining the Confederacy. Daniel W. Crofts, in a study of those Upper South Unionists, as discussed in Chapter 2 of this volume, insists that Lincoln's call for troops after the firing on Ft. Sumter forced the hand of those leaders and they became Confederates. In that earlier chapter I was concerned with the Unionists' reasons for opposing secession and rejecting a separate Confederacy to set the scene for their anti-Confederate behavior.[20] In this chapter I want to look more closely at how they performed during the war itself. Clearly, both the Lower and Upper South Unionists who joined the Confederacy lacked the zeal for the permanent separate nation of their former adver-saries. Many of those equivocators proved to be Confederates against the Confederacy.

Although he never acknowledged his opposition, William C. Rives did indeed turn on the Confederacy. Descendent of an old Virginia family, Rives had long served his state and nation ably in public office. A former diplomat, congressman, and United States senator—and a brilliant law-yer—Rives certainly knew the perils of defying such a power as the United States. James Madison's official biographer as well as his former secretary, Rives began his career as a nationalist but turned defender of local rights. Even though Rives owned slaves and a plantation, he also had many busi-ness dealings with the Northern states. As a Richmond lawyer and busi-nessman, he had benefited from commercial ties of the Upper South with the North. Two of his sons lived in the North and Rives did much business with them. He opposed secession because he believed the Republican party had no designs on slavery. After joining the Confederacy, Rives vowed to take no part in the war.[21]

Unfortunately for the Confederacy, Rives was unable to keep his prom-ise. Although a number of Virginia's Secessionists opposed him, the leg-islature eventually sent this experienced political leader to the Confederate

Congress. There he voted for most of the administration's war measures and became a loyal supporter of the Davis government. He never really took a leadership role in Congress, however. Throughout the war, Rives lamented the terrible costs to his native state. As the war ground on, Rives eventually supported a peaceful solution. He aligned with the congressional peace leaders and thus lent his prestige to a reconstruction he hoped would be favorable to the South. Rives could not wait to retire from what he believed had become a terrible mistake.

Enough confusion over Rives's wartime performance exists to warrent a closer look. When the war began, friends spoke out to "vindicate" his hesitation to go along. Rives had said that he would accept the "consequences" of war. In May 1861 he employed nearly biblical language to "devote all that I am and all that I have in service of my native and honored commonwealth." As a member of the provisional congress, he supported a home guard. He even ran afoul of Alexander Stephens as he petulantly spoke in favor of suspension of the writ of habeas corpus when Stephens and other friends opposed it. As late as March 1865, in a letter to fellow Virginian and house speaker Thomas Bocock, the ill Rives desired "success of the great cause."

A personal side to Rives's war weighed heavily on his patriotism. His brother and close friend, Alexander, supported the Union, even at personal peril, and Rives seemed proud of him. When Confederate authorities condemned his sons for living and profiting in the North, Rives defended them as "loyal and devoted" to the cause. He wondered, should they be? To his friend James Holcombe, in April 1862, he condemned as "demoralizing" the administration policy of retreating toward Richmond and abandoning land. When Governor John Letcher proposed to draft Charlottesville farmers, Rives exploded and said they were needed at home to feed their people. Rives also wrote, often anonymously, to Richmond newspapers of his opposition to government policies, and he especially criticized currency inflation. More, Rives kept in close touch with Alexander Stephens's peace movement in Virginia. When Undersecretary of War John Campbell openly favored peace, Rives applauded him. Buried in Rives's private papers in his own hand is a May 1864 *Prospectus of the Society for Promoting the Cessation of Hostilities in America*. If his public stance was to move cautiously for peace, in private, and in his mind, this able leader, by 1864, had given up on the Confederacy.[22] In private Rives had taken the measure of the "consequences" of war for Virginia and the South. Had this leader ever really been a Confederate?

Another former Upper South Unionist, Robert Hatton of Tennessee volunteered for Confederate military service and rose to the rank of brigadier general before his untimely death. (It has been my intention to avoid commentary on the military, especially the professional soldiers who perhaps knew exactly what the Confederacy was getting into. Hatton is an exception in that he came from civilian life and his story ably contributes to this essay.) Hatton had supported John Bell for president and Bell's peace initiatives, and Hatton's constituents regarded him as a politician of great personal integrity. He kept a diary of the events surrounding secession and of his war duties, and in it he wrote that "disunion is ruin to both sections." The Christmas season of 1860 became the gloomiest time of his life, as he remained in Washington to support the forces of peace. Hatton knew from his national political experience that secession would lead to a horrible civil war that his beloved South could never win. Publication and circulation of his Unionist pamphlet led for demands that he defend his position back home in Lebanon. There, a mob of unruly college students hissed him, someone fired a shot that carried close to his ear, and one night on a walk he saw himself burned in effigy. When he joined the state volunteers, this loyalist vowed to fight only in defense of Tennessee.[23]

Hatton certainly "discharged his duty," but his wartime letters reveal him to have been a reluctant Confederate. The anguish of one whose loyalties to the Confederate cause stretched thin finally led him to the breaking point. At the start of the war he had written to his wife "I have a high, and as I regard it, a sacred obligation imposed upon me." He managed to fulfill this obligation while fighting in Kentucky and Tennessee. Then, upset after the needless death of General Felix Zollikoffer in Kentucky, he wrote to friends that few people in the border states of the South supported the Confederacy. Hatton believed this disloyalty disastrous to the cause but understandable. Then his superiors in Richmond transferred him to western Virginia to defend that region against local Unionists, a duty he found unnerving. Those Unionists, he believed, were guilty only of defending their rights as loyal Americans. Hatton watched as a number of Virginians turned against the Confederate war. His observations of that war within a war led him to ask for transfer back home. Over and again, in his diary and letters, to the point of excessiveness, he vowed to do his duty. In April 1862 he learned that his home in Lebanon was under Federal siege. He feared for his family's safety and cursed the war that had caused such disruption of people's lives. In May he wrote "I go along, and do what I conceive to be my duty, and trouble myself but little about anything taking place around me." He had become morbid, and said that he never again expected to see his family.[24] On May 31, 1862, 500 miles from his beloved Tennessee, he gave the greatest sacrifice—his own life—for a cause he certainly had questioned. No one doubts his loyalty, but who will say that Hatton was not disloyal in his thoughts? The final most desperate act of disloyalty, of a Confederate in opposition, was to give up, and that General Hatton had done. One wonders how many other Hattons there were who served so reluctantly?

Unlike Hatton, North Carolina's Unionist leaders who joined the secession forces constituted a most treacherous group of anti-Confederate resisters in many ways and for many reasons. Two of the most important members of that group, Zebulon B. Vance and William W. Holden, illustrate this opposition in action. Their wartime careers have been studied extensively. For the purposes of this book, they require separate comments. After the war had begun, Holden sided with the Confederacy and for a time devoted his paper, the *Raleigh Standard*, to the cause. When the Confederate government used strong and coercive measures to protect the state's east coast from Federal invasion and control, he questioned both the abilities and the actions of the Confederacy. In his editorials Holden missed few opportunities to accuse Confederate leaders of usurping popular liberties. Perhaps frustrated about the many escaped coastal slaves, and worried about slave uprisings, he charged Confederate authorities with the heinous crime of failure to protect slave society. Tellingly, he predicted that the slave states rebellion would "end either in anarchy or despotism."[25] Still, Holden insisted that he remained loyal to the Southern nation, but by 1863 that former Unionist and supposed loyalist refused to assist the Confederate government in any of its activities.

Like Holden, after the war started Vance joined the Confederate cause. As governor, Vance early supported the Confederate war effort and committed North Carolina resources to the cause. As the war turned sour and as it became clear that North Carolinians would have to make major sacrifices to sustain the war effort, the governor refused additional aid to the national government. Vance then joined other leaders who advocated a separate peace. Yet he insisted he favored a separate Southern nation.[26] The words and deeds of Holden and Vance brand them as men who, despite their ostensibly patriotic words, had turned against the Confederacy.

Another former North Carolina Unionist, William A. Graham, served ably in the Confederate Congress. A former governor, congressman, and secretary of the navy, he joined the cause after Fort Sumter, stating "blood is thicker than water." As a member of the North Carolina legislature in

1861–1862, however, he vigorously opposed the Confederate government's tax-in-kind proposal. He then covertly joined the North Carolina peace movement. To Governor Vance Graham suggested that loyalty to the central government must give way to state sovereignty, and that "self defense was the first law of nature." Elected in 1863 to the Confederate Senate as a peace leader, he nevertheless supported some government military initiatives, yet he also resisted "further effusion of blood" for a cause that had died.[27] In Graham's service at Raleigh and Richmond was little cause for Confederate celebration.

Graham had not deserted the Confederacy just because of military reverses, but because those reverses had affected government behavior. The way the government fought the war destroyed everything he held sacred, his very values as an independent Southerner. This is best seen in his explosion over the Confederacy's imposing a test oath on all who held public office. Holden published his forceful speech against the bill in the *Raleigh Standard* and then printed and circulated it as a pamphlet. Graham's *Speech . . . on the Ordinances Concerning Test Oaths and Sedition* shocked many who believed he had become a devout Confederate. He called the test oath oppressive and despotic and raised fears among Carolinians when he insisted that the government meant to expel all Southerners who refused to sign it. He decried the Confederate policy of instituting criminal proceedings against all it deemed disloyal. Graham declaimed with wringing condemnation, "I am free born—what do you take away?" What, he queried, were North Carolinians to do to those who had become dissatisfied with constitutional controls over personal lives? The absence of a bill of rights he now knew meant that the South will "become a despotism by legislation." He feared that with the test oath the Confederate government had been "brought into contempt and collision with the people." Graham added that, the people of North Carolina looked upon the Civil War as a contest between the nations, but the test oath had made "a civil and social war, in which no man is to be trusted." For Graham, the Confederacy to which he had given support had thrown away personal liberties in the struggle to preserve them.[28]

To judge by the letters from all over the South in praise of his pamphlet, Graham had indeed struck a cord of fear. But he had done much more. Unionists, Union sympathizers, the growing number of peace advocates, and others who resisted the Confederacy's policies had rallied around Graham as their leader.[29] The North Carolinian, however, resisted all entreaties to form a Union and peace party.

As a member of the second Confederate Congress Graham claimed to support the cause of a separate republic, but his actions tell a different story. Never did he forget his own stirring words against those he accused of taking away popular rights, and he voted against all measures he felt coercive. Even though his votes against the government harmed the war effort, Graham maintained that he was only trying to protect the interests and values of his constituents. After the war had ended, he described his peculiar support for the Confederacy. He wrote that he had always defended the Southern people, but that he had never really believed in a separate nation. He had had to be careful because to live in the Confederacy and to oppose it openly was suicidal.[30] This plea marks Graham as a disloyal Confederate whose deeds and words undermined support for a separate nation.

Graham, the former Upper South Unionist, like some of his colleagues (the example of Henry S. Foote of Tennessee has been described in detail in Chapter 4), found that he had much in common with former Unionists from the Lower South who supported the Confederacy and held high leadership positions. Radicals in the Lower South attacked antisecessionists because they equivocated on forming a Confederate government. Many Unionists were vilified as reconstructionists who never supported a permanent Confederacy. Although a number of them insisted that they would do what was best for the interests of all the Southern people, they also ran afoul of the Confederate war effort in many ways and thus belong to the ranks of those Confederates who opposed the Confederacy. A few of the most prominent will be looked at to see how their words and deeds sometimes contradicted each other.

One such Lower South Unionist was the Alabama leader John A. Campbell. Campbell had been a member of the United States Supreme Court, where he voted in favor of the Dred Scott decision, and so his Southern credentials should never have been in doubt. When the war began, he resigned from the court and went home. In a letter to President Jefferson Davis dated April 23, 1861, Campbell volunteered his considerable talents to the new Richmond government. In that letter he revealed his true interests. He told the president that he favored the reconstruction of the Union based on Federal adoption of a slave protection clause in the Constitution. Campbell lived in New Orleans for a time and was there when the city fell to the Union. He made his way to Richmond and, despite opposition from those who insisted that Campbell opposed a permanent separate republic, Davis put his talents to use. Although he never held official appointment to the office, Campbell served as an undersecretary of war with the unorthodox but loyal George W. Randolph. Certainly

Campbell worked long and hard at his job, and he pursued a vigorous war policy, although he often sided with generals out of favor in Richmond government circles. On the other hand, he talked of schemes for peace, sometimes a separate peace and sometimes a restoration of the Union.[31] Even though he knew President Davis opposed a peace movement and merely used peace advocates for his own purposes, late in 1864 Campbell joined the peace contingent of Vice President Alexander Stephens and Senator R.M.T. Hunter to meet with the Federals at Hampton Roads. After negotiations had failed, Campbell aligned with peace politicians who had given up on a separate Confederacy.

Another Lower South prewar Unionist who had resisted secession and yet served as a Confederate political leader was the Alabamian William R. Smith. A former newspaper editor, an author of popular novels (see Chapter 2), and a member of the U.S. House of Representatives, Smith had opposed secession at the Alabama convention. Nevertheless, the convention leaders hired him to edit the proceedings and publish them for all to know why Alabama had seceded. The new Confederate state government sent many copies of his rendition of the proceedings to important public figures. Perhaps the government should have looked carefully at what Smith had written, for in his report of the proceedings Smith praised the integrity of Alabama Unionists such as Robert Jemison, Jr., a friend who had refused most stridently and publicly to sign the secession ordinance.[32]

Once he had finished his task of publishing the proceedings, and before he took his seat in 1862 in the first Confederate Senate, Smith behaved in ways peculiar for one who had gained the confidence of his state's Secessionist leaders. He intrigued with Jemison and other north Alabama Unionists to build a resistance group in that region. Along with his former Unionist friends, he accused the fire-eater William L. Yancey of raising a private vigilante army to wipe out Unionists in the Tuscaloosa region. Smith said he acted because the scandal of Alabamians against Alabamians was harmful to the fledgling Confederate government's position that all slave state people had united in behalf of a separate nation. He joined the Confederate army and rose to the rank of colonel. Transferred to the Upper South, he fought in western Virginia. After the Southern victory at First Manassas, Smith's true colors emerged, as he complained that Northern Virginia had been lost to Federal occupation unnecessarily. As for his own Lower South, Smith warned that young enlistees had become "stragglers" dangerous to property holders. When a good friend and ally was arrested in Richmond for disloyalty to the new government, the former editor wrote that the Confederacy had assumed the "dimensions" of the French Revolutionary government.[33] Then former Unionists back home sent him to the Confederate Senate.

In Congress Smith often opposed the government's war policies while in speeches on the floor of the Senate he defended the Confederacy. He also questioned the government's abilities. As a member of the Foreign Affairs Committee, he accused the leadership of inept diplomatic negotiations. Smith believed that only European intervention could save slave society, and he called on diplomats to promote that labor system as beneficial to the business world across the Atlantic. In addition, he talked to fellow congressmen about how the leadership had violated individual rights and thus had alienated many of its loyal supporters.[34] There is tension in Smith's words and deeds between individual liberty and the necessity to force support for a new government.

Smith also showed his anxieties through his facile pen. In his comic play on the results of First Manassas, the *The Royal Ape*, Smith revealed his own complex feelings about Confederate success. In *The Royal Ape*, Lincoln, his wife, his son Robert, and General Winfield Scott, to be sure, are all depicted as inept and cowardly. Generals Beauregard and Joseph Johnston, as well as President Davis, are seen as heroic conquerors. A closer look at the language and images in the play reveals the author's ambivalence about that Confederate victory. For example, Winfield Scott mouths a parody of Hamlet with "Oh, what a coward slave am I." But there also is a poignant moment when, in reference to Virginia, Scott says, "and my eyes do strain their nerves to find a spot of earth which I could call my home!" General Beauregard is given lines that make him appear pompous. President Davis, himself, goes to the battlefield on a horse as large as three elephants, dressed all in white, and bellows that any mortal must yield to him. Later in the script Lincoln is depicted as a coward frightened of Davis's coming to Washington, but another character sarcastically insists that Lincoln need have no fear.[35] The play shows us a homeland shrouded in lost causes and an avenging angel who goes nowhere, having passed up the opportunity, according to the Confederate press and to the play, to capture Washington and win the war early. One must wonder whether Smith himself yearned for a peaceful early return to a different "spot on earth," free of the enormous costs of the war.

No less conflicted a leader than Smith was the Mississippi prewar Unionist James L. Alcorn, whose ambivalent war career has been well documented. His biographer gives him too much credit for practical politics and fails to analyze why he opposed the Confederacy. Alcorn cast his vote for secession reluctantly and then he raised a regiment to fight in Tennessee, he said, to save Mississippi from invasion. As a member of the Mississippi state legislature, after his fighting career had ended under a cloud, Alcorn voted to raise troops to defend the state. When Northern troops invaded his homeland, Alcorn refused to take a oath of loyalty to the Union.

Still, his wartime career betrays a pattern of disloyalty worth looking at. During the Mississippi secession convention he supported separation in hopes that the new government would be able to protect slavery. He broke with President Davis as early as 1862, and for all practical purposes, save for some service at the state level, he sat out the rest of the fighting. Instead, Alcorn took up a fight of another kind. He wrote and spoke out against a failed Confederate government unable to protect its people. He said that he trusted the slaveholders to protect themselves more than he trusted the government. Like many another Lower South planter, he attempted to save his own wealth and property in slaves by selling cotton to the North, cotton that was used against the Confederacy. At war's end he quickly moved to rejoin the Union, and he even advocated the abolition of slavery.[36] Thus, Alcorn had supported the cause but questioned the leaders and their policies. He regarded the Confederacy as unable to protect his and his friends' interests as they understood them.

The performances of those Lower South ex-Unionists, who in their ways supported the Confederacy, pales before the confused, or perhaps calculated, activities of Georgia's Alexander H. Stephens, vice president of the Confederacy. A major leader in the Federal Congress before the war, this shriveled, emaciated, but proud Southerner had enjoyed the confidence of many national figures as well as Georgia's most important public men. During the secession crisis Stephens and his brother Linton led the state's antisecession forces, as they attempted to delay Georgia's secession. When secession became obvious, Stephens joined the cause. Sent to Montgomery to form the Confederate government, he made major contributions to the preliminary constitution, and the delegates chose him as vice president of the fledgling Confederacy. Back in Georgia, Stephens gave an address that summed up why he joined the new nation. In the famous "cornerstone speech" he insisted that the people supported the Confederacy to defend slave society.[37] Although a number of Southern radicals damned him as a closet reconstructionist, the Davis government expected much from him as a talented political leader.

Within a few months Stephens became part of the fledgling anti-Davis faction in Congress. As president of the Confederate Congress, the vice president often opposed administration measures. Soon Stephens tired of the fray and went home to Georgia, rarely ever to return to Richmond. At home he sulked, but he also intrigued against the Davis government. Along with his brother Linton and Governor Joseph E. Brown, supposedly a staunch secessionist, he labored to protect the interests of Georgia above those of the new Confederate nation. A former Whig who once had believed in a strong central government, Stephens had joined the forces of state particularism. To call him a defender of state rights, however, is to miss his real contribution to the cause of those ex-Unionists who had turned on the Confederacy. Certainly he doubted the Confederacy's ability to protect the people's interests and to win the war. To save the "cornerstone," Stephens joined the peace movement. Even the relationship he had with the invader General William T. Sherman remains clouded in mystery. Was he intriguing to save slavery or to minimize the destruction of Georgia? As the war ground to its inexorable conclusion, one might ask, just whose side was Stephens on?[38]

A brilliant student of politics and governance, as soon as the war ended Stephens defended the Confederate cause and explained his own peculiar wartime activities. Later scholars have regarded his nearly unreadable *A Constitutional View of the Late War Between the States*, a dialogue between a Northerner and a Southerner, as a defense of the rights of states. They have viewed that work as a major testimony to the forces in the South who opposed the excessive behavior of central government. Indeed, the work is a revisionist nightmare in which Stephens attacks both Federal and Confederate centralism. It is also much more, for in it Stephens attempted to explain his own peculiar opposition to the Confederacy. He wrote that "two-thirds, at least of those who voted for the Ordinances of Secession, did so, I have little doubt, with a view to a more certain reformation of the Union."[39] He said this was so because the Confederate government had failed to understand the true interests of the Southern people. In his autobiography, *Recollections*, he augmented the view that the Confederate president "did not understand the popular sentiment which was not directed so much to disunion as to security of rights." In an October 1865 letter written from prison, Stephens discussed what he personally had accomplished during the war. "I did all I could to avert the monster evil in the beginning," he said, "and after it was upon us, I did all I could to mitigate its horrors and to end them as speedily as possible."[40] This former Unionist turned Confederate concluded that he had never really believed the Confederacy protected the Southern way of life. (Thus, in his postwar writings, Stephens contributed to historians' future misunderstanding of the importance of Confederates who opposed the Confederacy as well as their reasons why.)

Another group of civilian leaders who supported the Confederacy but later turned on it, some of whom had been Unionists before the war and some who had been committed secessionists, serve as a transition to the activities of the third group of Southerners who turned on the Confederacy. From the war's outset a number of business and planter leaders displayed a wariness toward the Confederacy's objectives and the government's means to achieve them. They seemed loyal only to their own interests. Some of them resisted Confederate government requests to grow corn and other foodstuffs in place of cotton, regarding that demand as detrimental to their full use of the labor system, their ability to trade on the open market, and their very profits. Others, especially after the Federal army penetrated into or moved close to their regions, traded with the enemy for personal profit and in defense of their labor system. Lawrence Powell and Michael Wayne have suggested that a number of them even changed sides and declared allegiance to the Union. Southern-born Union general Walter Q. Gresham well understood the true loyalties of those people with whom he did business. He insisted that most of the planters who sold cotton to the Federals did so in hopes of preserving slave society. He also questioned their allegiances to any government. Ludwell Johnson, in his work on the Red River campaign, also discovered evidence of planter disloyalty. Some of the planters in that region, Johnson said, insisted that they sold cotton to the Yankees to gather much-needed specie for the war cause, but the Confederate authorities saw precious little of that currency.[41] Quite obviously those planters had personal priorities that hardly included the aims of the new nation.

No doubt many disloyal Confederate businessmen and planters believed that personal safety and personal gain went hand in hand. Former South Carolina governor and United States Senator James Henry Hammond, a staunch conservative and antisecessionist (discussed in Chapter 1), like other planters, behaved badly toward the Confederacy. Old and sick during the war, and worried about his family, Hammond also refused to plant needed corn for the Confederate troops and civilians behind the lines. He had hoped to profit by smuggling cotton through the Union blockade and to serve the Confederacy by trading with England. His frustration led to an explosion at incompetent local authorities who represented the Richmond government. Although he died believing himself loyal to the Confederacy, Hammond's lack of confidence in government policy and his personal selfishness, like that of other planters and businessmen, under-mined Confederate resolve.[42]

A critical observer of the planters and the businessmen's resolve was the Northern-born commissioner of ordinance, Josiah Gorgas. He fulminated against the Charleston commission firm of John Fraser and Company for overcharging and cheating the Confederacy. Gorgas never actually accused them of disloyalty, but his frustration often boiled over. Ruefully, he ru-minated, "must we conclude that we are, after all, wrong?" "If our own people gouge us, then what are we to expect?" Gorgas particularly criti-cized those Charlestonians who lived in the lap of luxury when others went hungry. "The sins of the people," he claimed, "may cause that city to fall." "Her fall will be looked on by many as righteous."[43] For Gorgas, if South Carolina, the heart of the secession movement, had turned on the Confederacy, what could one expect from other planter and business lead-ers?

Despite Gorgas's frustrations, many entrepreneurs did put their talents to work on behalf of the Confederacy. There is merit in Emory Thomas's assertion that business leaders created a Confederate military-industrial complex.[44] But their selflessness often turned to selfishness as the war ground down many around them. A number of manufacturers, by 1863, had refused to accept Confederate currency. Railroad managers, too, as Mary De Credico has shown, undermined the transportation system. At first those men praised the cause and devoted their talents to it, but they soon turned sour. No longer "wedded to vague principles or abstractions," they raised transport charges and refused to lay more tracks without ad-vance payment.[45]

Many of the interior and Mississippi river towns' commercial and ag-ricultural leaders, such as Atlanta and Natchez, never enthusiastically sup-ported secession. In fact, the towns were Lower South centers of Unionist activity. Of course, when war started, some local businessmen labored mightily to maintain a separate nation, but towns like Atlanta soon showed cracks. As James W. Russell has pointed out, in Atlanta speculation ran rampart and privation made the locals anxious. Some leaders made matters worse when they charged that city institutions failed to "deliver essential services to many people." In short, those business leaders knew that the critical infrastructure had collapsed and they refused to help resuscitate it. Some urban business leaders left for Europe or the North. Others simply struck out on their own for protection and profit.[46] Certainly those once-loyal business leaders by their words and deeds undermined the war effort. Perhaps Douglas Ball's cynical comment that "the Confederacy's survival was incompatible with the interests of the southern people" is an accurate assessment of those planter and business leaders who had once professed faith in the new nation.[47]

Another group of disgruntled, disloyal business leaders volunteered their services to the Confederate government. One who had opposed secession but still served the new nation was William M. Wadley, a railroad engineer from Savannah. Born in New Hampshire, Wadley had settled in Georgia and entered the railroad business. He became President Davis's superintendent of transportation. In that capacity he oversaw all government railroad agents and employees on the lines. Wadley ran afoul of his superiors when he resisted army impressment of railroad equipment and bickered with private railroad executives. In April 1863 the Confederate Senate rejected his reappointment as superintendent because his plans to centralize the railroad authority were drawn poorly. Fellow transportation executives told their friends in Congress that Wadley had behaved erratically because he had never believed in the Confederacy.[48] Even if his private views led him astray, Wadley's talents were lost to a Confederate government desperately in need of such skills.

Similar charges of disloyalty were lodged against Georgia's Gazaway B. Lamar, Confederate banker, intelligence agent, and blockade runner. From an old Georgia family, the talented Lamar had prewar business and banking experience. Even though he had resisted secession, for a time he was a useful servant of the Confederate cause. Then, in what appears as self-sacrificial, he leaked to the Richmond newspapers information about Confederate business dealings with New York mayor and Southern sympathizer Fernando Wood, which destroyed one major Northern source of Southern aid. Broken in confidence, and put on the shelf, when Sherman occupied Savannah, Lamar took the oath of allegiance to the United States government and was sent to a Federal prison. But long before that he had been lost to the Confederacy.[49] Two men with business experience, Wadley and Lamar, obviously did not sacrifice enough for the cause.

The conduct of former Unionists who served the Confederacy's business interests, yet in different ways turned on it, perhaps may be explained as lack of real commitment to the cause. What of the planters and businessmen who had been prewar Secessionists? More important, what of the staunch Secessionists, the third group under consideration here, who served the Confederacy throughout, but by their words and deeds undermined the war effort? Those men declared loyalty to the cause to the bitter end, even if their activities belied that devotion. Some historians have explained this group of disloyal Confederates' actions as jealousy, ambition, territorialism, and hatred for President Jefferson Davis. The attacks on Davis have been tied to charges of the president's lack of veracity, favoritism, and plain poor planning; in short, his incompetence. Some radical Secessionists who turned on him even suggested that Davis did not have his heart in a separate nation.[50] But Davis's behavior appears to have been an excuse for those hardcore leaders' opposition to the Confederacy. Their actions and their contributions to the personal rumor mill, as Mary Chesnut so vividly reconstructed in her book, indeed helped to wreck the Confederacy. The activities of some of the key leaders who proclaimed their ardent support for the Confederacy reveals the harm they did to the Confederacy and perhaps explains why they turned on their new nation.

From the Upper South no one brought better leadership skills and commitment to the Confederate cause than Virginia's Robert Mercer Taliaferro Hunter. Even his dislike of South Carolina's precipitate Secessionist action was because he wanted a united front for the separate nation. A brilliant student of political economy, he also had practical experience as chairman of the Senate Finance Committee. Much, then, was expected of this skilled leader. Hunter's Confederate career started off tumultuously, however, and turned out unsatisfactorily. As President Davis's first secretary of state, he presided over a number of foreign policy fiascos. He resigned his office, believing that he had lost the confidence of the president. Even some who respected him regarded Hunter as too conservative to lead a revolutionary movement.[51]

For a while Hunter complained that he had been forced to resign from government. But he soon reentered the fray, gained election to the Confederate Senate and became chair of the important Committee on Financial Affairs. Then Hunter clashed with Secretary of Treasury Christopher G. Memminger and the president, and he did little to lead the Senate in fiscal policy. Though he voted for most administration policies, he never helped to refine those policies, especially financial ones, or to persuade fellow senators to take leadership positions themselves. Often he exacerbated tensions between the executive and legislative branches of government. As the war turned sour, he behaved with increasing petulance. A close friend of Secretary of War James A. Seddon, Hunter rebelled over Davis's treatment of Seddon. After Seddon was forced to resign, Hunter went into opposition to the administration. At the crucial moment when the president called on him to take charge of the effort to enlarge the army through the use of slave soldiers, Hunter resisted. In fact, he led the movement against arming the slaves and argued that slavery would be undermined by such action. Despite Hunter's resistance to administration policies, Davis sent him to the Hampton Roads peace conference. The senator came away from the meeting committed to peace and furious with the president for scuttling an opportunity to end a lost war. Friends believed that he had become a reconstructionist. His most recent biographer says Hunter was no peace advocate, but that "once independence seemed unachievable, he would salvage what he could from the wreckage."[52] There is evidence, however, that Hunter had turned against the Confederacy long before victory was in doubt. Even so, in the postwar period Hunter remained unreconstructed, and he fervently insisted that he had been a committed Confederate.

Hunter professed but did not practice loyalty. North Carolina's Secessionist leaders, in contrast, were active in their disloyalty. They turned against the Confederate war effort over the personal costs of war, how it was conducted, and finally, whether it ever was winnable. The correspondence of North Carolina's elder Secessionist statesman, Thomas Ruffin, reveals a creeping loss of confidence in the war. Already seventy-four when the war began, Ruffin hardly could have been expected to shoulder much of the state's wartime burden, but he tried, especially early in the war. Ruffin embraced the Confederacy, contributed funds, raised troops, and endorsed Secessionists for leadership roles. By Christmas 1862, however, he had concluded that Confederates were too divided to achieve victory. Though he despised the Unionist Holden, in 1864 Ruffin supported Vance, the peace leader, for governor. When Congressman William T. Dortch, a peace advocate, solicited Ruffin's aid in calling a state peace convention, the old Secessionist assisted him.[53] Ruffin knew that North Carolinians had to protect themselves against the consequences of a lost war.

Ruffin's wartime changes in loyalty were much like those of other committed North Carolina Secessionists. Former congressman and stauch upcountry Secessionist Thomas J. Clingman became an important wartime leader. He expected to follow his prewar political career, but his dislike for President Davis led him instead to volunteer for military service. He served ably, with most of his duty in defense of North Carolina. Still, as Thomas E. Jeffrey points out, Clingman's hatred for Davis probably kept him from giving the best service he could to the Confederacy.[54]

From the Lower South, the Davis administration expected much support. There were diehard Confederates in South Carolina, like Wade Hampton and James Chesnut. In contrast, as Mary Chesnut wrote derisively, that symbol of secession and resistance to the Yankees, Robert Barnwell Rhett, early devoted his newspaper, the *Charleston Mercury*, to radical opposition. By 1862 Rhett father and son roused public dissent against the war policies of Jefferson Davis. Radical warhawks, the Rhetts accused Davis of criminal incompetence for refusing to take their advice. Rhett called on Congress to force Davis out and, in a *Mercury* editorial, even supported Henry S. Foote's demand for a change in government personnel. In 1863 Rhett wrote about a revolutionary scheme to depose Davis and set up a military dictator committed to victory. Inconsistently, Rhett also insisted that Davis had violated South Carolina's individual rights with excessive wartime measures.[55] Still, in 1863, Rhett continued to call for independence, even if he opposed excessive central government.

Rhett ran for Congress in 1863 on the very same warlike platform on which he had been elected to the provisional congress. This time he lost to the conservative Lewis M. Ayer, who also questioned the Davis government's commitment to Southern rights. Perhaps that defeat unhinged Rhett, for he turned into an even testier reviewer of administration policies. He grew despondent and defeatist because of the inaction of the federal government. Rhett even praised the forces in the state that called for a separate peace. After General Sherman's troops marched into South Carolina, the editor believed that "everything had gone wild." When the administration advocated arming the slaves as a last-ditch measure to strike for freedom, Rhett exploded. He called for Davis's impeachment. To arm slaves, he exclaimed, was to free them. What had the Confederacy been fighting for except to preserve slavery?[56] So far had this Secessionist's patriotism declined that he even came to doubt his original objectives. By pounding away day after day against the administration, could it be doubted that this most radical of Southern editors had undermined South Carolinians' confidence in the Confederacy?

An even more perplexing turncoat was the South Carolina political leader James L. Orr, at one time a moderate national Democrat. A man of political stature, Orr had been swept up in the state's secession hysteria and had led his conservative followers out of the Union. Though radical Secessionists once had distrusted him, because of his reputation and experience they sent him to the Confederate Senate, where he served throughout the war. He had defeated James Chesnut for that office, and as one would expect he raised the ire of the diarist Mary Chesnut. He incurred more of her wrath after he joined the anti-Davis government forces. Early in the war, this loyal Confederate had ably served the cause as chair of the important Foreign Affairs Committee. By mid-1862, however, war measures such as the conscription bill sent him into opposition.

When the Davis government wanted to punish what it called malingerers, Orr questioned its authority to do so and praised what he called "noble conspiracies" against a faltering government. A friend and ally of General Joseph E. Johnston, Orr opposed those who diminished the general's reputation. The senator came to loathe fellow South Carolinian Lucius B. Northrup, a friend of Davis whom Orr considered a failed commissary general. Then, when the Davis government talked of arming slaves, Orr feared for the future. He rejected the government's use of slave labor and told his constituents that slaves were too valuable to take from their masters for any reason. In December 1863, because of military reverses, he covertly began a peace movement. Along with Senator Graham of North Carolina and Congressman Henry S. Foote of Tennessee, he proposed that Congress begin negotiations with the Union. In March 1865 the Confederate Senate named Orr, Hunter, and Graham to consult President Davis on a peace initiative. After the movement failed, Orr blamed Davis.[57]

What had moved this Secessionist patriot to support reunion? Orr's biographer believes that the senator hated the president because of his incompetence, but there is more to his opposition than just anti-Davisism. Early in the war Orr resisted what he called overt government interference with individual rights, but he remained a Southern nationalist and rarely spoke as a states'-righter. He went into opposition because of his hypersensitive defense of slaveholders' rights. He supported slavery at all costs, and he doubted that the president did. In fact, Orr's peace movement was based on the misjudgment that reconstruction of the Union would keep abolition at bay.[58] For Orr the Confederate war effort eventually posed a threat to slave society.

Other former radical Secessionists who had prewar national political status and in their own ways turned on the Confederacy were the brilliant Georgians Howell Cobb and Robert Toombs. So famous were they at home that their support for secession doomed Georgia to join the Confederacy. Both men assisted in drafting the Confederate constitution, and both were candidates for president of the Confederacy. Both ably served in government, ran afoul of President Davis because of their ambition, entered the military, and resigned from the army out of frustration at defeat and failure to get promoted. Both Cobb and Toombs insisted they remained loyal Confederates throughout the war, at least as they understood loyalty.

The conflicted Toombs's anti-Confederacy efforts stand out. Hard drinker, gifted speaker, and political manipulator, the bulky leader knew how to command and draw people to his cause. Davis with some confidence named him secretary of state in the provisional government, but Secretary of the Navy Stephen Mallory became suspicious of the Georgian's belligerent attitude toward the president. Others felt him too ambitious, or at least too critical of what he called a timid military agenda. Determined to take matters into his own hands, Toombs resigned as secretary, acquired a military commission from the president, and fought well if erratically, but he resigned from the army because his views were not accepted. Then Governor Joseph E. Brown appointed that amateur student of military strategy to the state militia, and he joined the governor's antiadministration forces. In a January 1864 address Toombs hinted darkly "at open resistance . . . for the preservation of liberty." General P.G.T. Beauregard did not take that threat lightly. He arrested Toombs and began court-martial proceedings. Other issues intervened, such as the Northern advance on Atlanta, and Toombs was famous, so Beauregard dropped the charges. Even arrest had not stopped Toombs, as he next united with Alexander A. Stephens and Brown to condemn Davis for suspending the writ of habeas corpus in Georgia. Still, Toombs refused to assist in the peace overtures of those Georgians who sought an audience with Northern General William T. Sherman. To the last, he "strongly urged the continuation of the war."[59]

Not all Georgia's Secessionist leaders urged the war's continuation. The most infamous Secessionist turned anti-Confederate, the federal government's greatest obstructionist, was Governor Joseph E. Brown. What motivated that Confederate who opposed the Confederacy? Thanks to Jefferson Davis and the historian Frank L. Owsley, Brown is known to history as the war's most outspoken defender of the rights of states. Davis in his memoirs wrote that Brown frequently obstructed "the government officials in the discharge of their duties," withheld "the assistance which he might be justly expected to render, and in the contemplation of his own views of the duties and obligations of the executive and legislative departments of the general government," lost "sight of those important objects, the attainment of which an exalted patriotism might have told him depended on the cooperation of the state and the Confederate governments." Writing of Brown's reputation, years after the war, Herber Fielder disputed Davis's view of the governor's wartime actions and insisted that Brown had responded negatively to the Confederate constitution as too weak to conduct a rebellion and too strong to work effectively with the states. Modern historians explained his wartime behavior as that of a populist leader who fought President Davis's privileged business and political friends. The governor believed that business leaders had sought protection and gain under Davis's central state authority at the expense of the ordinary people.[60]

In those efforts to explain Brown's actions was born the populist man of the people as radical states'-righter. The rights of the states had, in his eyes, say many, replaced his desire for a separate nation. Brown had begun the Civil War as a committed Secessionist who led his state out of the Union. He early swore fealty to the new nation, though indeed he viewed the constitution as anything but a revolutionary document. He encouraged Georgians to support the war, raised troops for the effort, and early on promoted the government's policies to finance the war. Contemporaries suggested that the governor wanted a large role in the war effort, and that he often spoke of the personal sacrifices necessary to protect Southern society.[61]

Brown turned against the central government not merely on account of the rights of states, but because the war undermined individual values and hurt the Southern people. As the representative of his state, he roused other state leaders, especially those governors under Federal siege in Alabama and Mississippi, to resist the faulty central government authorities. Unfortunately for Brown, he had only one state's powers to use against the administration. When, later in the war, he refused to send Georgians to the Upper South, he said that they would be abused and deployed in the wrong places. When he opposed the tax in kind and other central Confederate fund-raising initiatives, he undermined the Confederacy's ability to pay for the war. The governor realized the foolishness of forcing people to support an unpopular cause. The Confederate central authorities, he said, had failed to protect the people and their possessions. He then accused the central government of undermining popular liberty. Of course, Brown had damaged morale and support for continuing to make personal sacrifices.[62] His attack on failed policies contributed to making the Confederate nation the enemy of its own people.

Another one-time staunch Secessionist who in his peculiar way turned on the Confederacy was the famed Alabama fire-eater William Lowndes Yancey. One of the South's most virulent and strident Secessionists, early on he was a radical exponent of the new nation and its government. Vigilant in his charges against others for insufficient loyalty, he struck out at the appointment of John A. Campbell as undersecretary of war, accusing his fellow Alabamian of wanting "the Southern people . . . restored, with the last measure of affliction, to that older government which he had never ceased to trust and venerate." In the Senate he mostly voted for vigorous war measures. On the other hand, Yancey grieved aloud against a failed Treasury Department. So feisty in debate that he often incurred the wrath and even the violence of his fellow lawmakers, Yancey became a most disruptive force in Richmond. When the Davis government attempted to organize a Supreme Court, Yancey fought the measure because the despised traitor John Campbell was to be named chief justice.[63] All the while he insisted on his loyalty to the cause, but could the Confederacy afford that kind of excessive loyalty? When he died in 1863, neither Davis nor many others shed a tear.

If Yancey the committed secessionist worried that the Confederacy's leaders undermined their own cause, Secessionists from the next state over, Mississippi, soon faced the more serious problem of Federal military occupation. Few state leaders made greater sacrifice to the cause than Mississippi's first Confederate governor, John J. Pettus, a committed Secessionist and Southern nationalist. So strongly had Pettus supported Mississippi's secession movement that he incurred the wrath of loyalist businessmen such as Benjamin Wailes, who believed that Pettus had done much damage to the state's financial future, and thus to the Confederacy's ability to protect the people and their interests. Pettus ignored Wailes's accusations and ably assisted the new government by calling for sacrifices from his followers. He always raised more troops than were required, personally donated funds to the government, and worked tirelessly on behalf of the slave states' interests.[64]

Pettus also saw his state come under increasing pressure from the Federal army, and he grieved as his fellow Mississippians suffered materially and became demoralized. When Confederate authorities accused farmers of trading with the enemy, Pettus lashed out, "our people must have salt." He allowed citizens to exchange cotton for salt and other commodities with the Union forces in nearby occupied New Orleans. Even his cousin dealt in contraband commerce, and Pettus supported him, especially as he aided the beleaguered city of Jackson. When Mississippi planters resisted Confederate impressment of their slaves, Pettus championed their accusations against the central government for mistreating slave property. He succumbed to pressure from Mississippi's large planters and opposed all Confederate government exacting of taxes from them. When he realized that Mississippi slaves contemplated revolt, he refused to send more troops from the countryside to the defense of besieged Vicksburg. Troops who escaped from that hellhole on the Mississippi River, rather than rejoin the Army of Tennessee, signed on to Pettus's home guard. The governor fulminated against failed Confederate western policy as the army lost town after town on the river. With the fall of Vicksburg, the loyal governor removed his administration into the state's interior to resist Northern invaders. More and more he conflicted with Confederate central authorities. In late 1863, after another Secessionist, Charles Clark, replaced him as governor, a tired Pettus supported his successor. By 1864 he and many other Mississippians expected no further assistance from Richmond.[65]

Pettus's resistance, then, had not been out of disloyalty or some vague ideal of states' rights. Oh, no! Pettus opposed the Confederacy to save his own besieged region. Richmond's accusations of disloyalty and of undermining the Confederate central government he called misguided. Pettus had turned against the Confederacy because the government had given too little assistance to his invaded southwestern state. Could the geography of occupation have been a factor in a Confederate turning against Confederate?

Even more of a problem for the Davis government than Pettus was the staunch Secessionist Texan Louis T. Wigfall. Early a personal friend and ally of the president, Wigfall served in the Confederate Senate throughout the war and insisted that he had never strayed from his fidelity to the cause. This member of the inner circle soon became a staunch enemy of the executive office and a most obstructionist congressman in the eyes of the administration. His somewhat sympathetic biographer, Alvy King, sums up Wigfall's contribution to the Confederacy thus: "Throughout the war he was continually in a military or political maelstrom."[66] Just what had that Texan done to undermine the Confederacy, and what made that declared ultrapatriot behave in such a disloyal way?

As a United States Senator, Wigfall had been a prewar leader of the secession forces in Washington. His hatred for the Unionist Andrew Johnson was real, and he untiringly undermined support for the Union among Southern political leaders. While living in Washington during the secession crisis, Wigfall spied on Federal authorities and informed the South Carolina government of Federal attempts to reprovision Fort Sumter. William Howard Russell, the perceptive English journalist who knew him, regarded the Texan as a raving, drunken radical. Whatever he imbibed, Wigfall's early friendship with Davis gave him real power in determining key Confederate officeholders. The ever-vigilant student of personal relations, Mrs. Chesnut, suspected tension between Varina Davis and Mrs. Wigfall, spats that would spill over into the men's relations. Slights were at issue, and indeed Wigfall sensed the president's loss of confidence in his recommendations for office and his none-too-subtle advice on war plans. The president had little choice in the matter—Wigfall, after all, accused him of failing the cause after First Manassas by not launching an attack on vulnerable Washington.[67]

Perhaps hell hath no fury like that of a spurned adviser. Loss of access to the president led Wigfall into harsher and harsher criticism of the administration's war policies on the floor of the Senate. Although the senator, and most of the other antis, voted for many war measures, as Alvy King pointed out, the language of dissent permeated the halls of Congress. King claims that Wigfall never had been a nationalist or a localist, but instead was a staunch militarist, certain he knew what was necessary to achieve freedom from the anti-slave North. The senator indeed toned down his wife's gossip about the Davises, favored many administration policies such as the twenty-slave rule, and even supported the president on the suspension of writs of habeas corpus. Whenever he felt the president's policies supported the generals, especially those fighting in the west, Wigfall led the cause in the Senate. But the Texan also wanted to organize a general staff system to work directly with Congress and bypass the president's crude system. After he regarded the west nearly lost, Wigfall went into open opposition. No longer content to argue in the relative privacy of the Senate chambers, he publicly took General Joseph E. Johnston's side against Davis. This action undermined the president's authority and certainly created morale problems in the army. Wigfall went even further and said that he doubted the president's military judgment. He then planned to undermine confidence in the President through belittling him in public. A hypersensitive Davis, prone to pouting and public outbursts himself, became the perfect foil for the clever Wigfall. When the senator blamed the president for the loss of Vicksburg, the president exploded. Policy issues, which heretofore had been kept secret, became public. Wigfall became a lightning rod for antiadministration activity. That ever-astute war clerk, John B. Jones, even uncovered a plot by the senator to remove the president from office. When the president moved to arm slaves, Wigfall aligned with powerful leaders Toombs, Hunter, Foote, and Brown to resist what he called turning the Confederate States into Santo Domingo. All who heard them knew exactly what they meant. Mrs. Chesnut in her diary despaired over Wigfall's success at undermining the president's policies. Undermine he did, as Wigfall remained in Richmond until the bitter end, urging removal of Davis and calling for one last great offensive to end the war.[68] As the war came to its conclusion, Wigfall, believing the United States government planned his execution, escaped in disguise and hid in

Texas and elsewhere. To the day he died, that recalcitrant, malcontent, and disloyal Texan believed he had given his unreconstructed all, even his life, to make a separate country.

Wigfall and his fellow Secessionist critics of Davis had undermined whatever chance there had been for a united war effort. Former Unionists turned Confederate, and of course the committed Unionists who never supported the new government, by their action and inaction contributed to the destruction of Confederate unity. Military historians point out pithily that the war was lost on the battlefield. They are surely correct, but the actions of civilian leaders influenced military officials' policies, the troops they received, the wherewithal with which to fight, and the behind-the-lines civilian aid. Those Confederate political state and national leaders who in various ways acted against the Confederacy had divided legislatures against executives, civilians against the military, the east against the west, and even had turned the defense of slavery into fear of race war. In their actions, both words and deeds, those leaders explained their disastrously divisive behavior.

Public officials' character, ambitions, and pettiness led them into opposition. Men who had grown used to the habit of command, who lived in a raucous political world of drink, vulgarity, and violence could hardly restrain themselves during the war. Reports of fights on the floor of Congress and of threatened duels circulated to the frustration of the citizenry, who desired calm and considered action. Spoiled ambitions led some to leave office, others to intrigue for gain, and still others to undermine superior authority. However violent and excessively sensitive Southern leaders were about their rights and sense of social order, it must be noted that some Northern political leaders behaved in a similar fashion, but the structure of Northern politics kept the leaders in order and certainly the leaders' behavior did not have such disastrous consequences.

That the war wore poorly on their constituents certainly turned some leaders against the Confederacy. From the beginning the North was on the offense, and that meant that the Southern people's lives constantly were disrupted. Politicos responded as one would have expected by going on the offense themselves. Especially the more radical Secessionsts wanted to drive the Federals from their soil. When they didn't get a military offensive, they went into opposition. That is why some intrigued with generals, played favorites among them, and became involved in geographical military politics. Of course, the North rarely was invaded and did not have that kind of military pressure. Still, arguments over pursuit of the war, either hard or soft, also divided Northerners, yet Northern leaders stood together enough to deny freedom to the Confederate nation. The Confederate leaders did not.

Clearly, from the war's beginning something was wrong in the Confederacy. That something contributed to Southern Unionism, antisecessionists turned anti-Confederate, and Confederates against the Confederacy, in various degrees of resistance. It was not merely a question of state fears that a central government would override powers or interests. Nor was it the national government's overly brief opportunity to organize and construct an effective governing system. Not even the failure to accustom the people to the idea of a separate new nation, or the leaders' inability or unwillingness to sell the nation to the people, caused the most harm. Some of the leaders, after all, were believed to have been reconstructionists bent on reuniting the sections once the Northerners realized the consequences of their actions. All those factors destabilized the leadership. They all point to the largest flaw that undermined leadership unity and loyalty.

What links the leaders who turned on the Confederacy, then, was the contradiction in the political values of slavery. Fierce individualists, they were also conservative at their core. Those conservative and freedom-loving beliefs coexisted warily in slave society, as Eugene Genovese and Kenneth Greenberg for different reasons and objectives have shown.[69] Those freedom-loving conservatives seceded, formed a Confederacy, and resisted the North's invasion, all to save their slave society. But secession meant revolution and some of those conservatives were anti-revolution, while others were counterrevolutionaries. Still, as long as the new Confederacy protected their way of life, they subverted their own freedoms for the cause. Once the cause became too costly, the government proved inefficient, and the war seemed unwinnable, those conservative individualists rebelled against excessive sacrifice, questioned the means used to resist the North, and even plotted for peace. The Confederates who turned on the Confederacy, even though they protested they had not, had gone into opposition because they had come to believe that their slave society, and thus their values, had become the victim of the pursuit of an independent nation. Those Confederates opposed the Confederacy because of the political contradictions in slavery itself and the Confederate States of America's inability to protect slave society.

Notes

CHAPTER 1: THE CHANGING LOYALTIES OF JAMES HENRY HAMMOND

1. For example, compare Harold S. Schultz, *Nationalism and Sectionalism in South Carolina, 1852–1860* (Durham, N.C.: Duke University Press, 1950), and Charles E. Cauthen, *South Carolina Goes to War* (Chapel Hill: University of North Carolina Press, 1950), with Eugene D. Genovese, *The World the Slaveholders Made* (New York: Pantheon, 1969), and Steven Channing, *Crisis of Fear* (New York: W.W. Norton, 1970).

2. Clement Eaton, *The Mind of the Old South* (Baton Rouge: Louisiana State University Press, 1964), pp. 36–37; Channing, *Crisis of Fear*, pp. 369–71.

3. Ralph A. Wooster, *The Secession Conventions of the South* (Princeton: Princeton University Press, 1962), chap. 2; Wooster, *The People in Power* (Knoxville: University of Tennessee Press, 1969), pp. 36–37.

4. Chalmers Gaston Davidson, *The Last Foray* (Columbia: University of South Carolina Press, 1971), *passim*; Lillian A. Kibler, "Unionist Sentiment in South Carolina in 1860," *Journal of Southern History* 5 (Aug. 1938): 356, 361. The term so-called Unionists is used to follow Kibler's characterization and connotes my skepticism about calling them Unionists. (In fact, few of them saw themselves as Unionists, even if a number of them eventually turned against the Confederate States of America.)

5. This biographical material is taken from Hammond's own self-analysis. See Hammond to William Gilmore Simms, July 8, 1848, Hammond Papers, Library of Congress (hereinafter cited HPLC); Hammond to Beaufort Taylor Watts, Nov.

24, 1845, and to Marcellus Hammond, Nov. 26, 1846, Hammond Papers, South Caroliniana Library, University of South Carolina (hereinafter cited HPSC); "Thoughts and Recollections," 1852–1853, HPSC. Also see Elizabeth Merritt, *James Henry Hammond* (Baltimore: Johns Hopkins University Press, 1923). Since Merritt's work, a number of studies have appeared on Hammond's life. Among the best are Drew Gilpin Faust, *James Henry Hammond and the Old South* (Baton Rouge: Louisiana State University Press, 1982); Carol Bleser, ed., *The Hammonds of Redcliffe* (New York: Oxford University Press, 1988); Clyde N. Wilson, ed., *Selections from the Letters and Speeches of Hon. James H. Hammond of South Carolina* (Spartanburg, S.C.: Reprint Co., 1978).

6. For an account of the political divisions in South Carolina, see Schultz, *Nationalism and Sectionalism*, chap. 7; and Laura A. White, "The National Democrats in South Carolina, 1852 to 1860," *South Atlantic Quarterly* 28 (Oct., 1929): 379.

7. See Laura A. White, *Robert Barnwell Rhett* (Gloucester, Mass.: Peter Smith, 1965), p. 147; Merritt, *Hammond*, pp. 139–41; Cauthen, *South Carolina*, pp. 58–59.

8. Hammond to Simms, Dec. 19, 1857, Jan. 20, Mar. 24, 1858, HPLC; also see J.H. Means to Robert Barnwell Rhett, July 20, 1857, Robert Barnwell Rhett Papers, Southern Historical Collection, University of North Carolina (hereinafter cited SHC).

9. Hammond to Simms, Feb. 7, Mar. 22, Apr. 5, 1858, HPLC; I.W. Haynes to Hammond, Apr. 17, 21, 1858, William Porcher Miles papers, SHC.

10. James Henry Hammond, *Letters and Speeches* (New York: Harper Bros., 1866), pp. 301, 303, 305, 307, 308, 311; for earlier plans, see *Russell's Magazine*, vol. 1 (April 1857), p. 77.

11. *Charleston Mercury*, July 26, Aug. 9, 1858; Hammond to Simms, July 3, 1858, HPLC. For reaction to the speech, see Milledge L. Bonham to his brother Libscomb Bonham, Aug. 14, 1858, Bonham Papers, South Caroliniana Library (hereinafter cited S.C.); John Cunningham to Hammond, Aug. 2, 1858, William Henry Trescot to Hammond, Aug. 15, 1858, and Governor John A. Means to Hammond, Oct. 9, 1858, HPLC.

12. Hammond, *Letters and Speeches*, pp. 328, 334, 335, 353, 356–57.

13. Lillian A. Kibler, *Benjamin F. Perry* (Durham, N.C.: Duke University Press, 1946), pp. 291–92; William P. Miles to Hammond, Nov. 10, 1858, Hammond to Marcellus, Nov. 28, 1858, HPLC; Maxcy Gregg, ed., *An Appeal to the State Rights Party of South Carolina* (Columbia, S.C.: State Press, 1858), pp. 25–36.

14. *Mercury*, Feb. 11, 1859; *Russell's Magazine*, vol. 3 (Apr. 1858), p. 96; R.B. Rhett, Jr., to Hammond, Nov. 5, 1858; James Gadsden to Hammond, Nov. 19, 1858, HPLC.

15. Congressional *Globe*, 35th Cong., 2d sess., p. 1525; Hammond to Simms, Apr. 22, July 30, 1859, HPLC; F.W. Pickens to Milledge Bonham, Apr. 2, 1859, Bonham Papers, S.C.

16. Trescot to Miles, Feb. 8, 1859, Miles Papers, SHC.; Orr to Hammond, Sept. 17, 1859, HPLC.

17. John Cunningham to Hammond, Oct. 14, 1859, HPLC. See letters to editor in *Mercury*, Aug.–Dec. 1859.

18. Hammond to Spann Hammond, Dec. 5, 1859, HPCS; Hammond to Watts, Dec. 6, 1859, Beaufort Taylor Watts Papers, S.C.; D.H. Hamilton to Miles, Dec. 9, 1859, Miles Papers, SHC.

19. Merritt, *Hammond*, p. 135.

20. Hammond to Miles, July 16, 1860, Trescot to Miles, May 8, 12, 1860, Miles Papers, SHC, Hammond to Simms, July 10, 1860, HPLC; also see *Mercury*, May 21, 1860.

21. Hammond, *Letters and Speeches*, pp. 365–68; also see *Charleston Daily Courier*, June 8, 1860.

22. Hammond to I.W. Hayne, Sept. 19, 21, 1860, Hammond to Marcellus, Aug. 30, 1860, HPLC; Hammond to Bonham, Oct. 30, 1860, Bonham Papers, S.C.; *Courier*, Nov. 7, 1860. Also see Merritt, *Hammond*, p. 140.

23. James Henry Hammond, "Rough of Letter to South Carolina Legislature," Nov. 1860, HPSC. The legislature supressed Hammond's letter.

24. Hammond to Simms, Dec. 12, 1861, HPLC; also see Edmund Ruffin Diary, vol. 4, 92–94, Library of Congress. (Hammond was wrong on Toombs, but his error was uncorrectable.)

25. Hammond to committee in Georgia, Nov. 22, 1860, HPLC; *Mercury*, Nov. 30, 1860. Also see C. Fitzsimmons to Hammond, Nov. 29, 1860, HPSC; Watts to Hammond, Dec. 1, 1860, Watts Papers, S.C.

26. Hammond *Diary*, p. 170, HPSC.

27. Eaton, *Mind of the Old South*, pp. 21–42; David Donald, "The Proslavery Argument Reconsidered," *Journal of Southern History* 37 (Feb., 1971): 3–18.

28. Because Hammond left no organized body of writings, it has been necessary to create a composite topical study of his theory. Hammond, *Letters and Speeches*, pp. 88–91, 217, 299–300; *Mercury*, Nov. 4, 1847; Hammond to Simms, Nov. 18, 1853, HPLC.

29. Hammond's views of how slavery freed the whites to form representative government become confused, because as a senator he said that he was willing to give up slavery in order to preserve the republican system. Until historians have studied the relation of government to slavery in the manner in which Eugene Genovese has studied the relation of the labor system to the social system, this important subject will remain confused. See Eugene D. Genovese, *The World the Slaveholders Made*, p. 136. For an interesting view, see George M. Frederickson, *The Black Image in the White Mind* (New York: Harper and Row, 1971), pp. 72–93; Hammond, *Letters and Speeches*, pp. 45, 129, 318; William Sumner Jenkins, *Pro-Slavery Thought in the Old South* (Chapel Hill: University of North Carolina Press, 1935), pp. 197, 286–88.

30. Hammond, *Letters and Speeches*, pp. 208–9, 227, 268; Nathaniel Bev-

erly Tucker, "Hammond's Eulogy upon Calhoun," *Southern Quarterly Review*, n.s. 4 (July 1851): 107–17; Richard A. Sterling, *Sterling's Southern Fifth Reader* (New York: Harper Bros., 1866), pp. 321–24; *College Lecture Book, 1822–1825*, HPSC; Hammond *Diary*, Jan. 2, 1851, HPSC; Hammond to Simms, Apr. 26, 1850, N. Bevery Tucker to Hammond, Apr. 19, 1851, Hammond *Diary*, 1846, pp. 3–9, 1850, pp. 63–69, 1852, pp. 119–26, *Occasional Thoughts*, Apr. 30, 1837, HPLC.

31. For the established role of some planter aristocrats in the secession movement, see Ralph A. Wooster, *Secession Conventions*, p. 20; Ralph A. Wooster, "An Analysis of the Membership of Secession Conventions in the Lower South," *Journal of Southern History* 24 (Aug. 1958): 362–68; Rosser Howard Taylor, "The Gentry of Antebellum South Carolina," *North Carolina Historical Review* 17 (Apr. 1940): 114. Hammond's own analysis of the leadership calls for further investigation of the entire movement. He identified three groups of political leaders: the established old-family planters, the self-made intellectual elite, and the newly ambitious young politicians. See Hammond, *Letters and Speeches*, p. 356; Hammond to George McDuffie, Dec. 27, 1844, Hammond Diary, 1851, pp. 55, 97, HPLC; Hammond *Diary*, pp. 38, 95, HPSC; and Francis W. Pickens to Beaufort T. Watts, Jan. 24, 1854, Watts Papers, S.C.

32. Hammond, *Letters and Speeches*, pp. 127, 213. Historians have accused Hammond of being a conservative political elitist; see Clement Eaton, *The Growth of Southern Civilization* (New York: Harper and Row, 1961), p. 21; James Petigru Carson, *Life, Letters and Speeches of James Louis Petigru* (Washington: American Historical Association, 1920), p. v; N. Beverly Tucker to Hammond, Dec. 29, 1846, HPLC. For Hammond's own countering of this argument, see Hammond to N.J. Cunningham, Dec. 29, 1833, Hammond to Simms, Jan. 1, Nov. 10, 1846, Sept. 22, 1848, Apr. 6, 1849, *Diary*, 1846, pp. 9–10, 1852, pp. 128, 131–32, HPLC; *Mercury*, Nov. 9, 1847; Hammond to Marcellus, July 24, 1832, Hammond, *Diary of European Trip*, Aug. 2, 1837, *Thoughts and Recollections*, 1852–1853, Mar. 13, 27, 1852, HPSC.

33. Those who have accused Hammond of agitating for elite education should examine Hammond, *Letters and Speeches*, pp. 70–75.

34. Hammond, *Letters and Speeches*, pp. 103, 182; *Southern Quarterly Review* 15 (July 1849): 274; Hammond to Simms, Oct. 11, 1851, Hammond *Diary*, 1851, p. 117, HPLC; Hammond to Harry Hammond, Sept. 11, 1855, HPSC.

35. Hammond, *Letters and Speeches*, pp. 63, 225; James Henry Hammond, *The Controversy between James Blair and James H. Hammond* (n.p., 1830), pp. 16, 19; Hammond, *Notes*, Aug. 25, 1837, Calhoun to Hammond, Apr. 18, 1838, Hammond to Simms, Feb. 19, 1846, Hammond *Diary*, 1850, p. 75, HPLC; Hammond to James L. Orr, June 19, 1854, Orr-Patterson Papers, SHC.

36. This article cannot begin to speak for all the Old South's so-called Unionists. Perhaps a fresh look at the political activities and the theoretical codes of

behavior of those men might reveal a more complex set of political alignments and lend some credence to the view that there were three groups of leaders on the eve of secession.

37. Bleser, *Hammonds of Redcliffe*; Hammond to Simms, July 17, 1861, p. 103, to Simms, Nov. 2, 1862, p. 110.

38. Bleser, *Hammonds of Redcliffe*; Edward Spann to Harry Hammond, "Last Moments of J.H.H.," Nov. 13, 1864, pp. 129–130.

CHAPTER 2: FEARS FOR THE FUTURE: A CONSIDERATION OF RELUCTANT CONFEDERATES' ARGUMENTS AGAINST SECESSION, THE CONFEDERACY, AND CIVIL WAR

1. Thomas J. Pressly, *Americans Interpret Their Civil War* (New York: Collier Books, 1962) has the most detailed analysis of this group of historians, many of whom came to fame in the years between World War I and World War II. They spawned a generation of postwar scholars whose works gave way to those trained in the wake of the civil-rights movement.

2. Daniel W. Crofts, *Reluctant Confederates: Upper South Unionists in the Secession Crisis* (Chapel Hill: University of North Carolina Press, 1989).

3. Ibid., pp. 130–163.

4. See also chapter 7 in this volume for more detail on the wartime activities of ex-Unionists of the Upper South. Also see the suggestions in George Rable, *The Confederate Republic* (Chapel Hill: University of North Carolina Press, 1994).

5. Dorothy Dodd, "The Secession Movement in Florida," *Florida Historical Quarterly* 12 (July and Oct. 1933): 3–24, 45–66; Thomas E. Schott, *Alexander H. Stephens* (Baton Rouge: Louisiana State University Press, 1989); Hiram Park Bell, *Men and Things* (Atlanta, Ga.: Foote and Davies, 1907); "From the Autobiography of Herschel V. Johnson, 1856–1867," *American Historical Review* 30 (Jan. 1925): 311–36.

6. Anne Easby-Smith, *William Russell Smith of Alabama* (Philadelphia: Dolphin Press, 1931); Rable, *Confederate Republic*, pp. 227, 292, 349; William Russell Smith, *Reminscences of a Long Life*, (Washington, D.C.: self-published, 1889). Fuller documentation of his wartime behavior may be found in chapter 7 of this volume.

7. James Vaux Drake, *Life of General Robert Hatton, Including His Most Important Public Speeches; Together with Much of His Washington and Army Correspondence* (Nashville, Tenn.: Marshall and Bruce, 1867), pp. 299–354.

8. Eugene D. Genovese, *A Consuming Fire: The Fall of the Confederacy in the Mind of the White Christian South* (Athens: University of Georgia Press, 1998), pp. 41, 44; William Mercer Green, *Memoirs of the Rt. Rev. James Hervey Otey* (New York: V.C. Pott, 1885), pp. 121, 128.

9. William C. Harris, *William Woods Holden: Firebrand of North Carolina Politics* (Baton Rouge: Louisiana State University Press, 1989); Crofts, *Reluctant Confederates*, pp. 25–26.

10. Crofts, *Reluctant Confederates*, p. 73; Max Williams and J.G. deRoulhac Hamilton, eds., *The Papers of William Alexander Graham*, 7 vols. (Raleigh: State Archives and History, 1971–1975), esp. vol. 6; Genovese, *A Consuming Fire*, p. 41; Lawrence Foushee London and Sarah McCulloh Lemon, eds., *The Episcopal Church in North Carolina, 1701–1959* (Raleigh: State Department of Archives and History, 1987), pp. 240–50.

11. Bruce S. Greenawalt, "Unionists in Rockbridge County: The Correspondence of James Dorman Davidson Concerning the Virginia Secession Convention of 1861," *Virginia Magazine of History and Biography* 73 (Jan. 1965): 78–102; Rable, *Confederate Republic*, p. 348; John Brown Baldwin to William Crawford, Apr. 24, 1863, L.C. Also see the papers of William C. Rives at the Library of Congress, which are cited more fully in chapter 7 of this volume.

12. For biographical information, see Thomas Alexander and Richard Beringer, *The Anatomy of the Confederate Congress* (Nashville, Tenn.: Vanderbilt University Press, 1968), and Jon L. Wakelyn, *Biographical Dictionary of the Confederacy* (Westport, Conn.: Greenwood Press, 1977).

13. Richard Keith Call, *Letter to John S. Littell* (Philadelphia: C. Sherman and Son, 1861), pp. 6, 7.

14. "Alexander H. Stephens' Unionist Speech," pp. 51–79 in William W. Freehling and Craig M. Simpson, eds., *Secession Debated: Georgia's Showdown in 1860* (New York: Oxford University Press, 1992), esp. pp. 55–56, 67, 74, and 78–79.

15. Alexander H. Stephens, "Cornerstone Address," pp. 402–12 in Jon L. Wakelyn, ed., *Southern Pamphlets on Secession* (Chapel Hill: University of North Carolina Press, 1996), esp. pp. 410, 412.

16. John A. Campbell, *The Administration of the Confederate States* (Washington, D.C.: n.p., 1861), p. 5; W.R.W. Cobb, *Personal Explanation* (Washington: W.B. Moore, 1861), pp. 4, 5; G.H. Martin, *A Sermon . . . Preached at Macon, Mississippi, on the 24th of December, 1860* (Macon: n.p., 1861), pp. 13–15.

17. William Russell Smith, *As It Is* (Albany, Ga.: Munsell and Rowland, 1860), pp. 37, 68, 88, 142, 260.

18. William Russell Smith, *The History and Debates of the Convention of the People of Alabama* (Atlanta: Wood, Hamleiter, Rice, 1861), pp. 63–64; Easby-Smith, *William Russell Smith*, p. 105.

19. William R. Smith, *History and Debates*, pp. iv, 184–86.

20. Smith to wife, Jan. 10, 12, 20, Mar. 10, May 7, 1861, in Easby-Smith Papers, Library of Congress.

21. Smith, *History and Debates*, iv–v.

22. Robert Hatton, *State of the Union* (Washington, D.C.: Office of Congressional Globe, 1861), pp. 7, 8.

23. Hatton, *State of the Union*, pp. 3, 4; for similar views, see James H. Thomas, *State of the Union* (Washington, D.C.: Office of Congressional Globe, 1861), pp. 2–7.

24. James H. Otey, *Trust in God the Only Safety of Nations* (New York: Daniel Dana, 1860), p. 26; James H. Otey, *Constitutional Government Founded upon the Recognition of God's Sovereignty* (New York: Daniel Dana, 1860), pp. 40–41; James H. Otey, *The Christian Ministry: A Sermon* (New York: Daniel Dana, 1860), p. 17.

25. Zebulon B. Vance, *To the Citizens of the Eighth Congressional District* (Washington, D.C.: Henry Polkinhorn, 1861), pp. 1, 4, 6, 7, 8.

26. Thomas Atkinson, *On the Causes of Our National Troubles* (Wilmington, North Carolina: Herald Book and Job Office, 1861), pp. 5, 14.

27. John A. Gilmer, *State of the Union . . . Jan. 26, 1861* (Washington, D.C.: Henry Polkinhorn, 1861), pp. 5, 7, 8. See also Warren Winslow, *The Critical Condition of the Country* (Washington: Henry Polkinhorn, 1861), p. 16; William N.H. Smith, *The Crisis, Its Responsibilities and Perils* (Washington, D.C.: W.H. Moore, 1861), p. 16.

28. Williams and Hamilton, *Papers of William A. Graham*, vol. 5, pp. 170–172, 224, speech of April 27, 1861, pp, 246–50.

29. William A. Graham, *Speech . . . on the Ordinances Concerning Test Oaths and Sedition* (Raleigh: W.W. Holden, 1861), pp. 4, 12–13, 18, 19. (In chapter 7 of this volume I look more carefully at the impact of this speech on Confederates who developed grievances against the Confederacy.)

30. John S. Millson, *State of the Union* (Washington, D.C.: Lemuel Towers, 1861), p. 8; William L. Goggin, *Speech . . . on Federal Relations, in the Convention of Virginia* (Richmond: Whig Book and Job Office, 1861), pp. 14, 19, 29; Samuel McDowell Moore, *Substance of a Speech Delivered . . . in the Convention of Virginia, on His Resolutions on Federal Relations, . . .* (Richmond: Whig Book and Job Office, 1861), pp. 1, 6, 15, 17, 21. Also see Bruce S. Greenawalt, "Unionists in Rockbridge County," *Virginia Magazine of History and Biography* 73 (Jan. 1965): 78–102 (p. 88 contains a letter of March 29, 1861, of Moore to James D. Davidson).

31. George H. Reese, ed., *Proceedings of the Virginia State Convention of 1861, Feb. 13–May 1*, 4 vols (Richmond: Virginia State Library, 1965), vol. 1, 129–248, esp. pp. 216, 225, 229, 230.

32. William C. Rives, *Speech . . . on the Proceedings of the Peace Conference and the State of the Union* (Richmond: Whig Book and Job Office, 1861), pp. 19–23; Bedford Brown to Rives, Jan. 17, 1861, Rives to George W. Summers, Apr. 15, 1861, Rives to H.B. Latrobe, Apr. 19, 1861, in William Cabell Rives Papers, Library of Congress. In that letter to Summers, a fellow Unionist, Rives continued to hope for a coalition of border free and slave states to stop the war and save slave society.

CHAPTER 3: THE SPEAKERS OF THE STATE
LEGISLATURES' FAILURE AS CONFEDERATE LEADERS

1. Edward Younger, ed., *Inside the Confederate Government: The Diary of Robert Garlick Hill Kean* (Baton Rouge: Louisiana State University Press, 1993), pp. 214–15; Allan Nevins, *The Statesmanship of the Civil War* (New York: Collier Books, 1954), chapter 3; David Donald, ed., *Why the North Won the Civil War* (New York: Collier Books, 1962), pp. 79–90. For another view of the leaders, see John M. Murrin, "The American Revolution Versus the Civil War," unpublished paper presented at the Washington Seminar, Washington Historical Society, May 1989.

2. For example, see William J. Cooper, "A Reassessment of Jefferson Davis As War Leader," *Journal of Southern History* 36 (1970); Thomas E. Schott, *Alexander H. Stephens of Georgia* (Baton Rouge: Louisiana State University Press, 1988); Rembert Patrick, *Jefferson Davis and His Cabinet* (Baton Rouge: Louisiana State University Press, 1954); Wilfred Buck Yearns, ed., *The Confederate Governors* (Athens: University of Georgia Press, 1985); William Morris Robinson, *Justice in Gray* (Cambridge: Harvard University Press, 1941).

3. Fletcher Green, *Constitutional Developments in the South Atlantic States* (Chapel Hill: University of North Carolina Press, 1930), pp. 84–88; Robert Stanley Rankin, *The Government and Administration of North Carolina* (Chapel Hill: University of North Carolina Press, 1955), p. 51; Ralph Wooster, *Politicians, Planters, and Plain Folk* (Knoxville: University of Tennessee Press, 1975), p. 44.

4. J. Mills Thornton, *Politics and Power in a Slave Society* (Baton Rouge: Louisiana State University Press, 1978), p. 116.

5. Yearns, *Confederate Governors*, pp. 7, 13; Charles E. Cauthen, *South Carolina Goes to War* (Chapel Hill: University of North Carolina Press, 1950), p. 161; John Edward Johns, *Florida During the Civil War* (Gainesville: University of Florida Press, 1963), pp. 81, 86; Charles R. Lee, *Confederate Constitutions* (Chapel Hill: University of North Carolina Press, 1963).

6. May Spence Ringold, *Role of State Legislatures in the Confederacy* (Athens: University of Georgia Press, 1966), pp. 56–57; Charles W. Ramsdell, *Behind the Lines in the Southern Confederacy* (Baton Rouge: Louisiana State University Press, 1944).

7. Ringold, *Role of State Legislatures*, p. 4.

8. For example, see Thornton, *Politics and Power in a Slave Society*.

9. Thornton, *Politics and Power in a Slave Society*; Ralph Wooster, *The People in Power* (Knoxville: University of Tennessee Press, 1969), pp. 3–47, 81–106; Lacy K. Ford, Jr., *Origins of Southern Radicalism* (New York: Oxford University Press, 1988), chapter 8.

10. Ringold, *Role of State Legislatures*, pp. 6, 100.

11. Reuben Davis, *Recollections of Mississippi and Mississippians* (Boston: Houghton Mifflin, 1889); Frontis W. Johnston, ed., *The Papers of Zebulon Baird Vance*,

3 vols. (Raleigh: State Archives and History, 1963), vol. 1, p. 347; Ramsdell, *Behind the Lines*, chapter 3; Yearns, *Confederate Governors*, pp. 5, 13, 224.

12. William J. Cooper of Louisiana State University, personal communication.

13. All biographical material and data computed on these speakers, except where otherwise noted, is taken from Charles Ritter and Jon L. Wakelyn, *Speakers of the State Legislatures, 1850–1910* (Westport, Conn.: Greenwood Press, 1989).

14. Ritter and Wakelyn, *Speakers of the State Legislatures*; James Daniel Lynch, *The Bench and Bar of Mississippi* (New York: Harper Bros., 1881).

15. Nevins, *Statesmanship of the Civil War*.

16. Ritter and Wakelyn, *Speakers of the State Legislatures*; John Lewis Poynton, *History of Augusta County Virginia* (Bridgewater, Va.: County Historical Society, 1953); Susan Braford Eppes, *Through Some Eventful Years* (Gainesville: University of Florida Press, 1968), xv–xvi.

17. Ritter and Wakelyn, *Speakers of the State Legislatures*; Lynch, *Bench and Bar of Mississippi*, pp. 450–52.

18. Jerome Dowd, *Sketches of Prominent Living North Carolinians* (Raleigh, N.C.: Edwards and Broughton, 1888).

19. Helen Lefkowitz Horowitz, *Campus Life* (Chicago: University of Chicago Press, 1987), p. 25; William T. Grant, *Alumni History of the University of North Carolina* (Chapel Hill: University of North Carolina Press, 1901).

20. Ritter and Wakelyn, *Speakers of the State Legislatures*.

21. Michael W. Fitzgerald, "Radical Republicans and the White Yeomanry During Alabama Reconstruction," *Journal of Southern History* 54 (Nov. 1988): 565–68; Paul D. Escott, *After Secession* (Chapel Hill: University of North Carolina Press, 1978); Carl Degler, *The Other South* (New York: Oxford University Press, 1974).

22. Emory Thomas, *The Confederacy As a Revolutionary Experience* (Englewood Cliffs, N.J.: Prentice-Hall, 1971), p. 111.

23. Ritter and Wakelyn, *Speakers of the State Legislatures*.

24. James Roger Mansfield, *A History of Early Spotsylvania* (Charlottesville: University of Virginia Press, 1900), pp. 97–99; 1860 census of Carroll County, Mississippi, manuscript returns, p. 54.

25. Thomas McAdory Owen, *History of Alabama and Dictionary of Alabama Biography*, 4 vols. (Chicago: S.J. Clarke, 1921), vol. 3, 422–24; Cauthen, *South Carolina Goes to War*, pp. 19, 21, 23.

26. Jon L. Wakelyn, *Biographical Dictionary of the Confederacy* (Westport, Conn.: Greenwood Press, 1977), p. 270.

27. Ritter and Wakelyn, *Speakers of the State Legislatures*; Bell I. Wiley, ed., *Letters of Warren Aiken, Confederate Congressman* (Westport, Conn.: Greenwood Press, 1975), pp. 31–33.

28. William S. Speer, ed., *Sketches of Prominent Tennesseans* (Nashville, Tenn.: A.B. Tavel, 1888), pp. 47–50; Robert M. McBride, ed., *Biographical Dictionary of the Tennessee General Assembly*, 2 vols. (Nashville, Tenn.: Vanderbilt University

Press, 1968), vol. 2, p. 484; Peter Maslowski, *Treason Must Be Made Odious* (Mill-wood, N.Y.: KTO Press, 1978), p. 14.

29. *Journal of the House of Representatives of the State of South Carolina: Being the Sessions of 1861* (Columbia, S.C.: state printer, 1861), pp. 294–95; Kenneth S. Greenberg, *Masters and Statesmen* (Baltimore, Md.: Johns Hopkins University Press, 1985), *passim*.

30. *Journal of the House of Commons of the General Assembly of the State of North Carolina at the Session of 1864–1865* (Raleigh, N.C.: state printer, 1866), pp. 24–30.

31. *House Journal 1861–1862 of the First Session of the Thirty-Fourth General Assembly of the State of Tennessee* (Nashville, Tenn.: state printer, 1957), pp. 7, 11.

32. Ibid., pp. 245, 259.

33. *A Journal of the Proceedings of the House of Representatives of the General Assembly of the State of Florida . . . November 21, 1864* (Tallahassee, Fla.: state printer, 1864), pp. 18, 92, 97, 100; *Journal of the House of Representatives of the State of South Carolina: Being the Session of 1861*, pp. 7–8; *Journal of the House of Representatives of the State of Georgia, at the Extra Session Convened Under the Proclamation of the Governor, March 10, 1864* (Milledgeville, Ga.: state printer, 1864), pp. 9, 118–119; *Alabama House of Representatives, Dec. 24, 1864, Joint Resolution on Impressment* (n.p., n.d.).

34. *Journal of the House of Representatives of the State of Mississippi, at a Regular Session . . .* (Jackson, Miss.: state printer, 1862), pp. 5–6; Donald, *Why the North Won*, p. 90.

35. *Journal of the House of Representatives of the State of Georgia, at the Extra Session, . . . March 10, 1864*, pp. 110–11; *House of Representatives of Georgia*, November 6, 1862, pp. 4, 17, 61, 68, 412–17.

36. *Journal of the House of Representatives of the State of Texas, Extra Session of the Eighth Legislature* (Austin, Tex.: state printer, 1861), pp. 4, 5; *Ordinances of the Constitution of the State of Alabama* (Montgomery, Ala.: state printer, 1861), p. 74; *Journal of the House of Representatives of the State of South Carolina . . . 1861*, pp. 199, 201, 204.

37. *A Journal of the Proceedings of the House of Representatives of Florida . . . November 17, 1862* (Tallahassee, Fla.: state printer, 1863), pp. 5–6; *Journal of the House of Representatives of South Carolina . . . 1862* (Columbia, S.C.: state printer, 1862), pp. 5–6; *Journal of the House of Representatives of Texas, . . . Eighth Legislature*, pp. 263–64; *Resolution of the Legislature, State of Mississippi, Apr. 5, 1864* (broadside).

38. Georgia Lee Tatum, *Disloyalty in the Confederacy* (Chapel Hill: University of North Carolina Press, 1934), viii.

39. Ritter and Wakelyn, *Speakers of the State Legislatures; Journal of the House of Commons of North Carolina . . . 1864–1865*, pp. 84, 108.

40. *Journal of the House of Representatives of the State of Georgia, at the Extra*

Session, . . . March 10th, 1864, p. 93; *Ordinances and Constitution of the State of Alabama,* p. 46; Ritter and Wakely, *Speakers of the State Legislatures.*

41. William J. Cooper, *The South and the Politics of Slavery, 1828–1856* (Baton Rouge: Louisiana State University Press, 1978); Thomas P. Alexander, "Persistent Whiggery in the Confederate South," *Journal of Southern History* 27 (1961): 305–29; also see Marc W. Kruman, *Parties and Politics in North Carolina, 1836–1865* (Baton Rouge: Louisiana State University Press, 1983), chapters 9 and 10.

42. Ritter and Wakelyn, *Speakers of the State Legislatures.*

43. Ritter and Wakelyn, *Speakers of the State Legislatures;* Dallas Herndon, ed., *Annals of Arkansas* (Chicago: S.J. Clarke, 1890), p. 175.

44. Ritter and Wakelyn, *Speakers of the State Legislatures;* Speer, *Sketches of Prominent Tennesseans,* pp. 47–50.

45. Davis, *Recollections of Mississippi and Mississippians,* p. 41.

CHAPTER 4: DISLOYALTY IN THE CONFEDERATE CONGRESS. THE CHARACTER OF HENRY STUART FOOTE

1. Edward Younger, ed., *Inside the Confederate Government: The Diary of Robert Garlick Hill Kean* (New York: Oxford University Press, 1957), pp. 44–45, 213–14, 215.

2. John B. Jones, *A Rebel War Clerk's Diary at the Confederate State Capital,* 2 vols. (New York: Old Hickory Book Shop, 1935), vol. 1, pp. 70, 81, 120, 150, 163.

3. Jones, *A Rebel War Clerk's Diary,* vol. 2, p. 257.

4. Jefferson Davis, *The Rise and Fall of the Confederate Government,* 2 vols. (London: Longmans, Green, 1881), *passim;* for affirmation of Davis's personality, see Varina Howell Davis, *Jefferson Davis, Ex-President of the Confederate States of America: A Memoir by His Wife,* 2 vols. (New York: Belford, 1890).

5. Davis, *Rise and Fall,* vol. 1, p. 479, and *passim.* The most recent view of Davis, a favorable one, is William J. Cooper, Jr., *Jefferson Davis, American* (New York: Alfred A. Knopf, 2000). Cooper generally agrees with Davis's view of congressional loyalty to the cause.

6. Edward A. Pollard, *Southern History of the War,* 4 vols. (New York: Charles B. Richardson, 1862–1866), vol. 1, pp. 231–32, vol. 2, p. 576, vol. 4, p. 457 and especially p. 473.

7. Max R. Williams and J.G. DeRoulhac Hamilton, eds., *The Papers of William Archibald Graham,* 7 vols. (Raleigh, N.C.: State Department of Archives and History, 1957–1976), vol. 5, p. 386, and *passim,* and vol. 6, p. 289.

8. Hiram Parks Bell, *Men and Things,* (Atlanta, Ga.: Foote and Davies, 1907), pp. 100–101; also see John Goode, *Recollections of a Lifetime* (New York: Neale Publishing, 1906), p. 91.

9. For detailed commentary on the Confederate Congress, see Thomas B. Alexander and Richard Beringer, *The Anatomy of the Confederate Congress: A Study of the Influence of Member Characteristics on Legislative Voting Behavior* (Nashville, Tenn.: Vanderbilt University Press, 1972); Wilfred Buck Yearns, *The Confederate Congress* (Athens: University of Georgia Press, 1954); Richard Franklin Bensel, *Yankee Leviathan: The Origins of Central State Authority in America, 1859–1877* (Cambridge: Cambridge University Press, 1990), chapter 2; George E. Rable, *The Confederate Republic: A Revolution Against Politics* (Chapel Hill: University of North Carolina Press, 1994).

10. Yearns, *Confederate Congress*, p. viii.

11. Alexander and Beringer, *Anatomy of the Confederate Congress*, pp. 26, 344; Yearns, *Confederate Congress*, pp. 255, 286.

12. For the politics of opposition, see Allan S. Bogue, *The Congressmen's Civil War* (Cambridge: Cambridge University Press, 1989), pp. 144, 147, 148.

13. Alexander and Beringer, *Anatomy of the Confederate Congress*, p. 26 and esp. p. 76; Yearns, *Confederate Congress*, p. 171; Rable, *Confederate Republic*, p. 271.

14. Office of Provost Marshall to Mrs. William R. Smith, March 1865, Easby-Smith Papers, Library of Congress; William R. Smith, *Reminiscences of a Long Life*, (Washington, D.C.: self-published, 1889), vol. 1, p. 308; Anne Easby-Smith, *William Russell Smith of Alabama* (Philadelphia: Dolphin Press, 1931), p. 161.

15. Cooper, *Jefferson Davis*, p. 463: Alexander and Beringer, *Anatomy of the Confederate Congress*, p. 86; Daniel Crofts, *Reluctant Confederates: Upper South Unionists in the Secession Crisis*, (Chapel Hill: University of North Carolina Press, 1989), pp. 288, 325.

16. Henry Stuart Foote, *Casket of Reminiscences* (Washington: Chronicle, 1874), *passim*; Reuben Davis, *Recollections of Mississippi and Mississippians* (Boston: Houghton Mifflin, 1889), pp. 101–2; John E. Gonzales, "Henry Stuart Foote: Confederate Congressman and Exile," *Civil War History* 11, no. 4 (Dec. 1965): 384–95.

17. Foote, *Casket of Reminiscences, passim*; Gonzales, "Henry Stuart Foote," pp. 390–91; Joseph Howard Parks, *John Bell of Tennessee* (Baton Rouge: Louisiana State University Press, 1950), pp. 221, 249, 394.

18. Cooper, *Jefferson Davis*, p. 195; R. Davis, *Recollections*, p. 314.

19. Ezra Warner and Wilfred B. Yearns, eds., *Biographical Register of the Confederate Congress* (Baton Rouge: Louisiana State University Press, 1975), pp. 86–87; R. Davis, *Recollections*, p. 322; Rable, *Confederate Republic*, pp. 185, 248, 360–61.

20. Jones, *Rebel War Clerk*, vol. 1, 238; *Journal of the Congress of the Confederate States of America*, 7 vols. (Washington: Government Printing Office, 1905–1906), vol. 4, pp. 155, 385, 386, 469–70.

21. Jones, *Rebel War Clerk*, vol. 1, p. 118; Edward McPherson, *The Political*

History of the United States of America During the Great Rebellion (New York: Da Capo Press, 1972), p. 617; Journal of the Confederate Congress, vol. 2, p. 260.

22. Thomas L. Connelly and Archer Jones, *The Politics of Command* (Baton Rouge: Louisiana State University Press, 1973), pp. 67, 85.

23. Jones, *Rebel War Clerk*, vol. 2, pp. 106, 113; *Journal of the Confederate Congress*, vol. 5, p. 11.

24. Jones, *Rebel War Clerk*, vol. 2, pp. 113, 116, 121.

25. Cooper, *Jefferson Davis*, p. 506.

26. Jones, *Rebel War Clerk*, vol. 2, p. 136.

27. The best early study on arming the slaves is Robert F. Durden, *The Gray and the Black: The Confederate Debate on Emancipation* (Baton Rouge: Louisiana State University Press, 1972); it has been supplanted by William W. Freehling, *The South Versus the South* (New York: Oxford University Press, 2001).

28. *Journal of the Confederate Congress*, vol. 4, p. 526, vol. 7, pp. 262, 312.

29. Yearns, *Confederate Congress*, p. 99; *Journal of the Confederate Congress*, vol. 7, p. 262.

30. Bell, *Men and Things*, pp. 100–101; Yearns, *Confederate Congress*, p. 171; *Journal of the Confederate Congress*, vol. 5, p. 385.

31. Jones, *Rebel War Clerk*, vol. 2, pp. 385, 389, 392; *Journal of the Confederate Congress*, vol. 6, pp. 8–9, 79–81, vol. 7, p. 312.

32. Jones, *Rebel War Clerk*, vol. 2, p. 392; Leroy P. Graf and Ralph W. Haskins, eds., *The Papers of Andrew Johnson* (Knoxville: University of Tennessee Press, 1967-), vol. 6, p. 657; *Journal of the Confederate Congress*, vol. 7, p. 49.

33. Gonzales, "Henry Stuart Foote," p. 391; For Foote's and other congressmen's views of the president, see Paul D. Escott, *After Secession: Jefferson Davis and the Failure of Confederate Nationalism* (Baton Rouge: Louisiana State University Press, 1978), and Michael B. Ballard, *A Long Shadow: Jefferson Davis and the Final Days of the Confederacy* (Jackson: University Press of Mississippi, 1986).

34. Crofts, *Reluctant Confederates*, p. 444.

35. Henry Stuart Foote, *Texas and the Texans*, 2 vols. (Philadelphia: Thomas Cowperthwait, 1841), vol. 1, p. 314.

36. Foote, *Texas and the Texans*, vol. 2, p. 388; also see pp. 379–87.

37. Foote, *Texas and the Texans*, vol. 2, pp. 388, 390.

38. Henry S. Foote, *Eulogy upon the Life and Character of James K. Polk* . . . (Washington, D.C.: Thomas Ritchie, 1849), pp. 11–14; Henry S. Foote, "*Oration . . . on the Fourth of July, 1850* . . . (Washington, D.C.: Henry Polkinhorn, 1850), pp. 12–13; Henry S. Foote, *A Lecture on the Value of the American Union* (Philadelphia: T.K. Collins, 1851), p. 18.

39. Henry S. Foote, *War of the Rebellion; or, Scylla and Charybdis* (New York: Harper and Bros., 1866), pp. 292–316; Crofts, *Reluctant Confederates*, pp. 325–326.

40. Foote, *War of the Rebellion, passim*; Foote, *Casket of Reminscences*.

41. Foote, *War of the Rebellion*, pp. 16, 22, 196.

42. Warner and Yearns, *Biographical Dictionary of the Confederate Congress*, pp. 87–88; Gonzales, "Henry Stuart Foote," p. 395.

43. Foote, *Casket of Reminiscences*, pp. 226, 319, 469–71.

44. Foote, *Casket of Reminiscences*, pp. 145–58; Foote, *War of the Rebellion*, p. 317.

45. Foote, *Casket of Reminiscences*, pp. 159, 319.

46. Foote, *Casket of Reminiscences*, p. 137; Foote, *War of the Rebellion*, p. 393.

CHAPTER 5: THE CONTRIBUTIONS OF THE SOUTHERN EPISCOPAL CHURCH TO CONFEDERATE UNITY AND MORALE

1. The best recent attempt to assess the contributions of religion to the Confederacy is Richard E. Beringer et al., *Why the South Lost the Civil War* (Athens: University of Georgia Press, 1986), chapters 5, 12, and 14. Also see James W. Silver, *Confederate Morale and Church Propaganda* (New York: W.W. Norton, 1967). I have found few references that link the religious faith of the military to wartime activities. For some hints on this matter, see Drew Gilpin Faust, *The Creation of Confederate Nationalism* (Baton Rouge: Louisiana State University Press, 1988), pp. 21–45. For the role of Episcopal leaders in the Confederacy, see Jon L. Wakelyn, *Biographical Dictionary of the Confederacy* (Westport, Conn.: Greenwood Press, 1977); *Addresses and Historical Papers Before the Centennial Council of the Protestant Episcopal Church of Virginia* (New York: Episcopal Publishing House, 1885), pp. 11, 18; Joseph Blount Chesire, *The Church in the Confederate States* (New York: Episcopal Publishing House, 1912). Studies of the lives of the clergy include Joseph Bamford Parks, *General Leonidas Polk* (Baton Rouge: Louisiana State University Press, 1950); William A. Clebsch, "Stephen Elliott's View of the Civil War," *Historical Magazine of the Protestant Episcopal Church* 31 (Mar. 1962): 1–22; Susan P. Lee, *Memoirs of William Nelson Pendleton* (Philadelphia: Longmans, Green, 1893); John Johns, *A Memoir of the Life of the Right Rev. William Meade* (Baltimore, Md.: Innes, 1867).

2. Ken Clark and Charlie Steen, *Making Sense of the Episcopal Church* (Harrisburg: Morehouse, 1996), *passim*; Rhys Isaac, *The Transformation of Virginia* (Chapel Hill: University of North Carolina Press, 1982); Jan Lewis, *The Pursuit of Happiness* (New York: Cambridge University Press, 1983).

3. William Meade, *Sermon at the Opening of the Convention of the Protestant Episcopal Church in Virginia, in Petersburg, May 15, 1828* (Richmond, Va.: J. Warock, 1828); William Meade, *Sermon Preached at the Opening of the General Convention . . . Philadelphia, Sept. 15, 1838* (Philadelphia: Episcopal Recorder Press, 1838); William Meade, *Ecclesiastical Law and Discipline: A Charge to the Clergy of the Protestant Episcopal Church of Virginia* (Richmond, Va.: H.K.E. Ellyson, 1850), pp. 21, 35, 56–57, 64, 68–70.

4. For the core beliefs of the church and Meade's comments, see William Meade, *Old Churches, Ministers and Families of Virginia*, 2 vols. (Philadelphia: J.B. Lippincott, 1861); Robert W. Prichard, *The Nature of Salvation: Theological Consensus in the Episcopal Church, 1801–1873* (Urbana: University of Illinois Press, 1997); and John Booty, *Mission and Ministry: A History of the Virginia Seminary* (Harrisburg, Pa.: Morehouse, 1997), esp. chapters 1 and 2.

5. Marshall DeLaney Heywood, *Lives of the Bishops of North Carolina* (Raleigh, N.C.: Alfred Williams, 1909), pp. 102–9; Lawrence Foushee London and Sarah McCulloh Lemmon, eds., *The Episcopal Church in North Carolina* (Raleigh: North Carolina Department of History and Archives, 1987); Peter Benedict Norhler, *The Oxford Movement in Context, 1760–1857* (Cambridge: Cambridge University Press, 1994); Robert Bruce Mullin, *Episcopal Vision/American Reality* (New Haven, Conn.: Yale University Press, 1986), pp. 146–57.

6. Joseph Blount Chesire, *Bishop Atkinson and the Church in the Confederacy* (Raleigh, N.C.: Edwards and Broughton, 1909), pp. 5–6; Heywood, *Lives of the Bishops*, pp. 144–55; William Mercer Green, *Memoirs of the Rt. Rev. James Hervey Otey* (New York: J.C. Potts, 1885), pp. 9, 57.

7. Lockert B. Mason, "Thomas Atkinson and the Separation and Reunion of the Church, 1860–1865," *Anglican and Episcopal History* 59, no. 3 (Sept. 1990): 345–365; also see Allen C. Guelzo, "Ritual, Romanism, and Rebellion: The Disappearance of the Evangelical Episcopalians," *Anglican and Episcopal History* 62, no. 4 (Dec. 1993): 551–77; Richard Rankin, *Ambivalent Churchmen and Evangelical Churchwomen: The Religion of the Episcopal Elite in North Carolina, 1800–1860* (Columbia: University of South Carolina Press, 1993).

8. William Mecklenburg Polk, *Leonidas Polk*, 2 vols. (New York: Longmans, Green, 1915), vol. 1, *passim*; Arthur Ben Chitty, *Reconstruction at Sewanee: The Founding of the University of the South and Its First Administration, 1857–1872* (Sewanee, Tenn.: Proctor's Hall Press, 1993).

9. James H. Otey, *Trust in God the Only Safety of Nations* (New York: Daniel Dana, Jr., 1860), pp. 19, 26; Chesire, *Bishop Atkinson*, p. 9; Thomas Atkinson, *Address Delivered Before the Historical Society of the University of North Carolina* (Raleigh, N.C.: Holden and Wilson, 1855), pp. 27–32; Polk, *Leonidas Polk*, vol. 1, p. 65; Johns, *A Memoir of the Life of the Rt. Rev. William Meade*, p. 494; Green, *Memoirs of James H. Otey*, p. 65.

10. Quoted in G. McLaren Brydon, "The Diocese of Virginia in the Southern Confederacy," *Historical Magazine of the Protestant Episcopal Church* 17 (1948): 387–88.

11. Green, *Memoirs of James H. Otey*, p. 96; Chesire, *Bishop Atkinson*, p. 21; London and Lemmon, *Episcopal Church in North Carolina*, pp. 238, 240, 245.

12. Polk, *Leonidas Polk*, vol. 2, pp. 306, 343; Parks, *General Leonidas Polk*, pp. 157–61.

13. William A. Clebsch, ed., *Journal of the Protestant Episcopal Church in the*

Confederate States of America (Austin, Tex.: Church Historical Society, 1962), p. 13.

14. Clebsch, *Journal of the Protestant Episcopal Church*, p. xii; Henry R. Jackson, *Eulogy on the Late Rt. Rev. Stephen Elliott* (Savannah: Purse and Sons, 1867).

15. Edgar Lee Pennington, "The Organization of the Protestant Episcopal Church in the Confederate States of America," *Historical Magazine of the Protestant Episcopal Church* 17 (Dec. 1948): 317, 321.

16. Johns, *Memoir of William Meade*, pp. 500, 506.

17. Silver, *Confederate Morale, passim*; Lawrence F. London, "The Literature of the Church in the Confederate States," *Historical Magazine of the Protestant Episcopal Church* 17 (Dec. 1948): 345–55.

18. Meade, *Old Churches, Ministers and Families of Virginia*, vol. 1, pp. 16, 18, 45, 61, 425, vol. 2, p. 489; Philip Slaughter, *Memoirs of the Life of the Rt. Rev. William Meade* (Richmond, Va.: Randolph and English, 1885).

19. *Church Intelligencer*, Sept. 16, 1861; Johns, *Memoir of William Meade*, pp. 500, 505.

20. Slaughter, *Memoirs of the Life*, p. 44; Clebsch, *Journal of the Protestant Episcopal Church, in the Confederate States of America*, p. 28; Judith W. McGuire, *Diary of a Southern Refugee During the War* (New York: E.J. Hale and Son, 1867), pp. 219–20.

21. Chesire, *Church in the Confederate States*, p. 71.

22. *Church Intelligencer*, June 13, 1862; Brydon, "Diocese of Virginia," pp. 390–402; McGuire, *Diary*, p. 201.

23. Brydon, "Diocese of Virginia," pp. 408–9; McGuire, *Diary*, pp. 292, 303.

24. Heywood, *Lives of the Bishops*, pp. 159–163; Chesire, *Bishop Atkinson*, pp. 10–14; Green, *Memoirs of Otey*, p. 121.

25. Clebsch, "Stephen Elliott's View," pp. 11–12; Pennington, "The Organization of the Protestant Episcopal Church," p. 332; *Church Intelligencer*, Sept. 16, 1861.

26. Henry Thompson Malone, *The Episcopal Church in Georgia, 1733–1957* (Atlanta: Church Historical Society, 1960), p. 107; Lawrence L. Brown, *The Episcopal Church in Texas* (Austin, Tex.: Church Historical Society, 1963), pp. 118–24.

27. See William Porcher DuBose, *Turning Points in My Life* (New York: Longmans, Green, Co., 1912), pp. 31, 36.

28. Polk, *Leonidas Polk*, vol. 2, p. 352; Green, *Memoirs of Otey*, p. 96; *Church Intelligencer*, July 18 and Aug. 2, 1861.

29. Thomas Lawrence Connelly and Archer Jones, *The Politics of Command*, (Baton Rouge: Louisiana State University Press, 1993), p. 129.

30. Parks, *Bishop Leonidas Polk*, p. 208.

31. Connelly and Jones, *Politics of Command*, pp. 52, 67, 146.

32. Polk, *Leonidas Polk*, vol. 2, pp. 225, 229–30; Parks, *Bishop Leonidas Polk*, pp. 280, 300, 342–44.

33. Polk, *Leonidas Polk*, vol. 2, p. 353.

34. Parks, *Bishop Leonidas Polk*, p. 383; Polk, *Leonidas Polk*, vol. 2, pp. 375, 392–93; Stephen Elliott, *Funeral Services at the Burial of the Rt. Rev. Leonidas Polk*, (Chapel Hill, N.C.: Academic Affairs Library, 1999).

35. Susas P. Lee, *Memoirs of William Nelson Pendleton*, pp. 16–88.

36. Lee, *Memoirs of William Nelson Pendleton*, pp. 78, 88, 104, 119; William Gleason Bean, *Stonewall's Man: Sandie Pendleton* (Chapel Hill: University of North Carolina Press, 1959), pp. 5, 12.

37. Lee, *Memoirs of William Nelson Pendleton*, pp. 138–42; Bean, *Stonewall's Man*, pp. 35, 42.

38. Lee, *Memoirs of William Nelson Pendleton*, pp. 272, 274.

39. Ibid., p. 336.

40. Ibid., pp. 206, 298–99, 381, 421.

41. Gardner H. Shattuck, Jr., *A Shield and a Hiding Place: The Religious Life of the Civil War Armies* (Macon, Ga.: Mercer University Press, 1987), pp. 40–41, 43; Heywood, *Lives of the Bishops*, pp. 163, 165; Mason, "Thomas Atkinson," pp. 364–65; Chesire, *Bishop Atkinson*, pp. 14–15; William Clebsch, *Christian Interpretations of the Civil War* (Philadelphia: Fortress Press, 1969), p. 14; Malone, *Episcopal Church in Georgia*, p. 109.

42. Bean, *Stonewall's Man*, pp. 227–28; Chesire, *Church in the Confederate States*, p. 77.

CHAPTER 6: "PERSONAL REMARKS ARE HAZARDOUS ON A CROWDED RIVERBOAT." MARY BOYKIN CHESNUT AND THE GOSSIP ON CONFEDERATE DIVISIVENESS

1. For a general overview of recent studies on Confederate women, see George C. Rable, *Women and the Crisis of Southern Nationalism* (Urbana: University of Illinois Press, 1989); Drew Gilpin Faust, *Mothers of Invention* (Chapel Hill: University of North Carolina Press, 1996); Catherine Clinton, *Tara Revisited: Women, War, and the Plantation Legend* (New York: Abbeville Press, 1995); Catherine Clinton and Nina Silber, eds., *Divided Houses* (New York: Oxford University Press, 1992). Quite useful to the present study has been Alice Fahr, *The Imagined Civil War: Popular Literature of the North and South, 1861–1865* (Chapel Hill: University of North Carolina Press, 2001).

2. For example, see Faust, *Mothers of Invention*, pp. 118–34; also see Victoria E. Bynum, *Unruly Women: The Politics of Social and Sexual Control in the Old South* (Chapel Hill: University of North Carolina Press, 1994), chapter 6.

3. Michael B. Chesson, "Harlots or Heroines? A New Look at the Richmond Bread Riot," *Virginia Magazine of History and Biography* 92 (Apr. 1984): 131–75.

4. For women in wartime public life, see Elizabeth Varon, *We Mean to Be Counted: White Women and Politics in Antebellum Virginia* (Chapel Hill: University of North Carolina Press, 1998), p. 170; Faust, *Mothers of Invention*, pp. 247–51.

5. Bynum, *Unruly Women*, chapter 6; Daniel E. Sutherland, ed., *Guerrillas, Unionists, and Violence on the Confederate Home Front* (Fayetteville: University of Arkansas Press, 1999); John C. Inscoe and Gordon B. McKinney, *The Heart of Confederate Appalachia: Western North Carolina in the Civil War* (Chapel Hill: University of North Carolina Press, 2000), pp. 117–20.

6. Judith W. McGuire, *Diary of a Southern Refugee During the War* (New York: E.J. Hale and Son, 1867), pp. 6–12.

7. McGuire, *Diary*, pp. 183, 212, 219–220, 303–4, 351.

8. John Q. Anderson, ed., *Brokenburn: The Journal of Kate Stone, 1861–1868* (Baton Rouge: Louisiana State University Press, 1955), pp. xix, 95, 320, 333.

9. Jesse Harrison, *Recollections Grave and Gay* (New York: Charles Scribner's Sons, 1911), pp. 148, 192, 219; also see Ada Sterling, ed., *A Belle of the Fifties: Memoirs of Mrs. Clay of Alabama* (New York: Doubleday, Page, 1905), 206.

10. I will follow the latest and most accurate of the many texts of Mary Chesnut's work. See C. Vann Woodward, ed., *Mary Chesnut's Civil War* (New Haven, Conn.: Yale University Press, 1981).

11. Woodward, *Mary Chesnut's Civil War*, pp. xv–lviii; William W. Freehling, *The Road to Disunion* (New York: Oxford University Press, 1990), pp. 246–49.

12. John B. Jones, *A Rebel War Clerk's Diary at the Confederate States Capital*, 2 vols. (New York: Old Hickory Book Shop, 1935), *passim*; Harrison, *Recollections*, p. 148.

13. See Elizabeth Muhlenfeld, *Mary Boykin Chesnut* (Baton Rouge: Louisiana State University Press, 1981); Faust, *Mothers of Invention*, pp. 92, 112, 150–64; Anne C. Rose, *Victorian America and the Civil War* (New York: Cambridge University Press, 1994), pp. 99, 101–2, 218–19, 230.

14. Sterling, ed., *A Belle of the Fifties*, p. 50; Eron Rowland, *Varina Howell, Wife of Jefferson Davis*, 2 vols. (New York: Macmillan, 1927, 1931), vol. 1, p. 291.

15. Muhlenfeld, *Mary Boykin Chesnut*, pp. 97–208; William J. Cooper, Jr., *Jefferson Davis: American*, (New York: Alfred Knopf, 2000) pp. 455, 478, 497.

16. Muhlenfeld, *Mary Boykin Chesnut*, p. 97; C. Vann Woodward and Elizabeth Muhlenfeld, eds., *The Private Mary Chesnut: The Unpublished Civil War Diaries* (New York: Oxford University Press, 1984), pp. 7, 14, 28.

17. Muhlenfeld, *Mary Boykin Chesnut*, pp. 113, 191, 223.

18. Woodward, *Mary Chesnut's Civil War*, pp. 217, 225.

19. Ibid., pp. 23, 32, 40; also see Edward A. Pollard, *The Lost Cause: A New Southern History of the War of the Confederates* (New York: E.B. Treat, 1867).

20. Sterling, *Belle of the Fifties*, p. 50; Woodward, *Mary Chesnut's Civil War*, p. 87.

21. Alvy L. King, *Louis T. Wigfall, Southern Fire-eater* (Baton Rouge: Louisiana State University Press, 1970), pp. 32–35; Woodward, *Mary Chesnut's Civil War*, p. 185.

22. Woodward, *Mary Chesnut's Civil War*, pp. 274–301; for Louisa McCord, see Elizabeth Fox-Genovese, *Within the Plantation Household: Black and White Women of the Old South* (Chapel Hill: University of North Carolina Press, 1988).

23. Woodward, *Mary Chesnut's Civil War*, pp. 304, 333, 352.

24. Ibid., pp. 501, 517. For James L. Orr, see Roger P. Leemhuis, *James L. Orr and the Sectional Conflict* (Washington: University Press of America, 1979).

25. Woodward, *Mary Chesnut's Civil War*, pp. 436–38; Richard D. Goff, *Confederate Supply* (Durham, N.C.: Duke University Press, 1969).

26. Woodward, *Mary Chesnut's Civil War*, pp. 519–20; Jon L. Wakelyn, *Biographical Dictionary of the Confederacy* (Westport, Conn.: Greenwood Press, 1977) pp. 103–4.

27. Woodward, *Mary Chesnut's Civil War*, pp. 600–625; Muhlenfeld, *Mary Boykin Chesnut*, p. 120.

28. Woodward, *Mary Chesnut's Civil War*, pp. 121, 185, 187, 687; Robert Nicholas Olsberg, "A Government of Class and Race: William Henry Trescot and the South Carolina Chivalry, 1850–1865," Ph.D. diss., University of South Carolina, 1972.

29. Woodward, *Mary Chesnut's Civil War*, pp. 186, 313, 480; Jones, *Rebel War Clerk*, vol. 2, pp. 38, 71.

30. Woodward, *Mary Chesnut's Civil War*, pp. 656, 666, 675, 785.

31. For the bickering of the generals about the abilities of their peers and competitors, the best source is Jones, *Rebel War Clerk*, and Woodward, *Mary Chesnut's Civil War*, pp. 468, 501, 600, 646, 688, 700, 709.

32. Woodward, *Mary Chesnut's Civil War*, pp. 154, 207, 219, 238, 325; information on Hammond is in Chapter 1 of this volume. For South Carolina's squabbles, see Manisha Sinha, *The Counter-revolution of Slavery* (Chapel Hill: University of North Carolina Press, 2000), pp. 221–58. South Carolina's betrayal of the Confederacy for a higher cause has yet to be told.

33. Woodward, *Mary Chesnut's Civil War*, pp. 253, 254, 301, 324.

34. Ibid., pp. 361, 370, 375, 387, 399; Muhlenfeld, *Mary Boykin Chesnut*, p. 117.

35. Woodward, *Mary Chesnut's Civil War*, pp. 597, 629, 687, 739; Charles E. Cauthen, *South Carolina Goes to War* (Chapel Hill: University of North Carolina Press, 1950).

36. Woodward, *Mary Chesnut's Civil War*, pp. 40, 331, 344, 759; on Jeremiah Clemens, see Jon L. Wakelyn, ed., *Southern Unionist Pamphlets and the Civil War* (Columbia: University of Missouri Press, 1999), pp. 330–40.

37. Woodward, *Mary Chesnut's Civil War*, pp. 517, 687, 706, 710; see Chapters 4 and 7 of this volume for comments on the failed peace conference.

38. Woodward, *Mary Chesnut's Civil War*, pp. 138–39, 199, 234, 737, 745.

39. Ibid., pp. 644, 733.

40. Ibid., pp. 341, 498, 499.

41. Ibid., pp. 208, 214; another memorialist who expressed the same reasons for writing down his observations is Thomas C. DeLeon, *Four Years in Rebel Capitals* (Mobile: Gossip Printing, 1892), pp. 5, 6.

CHAPTER 7: A CONSIDERATION OF THE CAUSES AND EFFECTS OF SLAVE STATES' LEADERS' DISLOYALTY TO THE CONFEDERACY

1. See Jon L. Wakelyn, ed., *Southern Unionist Pamphlets and the Civil War* (Columbia: University of Missouri Press, 1999), pp. 1–15.

2. Daniel W. Crofts, *Reluctant Confederates: Upper South Unionists in the Secession Crisis,* (Chapel Hill: University of North Carolina Press, 1989), *passim*; see Chapter 4 in this volume.

3. James Welch Patton, *Unionism and Reconstruction in Tennessee, 1860–1869* (Chapel Hill: University of North Carolina Press, 1934); Georgia Lee Tatum, *Disloyalty in the Confederacy* (Chapel Hill: University of North Carolina Press, 1934).

4. William W. Freehling, *The South Versus the South: How Anti-Confederate Southerners Shaped the Course of the Civil War* (New York: Oxford University Press, 2001); Daniel E. Sutherland, ed., *Guerrillas, Unionists, and Violence on the Confederate Home Front* (Fayetteville: University of Arkansas Press, 1999); Wayne K. Durrill, *War of Another Kind: A Southern Community in the Great Rebellion* (New York: Oxford University Press, 1990); John C. Inscoe and Robert C. Kenzer, eds., *Enemies of the Country: New Perspectives on Unionists in the Civil War South* (Athens: University of Georgia Press, 2001); Ira Berlin, et al., eds., *Freedom: A Documentary History of Emancipation, 1861–1867* (New York: Cambridge University Press, 1990); and Richard N. Current, *Lincoln's Loyalists: Union Soldiers from the Confederacy* (Boston: Northeastern University Press, 1992).

5. Carl N. Degler, *The Other South: Southern Dissenters in the Nineteenth Century* (Gainesville: University of Florida Press, 2000). Degler looks back on his study of 1974 and states, "I failed to recognize that within the Confederacy there was substantial dissent." The best study of anti-Davis sentiment is Paul Escott, *After Secession* (Chapel Hill: University of North Carolina Press, 1983).

6. Richard E. Beringer, et al., *Why the South Lost the Civil War.*

7. Freehling, *The South vs. the South*, pp. 64, 68, 81, 147, 202.

8. John J. Crittenden, *The Union, the Constitution, and the Laws* (Washington: William H. Moore, 1860); Lazarus W. Powell, *Speech . . . on the State of the Union* (Washington: Congressional Globe Office, 1861). Also see Albert J. Kirwin, *John J. Crittenden: The Struggle for the Union* (Lexington: University of Kentucky Press, 1962).

9. Lazarus W. Powell, *Speech on Executive Usurpation* (Washington: Congressional Globe, 1861); Kirwin, *Crittenden*, pp. 465–466.

10. Hamilton Rowan Gamble, *Message to the Missouri State Convention* (Jefferson City, Mo.: J.P. Ament, 1863); Kirwin, *Crittenden*, pp. 98, 279, 408, 437.

11. See, for example, Robert J. Breckinridge, *The Civil War: Its Nature and End* (Cincinnati: Office of the Danville Review, 1861); for unkind, but valuable, comments, see E. Merton Coulter, *The Civil War and Readjustment in Kentucky* (Chapel Hill: University of North Carolina Press, 1926).

12. Durrill, *War of Another Kind*; Freehling, *The South vs. the South*; Inscoe and Kenzer, *Enemies of the Country*.

13. Jon L. Wakelyn, ed., *Southern Pamphlets on Secession, Nov. 1860–Apr. 1861* (Chapel Hill: University of North Carolina Press, 1996), pp. 400–401; Wakelyn, *Southern Unionist Pamphlets*, pp. 82–104, 304–29; Jon L. Wakelyn, "The Politics of Violence: Unionist Pamphleteers in Virginia's Inner Civil War," in Sutherland, ed., *Guerrillas, Unionists, and Violence*, pp. 59–74.

14. Wakelyn, *Southern Unionist Pamphlets*, pp. 105–19, 255–72; Stephen V. Ash, ed., *Secessionists and Other Scoundrels: Selections from Parson Brownlow's Book* (Baton Rouge: Louisiana State University Press, 1999); Hans L. Trefousse, *Andrew Johnson: A Biography* (New York: W.W. Norton, 1989).

15. Trefousse, *Andrew Johnson*.

16. Trefousse, *Andrew Johnson*; Wakelyn, *Southern Unionist Pamphlets*, pp. 255–72.

17. For a hostile, but detailed, recounting of Brownlow's Northern adventures, see E. Merton Coulter, *William G. Brownlow: Fighting Parson of the Southern Highlands* (Chapel Hill: University of North Carolina Press, 1937). Brownlow needs a modern study. His wartime activities on behalf of the Union will be included in my future study of the Southern Unionists, currently titled *The Men in the Attic: Southern Unionists and the Civil War*.

18. Wakelyn, *Southern Unionist Pamphlets*, pp. 120–47. Only a few facts of Wood's life are known, but see Lillian A. Pereyra, *James Lusk Alcorn* (Baton Rouge: Louisiana State University Press, 1966).

19. Wakelyn, *Southern Unionist Pamphlets*, pp. 238–54, 378, 379; John L. Waller, *Colossal Hamilton of Texas* (El Paso: Texas Western Press, 1968).

20. Crofts, *Reluctant Confederates*, pp. 137, 235, 287, 336–37, 359.

21. Wakelyn, *Southern Pamphlets on Secession*, pp. 349–72; Robert G. Gunderson, "William C. Rives and the 'Old Gentlemen's Convention,' " *Journal of Southern History* 22 (Nov. 1956): 459–76.

22. Unfortunately, Rives and other important second-tier Southern leaders have never been studied in depth. See Drew McCoy, *Last of the Fathers: James Madision and the Republican Legacy* (New York: Cambridge University Press, 1989), pp. 338–59. Also see Rives to John Janney, May 1, 1861; Rives to Gov. John Letcher, Apr. 25, 1862; Rives to Thomas A. Bocock, Mar. 1, 1865; *Prospectus of the Society for Promoting the Cessation of Hostilities*, in Rives's hand (May 1864), all in Rives Papers, Library of Congress.

23. Wakelyn, *Southern Pamphlets on Secession*, p. 398; Crofts, *Reluctant Confederates*, pp. 1–7, 73–74, 252, 352; James Vaux Drake, *Life of General Robert Hatton, Including His Most Important Public Speeches; Together, with Much of His Washington*

and Army Correspondence (Nashville, Tenn.: Marshall and Bruce, 1867), pp. 301, 354.

24. Drake, *Life of Hatton*, pp. 414, 415, 416–17, 418; Charles M. Cummings, "Robert Hopkins Hatton: Reluctant Rebel," *Tennessee Historical Quarterly* 23 (1964): 169–81.

25. William C. Harris, *William Woods Holden: Firebrand of North Carolina Politics* (Baton Rouge: Louisiana State University Press, 1987), pp. 91, 98, 106, 142.

26. Frontis W. Johnston, ed., *The Papers of Zebulon Baird Vance* (Raleigh, N.C.: State Archives and History, 1963), 99–100; Harris, *Holden*, p. 137.

27. Ben Ames Williams and James G. De Roulhac Hamilton, eds., *Papers of William Alexander Graham*, 7 vols. (Raleigh, N.C.: State Archives and History, 1971–1976), vol. 5, pp. 459–60, 530, 531, 532.

28. William Alexander Graham, *Speech . . . on the Ordinance Concerning Test Oaths and Sedition* (Raleigh, N.C.: Office of the Raleigh Standard, 1861), pp. 7, 41; Williams and Hamilton, *Papers of Graham*, vol. 5, pp. 311, 337.

29. Williams and Hamilton, *Papers of Graham*, vol. 6, pp. 20, 31, 160, 206, 224–25.

30. Williams and Hamilton, *Papers of Graham*, vol. 7, pp. 330–37 to Andrew Johnson, July 25, 1865.

31. "Papers of John A. Campbell, 1861–1865," *Southern Historical Society Papers*, n.s. 4; (Oct. 1917): 26–29; George Green Shackleford, *George Wythe Randolph and the Confederate Elite* (Athens: University of Georgia Press, 1988), pp. 111–13.

32. William R. Smith, *History and Debates of the Convention of Alabama* (Montgomery, Ala.: White, Pfister, 1861), p. 63.

33. W.R. Smith to his wife July 21, 1861, Easby-Smith Papers, Library of Congress; Anne Easby-Smith, *William Russell Smith of Alabama*, p. 130.

34. Smith to his wife, Sept. 10, 1862, May 12, 1864, Easby-Smith Papers, Library of Congress.

35. Smith to his wife, Apr. 18, 1863, Easby-Smith Papers, Library of Congress; William Russell Smith, *The Royal Ape* (Richmond, Va.: West and Johnston, 1863), pp. 28, 37, 64, 70–75.

36. Pereyra, *Alcorn*, pp. 50, 61, 62, 69, 72.

37. Wakelyn, *Southern Pamphlets on Secession*, pp. 402–12; Thomas Schott, *Alexander H. Stephens of Georgia* (Baton Rouge: Louisiana State University Press, 1988), pp. 306, 323, 334.

38. James D. Waddell, ed., *Biographical Sketch of Linton Stephens* (Atlanta: Dodson and Scott, 1877), pp. 257, 266, 285, 287; Schott, *Stephens*, pp. 372, 376, 395, 427.

39. Alexander H. Stephens, *A Constitutional View of the Late War Between the States: Its Causes, Character, Conduct and Results*, 2 vols. (Philadelphia: National Publishing, 1868, 1870), vol. 1, pp. 18, 19–20, vol. 2, pp. 321, 356.

40. Myrta Lockett Avery, *Recollections of Alexander H. Stephens* (New York: Doubleday, 1910), pp. 328, 528.

41. See most recently Thomas G. Dyer, *Secret Yankees: The Unionist Circle in Confederate Atlanta* (Baltimore, Md.: Johns Hopkins University Press, 1999); Lawrence N. Powell and Michael S. Wayne, "Self-Interest and the Decline of Confederate Nationalism," pp. 29–45 in Harry P. Owens and James J. Cooke, eds., *The Old South in the Crucible of War* (Jackson: University Press of Mississippi, 1983); Ludwell H. Johnson, *Red River Campaign: Politics and Cotton in the Civil War* (Baltimore, Md.: Johns Hopkins University Press, 1958), pp. 71–72; Mary A. De Credico, *Patriotism for Profit: Georgia's Urban Entrepreneurs and the Confederate War Effort* (Chapel Hill: University of North Carolina Press, 1990).

42. See the end of Chapter 1 in this volume.

43. Sarah Woolfolk Wiggins, ed., *The Journal of Josiah Gorgas, 1857–1878* (Tuscaloosa: University of Alabama Press, 1995), p. xviii; Frank E. Vandiver, ed., *The Civil War Diary of General Josiah Gorgas* (University, Alabama: University of Alabama Press, 1947), pp. 51, 58.

44. Emory Thomas, *The Confederacy As a Revolutionary Experience* (Englewood Cliffs, N.J.: Prentice-Hall, 1971), *passim*; also see Richard Bensel, *Yankee Leviathan* (New York: Cambridge University Press, 1990), chapter 2.

45. De Credico, *Patriotism for Profit*, pp. 76, 80, 85, 95, 97, 99.

46. James Michael Russell, *Atlanta 1847–1890: City Building in the Old South and the New* (Baton Rouge: Louisiana State University Press, 1988), p. 108.

47. Douglas B. Ball, *Financial Failure and Confederate Defeat* (Urbana: University of Illinois Press, 1991), pp. 264, 268.

48. Richard N. Current, ed., *Encyclopedia of the Confederacy*, 4 vols. (New York: Simon and Schuster, 1993), vol. 3, pp. 1296–1297; Goff, *Confederate Supply* (Durham, N.C.: Duke University Press, 1969), *passim*.

49. Edward B. Coddington, "Activities and Attitudes of a Confederate Businessman: Gazaway Bugg Lamar," *Journal of Southern History* 9 (Feb. 1943): 3–36; Ball, *Financial Failure and Confederate Defeat*, p. 30.

50. See Chapter 6 and Mary Chesnut's comments on the destructiveness of personal attacks on President Davis. Escott, *After Secession* (Chapel Hill: University of North Carolina Press, 1983); John B. Jones, *A Rebel War Clerk's Diary at the Confederate States Capital*, 2 vols. (New York: Old Hickory Book Shop, 1935) esp. vol. 2.

51. Henry Harrison Simms, *Life of Robert M.T. Hunter: A Study in Sectionalism and Secession* (Richmond, Va.: William Byrd Press, 1935), pp. 187–92; C. Vann Woodward, ed., *Mary Chesnut's Civil War*, (New Haven, Conn.: Yale University Press, 1981), p. 80.

52. Simms, *Life of Hunter*, pp. 196, 197, 200; Woodward, *Mary Chesnut's Civil War*, p. 550; James Scanlon, "Life of Robert M.T. Hunter," Ph.D. diss., University of Virginia, 1969.

53. James G. De Roulhac Hamilton, ed., *The Papers of Thomas Ruffin*, 4 vols. (Raleigh, N.C.: Edwards and Broughton, 1920), vol. 3, pp. 368, 413.

54. Thomas E. Jeffrey, *Thomas Lanier Clingman: Fire Eater from the Carolina Mountains* (Athens: University of Georgia Press, 1998), p. 181.

55. Laura A. White, *Robert Barnwell Rhett: Father of Secession* (New York: American Historical Association, 1931), pp. 224–25; also see Mary Chesnut's pithy comments on Rhett in chapter 6 of this volume.

56. Ibid., pp. 236, 240.

57. See Mary Chesnut's comments on Orr in Chapter 6 of this volume. Also see Roger P. Leemhuis, *James L. Orr and the Sectional Conflict* (Washington, D.C.: University Press of America, 1979), pp. 93–94; *Journal of the Congress of the Confederate States of America* (Washington, D.C.: Government Printing Office, 1904–1905), vol. 4, pp. 143, 284.

58. Leemhuis, *James L. Orr*, p. 94.

59. William Y. Thompson, *Robert Toombs of Georgia* (Baton Rouge: Louisiana State University Press, 1966), pp. 173, 205, 210, 211, 214, 217.

60. Jefferson Davis, *Rise and Fall of the Confederate Government*, 2 vols (London: Longmans, Green, 1881), *passim*; Frank L. Owsley, *State Rights in the Confederacy* (Baton Rouge: Louisiana State University, 1994); George Rable, *The Confederate Republic* (Chapel Hill: University of North Carolina Press, 1994), pp. 191, 244, 256–62; Thomas Beringer et al., *Why the South Lost the War* (Athens: University of Georgia Press, 1986), p. 455.

61. Rable, *Confederate Republic*, pp. 65, 91; Joseph Howard Parks, *Joseph E. Brown of Georgia* (Baton Rouge: Louisiana State University Press, 1977), pp. 123–72.

62. Herbert Fielder, *A Sketch of the Life and Times and Speeches of Joseph E. Brown* (Springfield, Mass.: Press of Springfield Printing, 1883), pp. 256, 267.

63. John Witherspoon DuBose, *The Life and Times of William Lowndes Yancey*, 2 vols. (New York: Peter Smith, 1942), vol. 2, pp. 690, 692, 712; Woodward, *Mary Chesnut's Civil War*, pp. 283, 300, 318, 321, 339.

64. Robert W. Dubay, *John Jones Pettus, Mississippi Fire Eater* (Jackson: University Press of Mississippi, 1975), p. 74; Bradley G. Bond, *Political Culture in the Nineteenth Century South: Mississippi 1830–1890* (Baton Rouge: Louisiana State University Press, 1995), pp. 118, 125, 133.

65. Dubay, *John Jones Pettus*, pp. 144, 164, 165, 189, 194.

66. Alvy King, *Louis T. Wigfall* (Baton Rouge: Louisiana State University Press, 1970), p. viii.

67. King, *Wigfall*, pp. 124, 128, 132; Woodward, *Mary Chesnut's Civil War*, pp. 138–39.

68. King, *Wigfall*, pp. 141, 156, 158, 176–84; also see Chapter 6 in this volume on Mary Chesnut's worries about Wigfall's dislike of Davis and Jones, *Rebel War Clerk*, vol. 2, pp. 353–54.

69. Eugene D. Genovese, *The Slaveholder's Dilemma: Freedom and Progress in*

Southern Conservative Thought, 1830–1860 (Columbia: University of South Carolina Press, 1992); Kenneth Greenberg, *Honor and Slavery* (Princeton, N.J.: Princeton University Press, 1996); and Manisha Sinha, *The Counter-revolution of Slavery: Politics and Ideology in Antebellum South Carolina* (Chapel Hill: University of North Carolina Press, 2000), esp. chapter 6.

Essay on Sources

Primary materials best capture the attitudes and activities of those Confederates who intrigued against Confederate policy while at the same time regarding themselves as loyal Confederates. Among the most important collections of letters, broadsides, unpublished writings, and commentaries of the participants are the papers of John A. Campbell in *Southern Historical Society Papers* and papers of James Henry Hammond, the Easby-Smith Papers (William Russell Smith), and the William Cabell Rives Papers at the Library of Congress. At the Southern Historical Collection in Chapel Hill, North Carolina, are the useful papers of William P. Miles and Robert Barnwell Rhett. There are also James Henry Hammond papers in the South Caroliniana at the University of South Carolina.

Printed collections include Leroy Graf and Ralph P. Haskins, eds., *The Papers of Andrew Johnson* (Knoxville: University of Tennessee Press, 1967–), Max Williams and James G. De Roulhac Hamilton, eds., *The Papers of William Archibald Graham* (6 vols. Raleigh, N.C.: Department of Archives and History, 1957–1976), and Frontis W. Jonston, ed., *The Papers of Zebulon Baird Vance* (North Carolina Department of Archives and History, 1963). Especially valuable are the Graham papers. Letters and sometimes writings may be found in the various life-and-times studies, often collected by members of the family or close friends. See James P. Carson, *Life and Letters of James L. Petigru* (Washington, D.C.: W.H. Lowdermilk, 1920); Susan P. Lee, *Memoir of William Nelson Pendleton* (Philadelphia: Longmans, Green, 1893); Clyde Wilson, ed., *Selected Letters and Speeches of James Henry Hammond* (Spartanburg, S.C.: Reprint Co., 1978); Anne Easby-Smith, *William Russell Smith of Alabama* (Philadelphia: The Dolphin Press, 1931); Reuben Davis,

Recollection of Mississippi and Mississippians (Boston: Houghton Mifflin, 1889); and John Johns, *A Memoir of the Life of the Rt. Rev. William Meade* (Baltimore, Md.: Innes & Company, 1867).

A handful of wartime newspapers have been of use. Especially see the *Raleigh Register* and the *Charleston Mercury*. In them, editors William W. Holden and Robert Barnwell Rhett come near to destroying local popular confidence in the Confederate government's ability to defend its people.

The prewar and wartime works of the most important Confederate leaders who resisted government policies are many in number. Among the most important pamphlets or documents that circulated widely and had lasting influence are Robert Hatton, *The State of the Union* (Washington, D.C.: Office of the Congressional Globe, 1861), Rt. Rev. James H. Otey, *Trust in God* (New York: Daniel Dana, Jr., 1860), and William A. Graham, *Speech . . . on the Ordinances Concerning Test Oaths and Sedition* (Raleigh, N.C.: Office of the Raleigh Standard, 1861). In a class by itself is William R. Smith, *History and Debates of the People of Alabama* (Montgomery, Ala.: White, Phister and Company, 1861). An important collection of antisecession pamphlets and writings that often reflected the author's wartime behavior are in William W. Freehling and Craig Simpson, eds., *Secession Debated: Georgia's Showdown in 1860* (New York: Oxford University Press, 1994). Also see my edition of *Southern Pamphlets on Secession: Nov. 1860–Apr. 1861* (Chapel Hill: University of North Carolina Press, 1996). In that volume I have commented on many antisecession pamphlets by authors who later supported the Confederacy with faintness of heart.

The most important printed government and private organization documents are *The Journals of the Confederate Congress* (Washington, D.C.: Government Printing Office, 1905–1906), in seven volumes of argument over policy, and William A. Clebsch, ed., *Journal of the Protestant Episcopal Church of the Confederate States of America* (Austin, Tx.: Church Historical Society, 1962). Wartime state legislative journals have been of much use. Especially see *Journal of the House of Representatives of Tennessee* (Nashville, Tenn.: State Printer, 1957), *Journal of the House of Representatives of Georgia* (Milledgeville, Ga.: State Printer, 1861), and surprisingly *Journal of the House of Representatives of South Carolina* (Columbia, S.C.: State Printer, 1861).

Wartime books by participants that cut to the heart of the differences among Confederates are many in number. Among the most important are John B. Jones's gossipy but informed *Rebel War Clerk's Diary* (2 vols. Philadelphia: J.B. Lippincott, 1866); Edward A. Pollard's carping and critical *Southern History of the War* (2 vols. New York: Fairfax Press, 1866); John Goode's political *Recollections of a Lifetime* (New York: Neale Publishing Company, 1906); and *The Diary of Robert Garlick Hill Kean* (New York: Oxford University Press, 1957), edited by Edward Younger. Those participants who wrote memoirs and their own personal accounts of the war and its disputants are also quite useful. Thomas C. DeLeon's *Four Years in Rebel Capitals* (Mobile, Ala.: Gossip Printing Company, 1890) recounts tensions among the leaders. Two perceptive and informed women memoirists are Judith W. McGuire, *Diary of a Southern Refugee During the War* (New York: E.J. Hale & Company, 1867), and Mrs. Burton Harrison, *Recollections Grave and Gray* (New York: Charles Scribner's Sons, 1911). Most provocative and informative on how to appear to support the Confederacy but actually undermine the war effort are found in the postwar memoirs of William R. Smith of Alabama and Henry Stuart Foote of Tennessee. See Smith's *Reminiscences of a Long Life* (Washington, D.C.: Self-published, 1889) and Foote's aptly titled *Casket of Reminiscences* (Washington, D.C.: Chronicle Publishing Company, 1874) and *War of the Rebellion* (New York: Harper & Brothers, 1866). In a class by itself and perhaps the most informative account of anti-Confederate activity written is the memoir in the form of a diary by Mary Chesnut. Although this profound work remains controversial for its veracity, a most accurate account is C. Vann Woodward's Pulitzer Prize edition, *Mary Chesnut's Civil War* (New Haven, Conn.: Yale University Press, 1981). Jefferson Davis's *Rise and Fall of the Confederate Government* (2 vols. London: Longmans, Green, 1881) is a paranoid account of his enemies by the president of the Confederacy. Also, Alexander Stephens's tortured *A Constitutional View of the Late War Between the States* (2 vols. Philadelphia: National Publishing Company, 1868–1870) reveals the level of self-deception even in the learned and political vice president of the Confederacy. Stephens's shift in viewpoint and explanations for why he came to oppose the government are most revealing of his revisionist mind.

Older secondary accounts have proved most useful for setting the causes of dissension. See, for example, Charles W. Ramsdell, *Behind the Lines in the Southern Confederacy* (Baton Rouge: Louisiana State University Press, 1944), and James Welch Patton, *Unionism and Reconstruction in Tennessee* (Chapel Hill: University of North Carolina Press, 1934). Also see Robert Gunderson, *The Old Gentlemen's Convention* (Madison: University of Wisconsin Press, 1961) for a glimpse into future anti-Confederate activities of the secession era compromisers. Perhaps the most important of these studies and a work never really surpassed is Georgia Lee Tatum, *Disloyalty in the Confederacy* (Chapel Hill: University of North Carolina Press, 1934). Tatum attempts to identify categories of dissidence, but like many others who have studied these people, she confuses outright Unionists with the vindictive Confederates who came to oppose the Confederacy.

Important modern studies also follow Tatum's dichotomy but have been useful for pointing out the level of dissent within the South. Some of the best recent work is found in biography. See, for example, William C. Harris, *William Woods Holden: Firebrand of North Carolina Politics* (Baton Rouge: Louisiana State University Press, 1989). Harris is a most careful student of Southern dissent. Also see the biography *Jefferson Davis: American* (New York: Alfred Knopf, 2000), by William J. Cooper. Cooper is not much concerned with the dissidents, but he understands how they riled President Davis.

The best synthesis of the anti-Confederates is Carl Degler's *Other South: Southern Dissenters in the Nineteenth Century* (Gainesville, University of Florida Press, 2000).

Thomas Alexander and William Beringer, *Anatomy of the Confederate Congress* (Nashville, Tenn.: Vanderbilt University Press, 1974), reveals more dissenting damage to the government than the book admits. While not necessarily interested in what Unionists will do as Confederates, Daniel Crofts, in *Reluctant Confederates: Upper South Unionists in the Secession Crisis* (Chapel Hill: University of North Carolina Press, 1989), has been most useful for understanding why those leaders would turn on the Confederacy. George Rable, *The Confederate Republic* (Chapel Hill: University of North Carolina Press, 1994), captures aspects of congressional contempt for the president's policies. Also on dislike of Jefferson Davis is Paul Escott, *After Secession* (Baton Rouge: Louisiana State University Press, 1978). Thomas Connelly and Archer Jones's book, *The Politics of Command* (Baton Rouge: Louisiana State University Press, 1973), reveals military and political intrigue against the administration for good reason. That book remains the best attempt to chronicle the regional discontent in the Confederacy that spilled over into policy disputes. Also useful for an understanding of the role of women's morale in upsetting Confederate unity is Drew Faust, *Mothers of Invention* (Chapel Hill: University of North Carolina Press, 1996). Problems in religious dissent are found in Gardner H. Shattuck, Jr., *A Shield and a Hiding Place: Religious Life of the Civil War Armies* (Macon, Ga.: Mercer University Press, 1987). Douglas B. Ball, in the perceptive *Financial Failure and Confederate Defeat* (Urbana: University of Illinois Press, 1991), shows how Southern businessmen turned on the Confederate government.

Recently a spate of books on Unionists and anti-Confederates among the Southern people have appeared. The best of these are Thomas G. Dyer, *Secret Yankees: Unionist Circles in Confederate Atlanta* (Baltimore, Md.: Johns Hopkins University Press, 1999); Daniel E. Sutherland, ed., *Guerrillas, Unionism, and Violence on the Confederate Home Front* (Fayetteville: University of Arkansas Press, 1999); and John S. Inscoe and Robert C. Kenzer, eds., *Enemies of the Country: New Perspectives on Unionists in the Civil War South* (Athens: University of Georgia Press, 2001). Again, Unionism and anti-Confederate sentiment are often merged in these studies.

In categories by themselves as works that have helped me to focus on the nature of anti-Confederate sentiment and activities of purported Confederates are a number of recent works. Manisha Sinha, *The Counter-revolution of Slavery* (Chapel Hill: University of North Carolina Press, 2000), and Daniel Greenberg, *Honor and Slavery* (Princeton: Princeton University Press, 1996), both suggest how support for slavery itself could have undermined confidence in the Confederacy. Though neither Sinha or Greenberg writes specifically about the war, their accounts of divisions over how best to support slavery inform my own judgments on how differing views on the defense of slavery undermined leadership support for the Confederacy. In an exchange quite useful for me over his paper "The American Revolution Versus the Civil War," given at the Washington Conference at the Washington Historical Society in 1992, I profited from the thoughts of John M.

Murrin. William W. Freehling, in *The South Versus the South: How the Anti-Confederate South Shaped the Course of the Civil War* (New York: Oxford University Press, 2000), has written brilliantly on the reality of dissent. He has so covered the actions of slaves and ordinary Southerners that I have been able to concentrate my efforts on the leadership classes. Last, perhaps the most profound student of the Old South of our time, Eugene G. Genovese, has weighed in on the divisions in the Southern mind and has helped to mold this present work. Though I am not sure what he will make of my use of his thoughtful efforts, almost everything he has had to say about Southern political and cultural thinking has informed my own views. See his *Consuming Fire: The Fall of the Confederacy in the Mind of the White Christian South* (Athens: University of Georgia Press, 1998). Especially a major, but I fear neglected, work, Genovese's *The Slaveholder's Dilemma: Freedom and Progress in Southern Conservative Thought, 1830–1860* (Columbia, S.C.: University of South Carolina Press, 1992), has suggested to me an insurmountable dilemma in the ways Southerners defended slavery. That dilemma was rife among Confederates who opposed the Confederacy.

Index

Bryan, George W., 113
Bunch, Bradley, 41

Calhoun, John C., xiii, 2
Call, Richard K., 14, 19; fears civil
  war, 19
Campbell, John A., 15, 21, 114, 115,
  129, 133–34, 146, 147; peace
  movement, 134; slave protection
  clause, 21
Campbell, Josiah A.P., 39, 42, 43, 50
Carlile, John S., 124
Chambers, Henry C., 66
Chesnut, James, 4, 6, 103, 105, 142;
  loses election, 106; Mary as gossip,
  115; sends Mary home, 108
Chesnut, Mary B., xiv, 141, 142, 148,
  149; biography, 102–103; diarist,
  103–18; veracity of diary, 101–102
Church Intelligencer, 87, 88
Clark, Charles, 148
Clay, Virginia, 103, 106
Clemens, Jeremiah, 113
Clingman, Thomas J., 142
Cobb, Howell, 20, 144
Cobb, Williamson R.R., 15, 21
Confederate Congress: evaluated, 53–
  58; modern historians on, 57–58
Confederate Constitution, 37
*Confederate States Book of Common
  Prayer*, 84, 87
Connelly, Thomas L., xiv–xv, 89
Crenshaw, Walter H., 39, 42, 45, 47,
  49, 50
Crofts, Daniel W., 13–14, 17, 128
Crutchfield, Oscar M., 39, 42

Danville Review, 123
Darnell, Nicholas H., 41, 47, 51
Davis, Jefferson, xiv, 11, 21, 35, 48,
  53, 57, 65, 75, 141; bread riots, 98;
  damage to, 117; despot, 17; and
  Leondias Polk, 88, 90; parodied,

135; pressure from Foote, 65–66;
  view of Congress, 55
Davis, Joseph, 60
Davis, Reuben, 61; on H.S. Foote,
  62
Davis, Varina Howell (friend of Mary
  Chesnut), 103, 107, 109, 114, 143
Degler, Carl, xi, 120, 181
Dell, Phillip, 39, 45
De Saussure, John, 111
Donald, David H., 35, 38, 46, 51;
  "died of democracy" theme, 51
Donnell, Richard S., 40, 50, 52;
  accused by Davis, 48, 49
Dortch, William T., 40, 41, 142

Elliott, Bishop Stephen, 78, 81; as ally
  of Bishop Polk, 83; attends funeral
  for General Polk, 90; supports Polk
  for general, 88; urges adoption of
  new prayer book, 87
Episcopal Church, south, xiv, 16;
  divisions within, 81; history of, 78–
  79
Eppes, Thomas J., 39, 45;
  commitment to Confederate cause,
  45

Fleming, Nathan N., lost to history,
  52
Foote, Henry S., xiii, xiv, 54, 56, 133;
  biography of, 60–62; bravery, 59;
  Chesnut mentions, 106; debate to
  arm slaves, 66–67; doubts future of
  Confederacy, 64; expelled from
  House, 68–69; explains secession,
  73; hostility to Davis, 61–62;
  loyalty analyzed, 58–75; on Lucius
  B. Northrop, 65; on Mexican War,
  60–61; on peace movement, 67–68,
  144; reflects on war activities, 69–
  76; on Texas, 70–71

About the Author

JON L. WAKELYN is Professor of History at Kent State University. He is the author of nine books, including *The Politics of a Literary Man, Southern Pamphlets on Secession, Leaders of the American Civil War*, and *Southern and Unionist Pamphlets and the Civil War*.